SOUTHERN COMFORTS

SOUTHERN LITERARY STUDIES

Scott Romine, Series Editor

SOUTHERN COMFORTS

DRINKING & THE U.S. SOUTH

EDITED BY CONOR PICKEN &
MATTHEW DISCHINGER

Louisiana State University Press
Baton Rouge

Published by Louisiana State University Press
Copyright © 2020 by Louisiana State University Press

All rights reserved
Manufactured in the United States of America
First printing

Portions of Hannah C. Griggs's essay, "Jim Crow, Mardi Gras, and the
Ojen Cocktail," first appeared in *The Atlantic* as "How New Orleans's Favorite
Mardi Gras Cocktail Was Saved from Extinction," in the February 23, 2017,
issue. Copyright © 2017 by Hannah C. Griggs.

DESIGNER: Michelle A. Neustrom
TYPEFACE: Whitman
PRINTER AND BINDER: Sheridan Books, Inc.

Cataloging-in-Publication Data are available at the Library of Congress.
ISBN 978-0-8071-7173-8 (cloth : alk. paper) | ISBN 978-0-8071-7330-5 (pdf) |
ISBN 978-0-8071-7331-2 (epub)

The paper in this book meets the guidelines for permanence and
durability of the Committee on Production Guidelines for Book
Longevity of the Council on Library Resources. ∞

CONTENTS

ACKNOWLEDGMENTS

Southern Comforts exists because of the excellent work of its contributors, who worked patiently with editors and reviewers while also presenting short versions of these essays at conferences organized by the Southeastern American Studies Association, the Society for the Study of Southern Literature, and the American Literature Association. The contributors' enthusiasm and generosity throughout the project made our work enjoyable, and their brilliant insights taught us much about our topic.

The editorial team at LSU Press guided us expertly throughout this process. James W. Long saw this project through from the early stages to its fruition. As editor of the press's Southern Literary Studies series, Scott Romine provided essential feedback and encouragement at every stage. A special thanks to Margaret Lovecraft for working with us early on. Our anonymous reviewer provided critically deft and helpful advice for revisions, so we want to offer our thanks for their work, as well.

We would also like to thank *The Atlantic* for allowing portions of Hannah C. Griggs's essay, "How New Orleans's Favorite Mardi Gras Cocktail Was Saved from Extinction," to be republished here. Finally, thanks to Jack Daniel's for allowing us to use its photo of Daniel and George Green in the collection's introduction.

SOUTHERN COMFORTS

Introduction

A Glass Half Full

CONOR PICKEN AND
MATTHEW DISCHINGER

The mythology that informs the consumption of one of the South's most famous liquors, Jack Daniel's Tennessee Sour Mash Whiskey, begins with the bottle's label. The left panel highlights words that summarize the process by which the whiskey is made ("*mellowed* for smoothness" and "*matured* for character"), how it is deemed ready for sale and consumption ("*tasted* for flavor"), and, finally, how it has been received by consumers ("*awarded* for quality"). A panel on the far right of the label characterizes the place occupied by Jasper Newton "Jack" Daniel in the company's mythology: "Here at the Jack Daniel distillery, we're proud to honor the independence & integrity of the man who established our distillery at the Cave Spring Hollow. True to Mr. Jack's whiskey-making tradition, we still mellow our whiskey drop by drop and stand by Jack's charge: 'Every day we make it, we'll make it the best we can.'" The company's story on its website supplements the label's emphasis on independence, integrity, and tradition with a pastoral image of a hazy morning in Lynchburg, Tennessee, that visualizes the brand's mythology. A sun tucked behind clouds illuminates a landscape of rolling hills and lush tree lines interrupted by aging warehouses.

These images and stories initiate the act of consumption, fulfilling a particular purpose for the Jack Daniel's brand. The production narrative of a bottle of Jack Daniel's appears simple and straightforward precisely because the images associated with its production suggest that a pastoral South is a peaceful one. This framework has plagued configurations of the region at least since the Agrarians called for returns to a pastoral South, which obscured "the fact that southern plantations and cash-crop monocultures were fundamental to industrial modernity" in the nation and beyond (Knepper 267). For Jack Daniel's, as ever, the pastoral hides an essential truth that illuminates much about the type of consumption the label encourages. Like many texts set in the South, the pastoral narrative put forth by Jack Daniel's "does not eviscerate hierarchy and racism but crystallizes them," revealing a connection between the longing for pastoral peace and nostalgia for the attendant power structures of such spaces and times (Yaeger 36).

Indeed, recent excavations from the Jack Daniel's vault by author Fawn Weaver and *New York Times* reporter Clay Risen unearth a muddled company history that is both essential to its success as a leading distiller and somewhat antithetical to its branded mythology. The company's recent rebranding, which incorporates a more complex narrative than the one put forth by the bottle label, reads as both admirable and perplexing, given the space between what Jack Daniel's has always been and what it now acknowledges.

Mr. Jack Daniel, it turns out, had help. Nearest Green, an enslaved man who previously ran a still at a nearby farm, both taught Jack Daniel how to distill whiskey and was employed as the company's first master distiller. That fact has only been acknowledged by Jack Daniel's since 2016 (Risen, "When Jack Daniel's Failed"). According to the narrative Jack Daniel's displays on its website (jackdaniels.com), after the Civil War, Daniel bought the still where Green toiled under slavery and used it to start selling his own whiskey. It was Green, however, who "worked side by side with Jack and taught the young distiller what would become his life's passion" and thus became the company's head distiller. The rest is history. Whose history, however, depends on the framing of these branded narratives and recovered histories.

The updated Jack Daniel's narrative clarifies that "Jack Daniel not only never owned slaves but he worked side by side with them as a hired hand to Dan Call," a reverend who eventually chose religion over whiskey after his wife and congregation pressured him to exit the distilling business. Before that, Call owned a still where Nearest Green was loaned as a slave. Thus, the company, owned by the publicly traded, multibillion-dollar liquor conglomerate Brown-Foreman, recasts its founder as a racial progressive. As is true of any other company with an image to create and protect, the branding of Jack Daniel's fulfills a particular purpose: mix two parts nostalgia with one part southern self-making and enjoy it on the way down. And the company has profited handsomely from the twinning of myth and product, with sales of close to 12.5 million cases in 2016 (thespiritsbusiness.com).

The story and the images that accompany it are, of course, a *myth* created to sell whiskey and its concomitant, regionally inflected lifestyle. The *history* of Jack Daniel and his distillery reads differently, however, when we consider what is omitted from the myth and what these omissions reveal about both a product and a region with revelatory drinking histories.

The holes in the story should make it collapse. Risen's recent *New York Times* article substantiates the company's claim, stating that, indeed, "Daniel never owned slaves and spoke openly about Green's role as his mentor" (Risen, "When Jack Daniel's Failed"). Illustrating the story of purported equality between the two men, a photograph hanging in Daniel's old office offers further proof of a harmonious black–white relationship between the two men (Risen, "Jack Daniel's Embraces"). In the middle of the photograph (figure 1), which captures Jack Daniel and his distillery crew from the late 1800s, sits a black man, next to Daniel himself. The man is believed to be either Nearest Green or his son, George, but that fact is now difficult to verify.[1]

The man occupies the picture's center like an absence, his dark skin and hat offset against that of the other men. The image illustrates what Thadious M. Davis refers to as "the work of the camera" in the poetry of Natasha Trethewey: "The aperture is the hole, gap, or split that limits the amount of light passing through a lens," an "absence that allows for presence," and, in so doing, serves as an apt metaphor for the "reclaiming of the South" as a black space (66). The narrative put forth by the distillery is one of absence, and the image of the man, who may or may not be Nearest Green, demands attention and narrative refocus. That is, what truly informs the story of Nearest Green is what has long remained untold, buried beneath 150 years of branding that covered over Green's central role in the company's founding—a role that Weaver is attempting to redress and to allow Green's family to reclaim.

Even so, the attempt to incorporate Green's absence still privileges a traditional, racially hierarchical southern narrative: the slave-owning reverend must turn away from the vice of immoral drink, encouraged by his pious, teetotaler wife and his sanctimonious congregation; his egalitarian protégé assumes control and, with the guidance of his trustful mentor, becomes the figurehead of the largest distillery in the world. But this new story needs to be consumed in moderation, considering the important fact that, initially, "the Green story [was] an *optional* part of the distillery tour, left to the tour guide's discretion" (Risen, "Jack Daniel's Embraces," emphasis added).

FIGURE 1. While Clay Risen's *New York Times* articles identify the man in the center of the photograph and seated to the right of Jack Daniel (who wears a white hat with a dark ribbon, a bushy mustache, and a bow tie) as "Nearest Green or one of his sons," the Jack Daniel's website states that "the man in the photograph above, we have reason to believe, is George Green." Jack Daniel's also identifies the man seated alone in the back row as Eli Green, another of Nearest's sons (Jansen). Courtesy Jack Daniels.

If the Jack Daniel's story has been incomplete all along, then why the reluctance to utter the new truth, one so fundamental to the distillery's history that it dates back to the years before its founding? The distillery's in-house historian was even quoted as saying "It's taken something like the anniversary for us to start to talk about ourselves" (Risen, "Jack Daniel's Embraces"). Even that admission consigns the moment of truth to a narrative of inevitable progress. It took the investigative labor by Weaver and prodding by journalists for the brand to acknowledge fully Nearest Green's central role in the company's history.

The subtexts that buoy this history are not unique. Pull at the threads connecting Nearest Green to Jack Daniel's, and the company's erasure of Green begins to look like a familiar type of omission—and one that this book seeks to correct. *Southern Comforts* builds from the premise that we should interrogate the mythologies of drunks, outlaws, and teetotalers that typify our considerations of drinking and the South. These frameworks strike a nostalgic pose, sacrificing specific accounting for comforting tales of the production and consumption of alcohol in the region. Furthermore, mythologizing comes at the expense of a rigorous, historical reckoning with what drinking has meant over time.[2]

To be clear, our book does not celebrate drinking. For the reader interested in figuring drinking through its most "traditional" or hip versions (increasingly, these two versions are becoming one), that sort of celebratory work is not difficult to find in the pages of popular print and online magazines. This book, instead, explores how our work can and should undercut popular myths—of hard-drinking authors, bootleggers, moonshiners, and distillers, to name but a few—that have long been accepted without scrutiny or rigor.[3] We see a reciprocal relationship between mythologies of drinking and the mythologies of region. Just as Lisa Hinrichsen, Gina Caison, and Stephanie Rountree read the televisual South as offering "stabilized and *stabilizing* narratives" (9, emphasis original), narratives of drinking in the South typically rely upon an already formed and constantly reified notion of the region. Thinking critically about drinking and the South, for us, means interrupting habits of consumption that have rarely been challenged.

One familiar framework is the frequently discussed paradox in how alcohol is consumed in the South, noted by foreign correspondent John Gunther during a tour of the region in the 1940s: "Dry as the South may be in some spots, it is also the hardest-drinking region I have ever seen in the world, and the area with the worst drinking habits by far. . . . [It is a place where] hypocrisy begets disorderly behavior" (Barr 253). This is but one of countless examples illustrating the ideological inconsistencies born of a combustible relationship between drinking and the South. Alcohol so soaks southern landscapes, real and imagined, that it becomes another means through which we perceive and define what "the South" actually is—in this formulation, a place framed through exaggeration. Drinking has become its own generic trope, glibly (and irresponsibly) bantered about as "something that happens there," ascribed to the region without reflecting critically on how we draw meanings from drinking and its narrative representations.

Gunther's provocative observation reinforces what he and many others surely suspected all along about a region defined through myriad forms of self-destruction. Indeed, while the drinking mythology Gunther serves up might well apply to representations of other regions, its geographical specificity corresponds, at least in part, to a region often still divided into dry and wet counties.[4] It should not be surprising to find the region's literary landscapes likewise enlivened by drinking or its absence.

As is often the case, popular national narratives of the region often orbit around excess. The most exaggerated versions of southern drinking—either the renegade moonshiner or the teetotaling fundamentalist—are the most commonly represented. *Southern Comforts* takes as its central premise the notion that a critical examination of how alcohol and drinking function throughout southern literature and culture can supplement and enrich these popular dichotomies—or render them useless. As the essays in this collection show, the very dichotomies alluded to by Gunther oversimplify the region's relationship to drinking by absorbing it into narratives of southern exceptionalism that persist to this day.

The list of southern authors with notoriously problematic relationships to alcohol fuels popular mythologies that relate artistic genius to inebriation. If criticism is to move beyond merely reinscribing the figure of the alcoholic southern writer, it must move beyond the author function as a mix of tall tales, intrigue, and focus. For that reason, just as Patricia Yaeger once wondered what it would mean to organize southern literature around Zora Neale Hurston rather than William Faulkner (*Dirt and Desire* 35), we wonder what it would mean to disentangle narratives of drinking from that of authors who drink. Simply identifying a correlation between drinker and region fails to interrogate how alcohol and drinking can both reify and destabilize southern identity. Those narratives have long relied on what Lori Rotskoff calls "cultures of drink," a term circumscribing "the physical setting, social rituals, and cultural meanings of a particular drinking style or situation. It encompasses questions of who drinks, when and where drinking occurs, what beverages are consumed, how drinkers understand their motivations to drink, and how drinkers pursue relationships with fellow drinkers (and often with nondrinkers as well)" (11).

Narrative representations of a southern "culture of drink," however, risk generalizing a complex series of signifiers that expose how such a culture merely perpetuates different forms of inequality. In other words, acknowledging that a culture of drink exists risks accepting a monolithic understanding of what this culture *means*, a dangerous proposition, given how alcohol and drinking, within many cultures, enact and deploy power in the South. Susan Zieger warns of this very effect in her assessment of the metaphoric power of "addiction" throughout nineteenth-century transatlantic cultures: "The central nineteenth-century metaphor of addiction, self-enslavement, activates an entire network of meanings involving chattel slavery, race, and modernity, [and] illuminating them requires a critical tool that does not preserve cultural nationalism. . . . For example, critiquing addiction from the standpoint of the inviolability of a 'drinking culture' would reinscribe the very modes of power that rituals of drinking and addictions more broadly deploy" (10). Indeed, reifying a culture of drink that has historically corresponded to the white, male, elite cultures risks undercutting the possibility of viewing it critically.

Symptomatic of prevailing (and perceived) cultures of drink in the South, both the fictional Jason Compson Sr. and the very real Faulkner struggled with alcoholism. One gesture with respect to how their diseases ultimately consumed them, and others like them, has been to essentialize the connection between the bottle and the person, to refashion alcoholism into its own southern culture of drink. This practice serves almost no critical purpose, and it consigns to alcohol little more significance than benign regional signifier. Anyone who has visited Faulkner's grave in Oxford, Mississippi, has surely seen a bottle of whiskey left by a Faulknerphile. These bestowers of booze gift according to the inflated mythology that reads the author's notorious benders with detached admiration, and not in a more startlingly realistic way that illuminates how hard drinking hindered his relationships and compromised his health—to say nothing of how it signaled his status within hierarchies of race, gender, and class. *Southern Comforts* builds from work in the fields of foodways, southern studies, and alcohol and addiction studies to strip from southern cultural narratives the veneer of nostalgia and myth and thus to uncover what lies hidden under regional signifiers that have received little focused critical attention.

Despite the obvious ways that the South has been understood relative to alcohol, the connection between region and drinking was not the focal point of early critical work in what has come to be called alcohol and addiction studies. Tom Dardis's pioneering work *The Thirsty Muse: Alcohol and the American Writer* (1990) keyed on the relationship between writing and drinking in many (mostly white, mostly male) canonical American modernists, showing how the physiological effects of alcoholism shortened the careers of Faulkner, Ernest Hemingway, F. Scott Fitzgerald, and Eugene O'Neill. Donald W. Goodwin's *Alcohol and the Writer* (1990) applies a psychiatric model to determine reasons behind the frighteningly high percentage of twentieth-century American writers afflicted with alcoholism. More recently, Olivia Laing updates both of these in her biocritical/autobiographical work called *The Trip to Echo Spring: On Writers and Drinking* (2013).

Biocriticism offers fascinating insight into how alcohol catalyzes and ultimately stymies artistic talent, though this critical lens is sometimes reductive and elliptical. Was Faulkner a genius who burned out because of alcoholism, or was alcohol the fuel that allowed him to tap into a heightened state of consciousness? More importantly, what do the answers to such questions tell us about cultural formations that move beyond the author's life? Too narrow a focus on literary biography subordinates texts and the cultures from which they emerge.

As later scholars in the field showed, it is in the *representations* of alcohol and drinking within these texts that revealing critical work can be accomplished. Indeed, John W. Crowley's *The White Logic: Alcoholism and Gender in American Modernist Fiction* (1994) bridges the gap between biographical and literary criticism in connecting disease paradigms of addiction to gendered constructions of alcoholism in canonical American modernist literature. His landmark study evolves the field well past biocriticism, even if it offers little consideration of how region shapes representations of drunkenness. Likewise, Zieger's *Inventing the Addict* (2008) traces how the concept of addiction evolved to mark certain deviant behaviors and populations in nineteenth-century British and American literature.

Biocriticism and southern alcoholic mythmaking fall short of these later works in showing the breadth of scholarly discourse possible in a study of drinking and the South; so too do recent popular investigations that casually graft alcohol and drinking onto hip, artisanal, and stylized portraits of the region. These publications reify cocktail culture as a harbinger of "southern identity," and they gloss over how artisan liquor—locally sourced though it might be—often whitewashes histories of inequality while trumpeting the community-affirming possibilities of a mixed drink. Herein lies a frequent conflict between foodways scholarship and that of southern studies: Consumption of food and drink might reenact community, but what kind of community is it?[5] And from where did that community arise? And who might be excluded from that community? Or, to put it another way, who but the palate-gifted elite invested in performing identity even *acquires* the taste for such consumption?[6]

Southern Comforts does not attempt to undermine the work of these publications or to dismiss their work as unimportant, but it does draw attention to how contemporary southern popular culture packages and sells alcohol and drinking in a way that privileges palatable consumption at the expense of historical, critical, and theoretical understanding. A proliferation of books, magazines, blogs, and reality television shows centralize drinking within southern culture, and many rely clumsily on loose references to the past to fuel their representations of southern drinking.

One popular online publication, *The Bitter Southerner,* narrates its genesis with a heavy emphasis on cocktail culture. In the site's mission statement, editor Chuck Reece recounts a week in New Orleans, spent among the city's most renowned bartenders. Feeling slighted that no New Orleans bars were featured that year in *Drinks International*'s World's 50 Best Bars list, Reece "decided somebody needed to show the world our region's drinking secrets." Emboldened, Reece set out to share the South "that we know: a South that is full of people who do things that honor genuinely honorable traditions. Drinking. Cooking. Reading. Writing. Singing. Playing. Making things." He promises that "over time, you'll see many pieces about bartenders, because (a) that's where we started and (b) we very much enjoy a great cocktail. After all, one Southern tradition worthy of honor is the act of drinking well."

To be fair, the mission statement is intended for readers committed to "throw[ing] our dishonorable traditions out the window," but claiming drinking as a "tradition worthy of honor" cloaks troubled histories related to alcohol's production, circulation, and consumption in romantic nostalgia, as if the cocktail represents the best hope for an always already-in-production New South. Even here, as the online publication distances itself from rebel flags and states' rights, it categorizes alcohol and drinking as an honorable tradition, a phrase that should itself raise red flags.[7] This branding of cocktail culture enlivens histories about southern drinking just enough to position them in the shadow of artisan bourbon bottles, blinding us to nefarious forces that have long informed southern cultures of producing and consuming alcohol. The fact that *The Bitter Southerner*'s mission statement invites interrogation of "the South" while celebrating drinking as a benign marker of "honor" raises questions rather than offering answers about whether it is possible to consume ideologies of southern honor free from the politically charged material we must associate with such a concept. We have found that the production, circulation, and consumption of alcohol have expanded and undermined the social orders of the region. Far from being ornamental objects in the many Souths, drinks help us to understand those Souths.

As the first book-length collection critically investigating the symbiotic relationship between drinking and the South, *Southern Comforts* seeks both to fill a void in contemporary scholarship and to redirect public criticism about southern foodways—an interdisciplinary field that garners attention from a variety of reading publics. In *Writing in the Kitchen: Essays on Southern Literature and Foodways,* David A. Davis and Tara Powell argue that "the self-conscious act of preparing or eating traditional southern food . . . is a deliberate act of performing southern identity," even if such consumption includes fried chicken mass produced and marketed globally (14).

Performing identity, of course, requires a commitment to a (real or imagined) set of rules pertaining to what is "southern," an inherently slippery slope for scholars working in the most recent iterations of southern studies. The turn to what critics have termed new southern studies was, in fact, typified by rejecting the notion that "southern" denotes anything beyond an imagined fantasy. Southern, in this formulation, is a longing to cohere. It is a set of desires that are historical—and very often exclusionary. The task for new southern studies has often been "to examine the sorts of present people actually live in, rather than to continue to consume fantasies overdetermined by symbolic investments in the future or the past" (Smith 30). In other words, reifying the cultural history of a cocktail does not inure us from the responsibility of admitting what *else* happened in the past. If a cocktail is another object that we treat as a signifier of identity formation, then we must "come to understand what leads [us] to seek out such objects . . . and invest so much in them" (34). Our critical investment in alcohol and drinking must do more than show cocktail culture in the South as merely another commodified libidinal investment in the past under the rubric of "bitterness." Critical analyses of alcohol and drinking should help bridge the disconnect between what southern studies sees as the myriad and meaningful complexities of the many Souths and how popular narratives often represent the region through benign portraits of consumption.

One path that clarifies the distance between critical and popular conceptions of the region focuses on the contrast between alcoholism and temperance. Whether these terms relate to states of sobriety or to ideological positions relative to social-political debates about public health and individual morality, both alcoholism and temperance illustrate how drinking in the South has long been a flash point for debate and division. Indeed, alcoholism and temperance have framed and signaled wider discourses about race, class, and gender in the South. Furthermore, the conditions under which these terms are deployed illuminate how the act of drinking has operated as a stand-in for other cultural ills in the region.

Each of the essays in part 1, "Alcoholism, Temperance, and the South," views alcohol and drinking, and the cultural politics inscribed onto them, as catalysts for social change. By focusing on lyrics by black blueswomen like Ma Rainey, Alison Arant shows how Prohibition-era songs about drinking upend our understanding of drinking as gendered activity. In so doing, Arant implores critics to see the restrictive racial and gendered structures of temperance movements. John Stromski reads the ideological tension in Charles Chesnutt's fictionalized representation of the Wilmington race riots to show how temperance politics of the day might be understood as a function of broader, racist power structures. Susan Zieger investigates how the temperance cause related to novelist and activist Frances E. W. Harper's black feminist political vision of a renewed public sphere. Harper's vision, Zieger writes, redirects our understanding of black temperance movements more generally. Orson Welles's 1958 *Touch of Evil* is the focus of Cara Koehler's essay, which argues that the film's discourses around alcohol abuse function as an allegory of power along the U.S.–Mexico border during the postwar years. Finally, Matthew Sutton reads the autobiographies of Johnny Cash and George Jones, two of country music's most notorious alcoholics, as examples of what he terms the "Tennessee Two-Step," a co-opting of language from Alcoholics Anonymous that downplays the dual self-portrayal of the southern hell-raiser and the reflective, repentant alcoholic. In each of these essays, discourses around temperance and alcoholism complicate our understanding of the broader social conditions in which the texts under investigation operate.

Narrative fictions of excessive drinking are a distinct genre unto themselves, and scholars in alcohol and addiction studies have traced how fictional representations of extreme drunkenness reflect broader concerns about drinking and public health.[8] Similarly, the essays in part 2, "Revising Narrative through Intoxication," centralize drunkenness in their analysis, examining how excessive drinking destabilizes the body politic by pointing to social-historical contexts and theories of literary form. In each of these essays, intoxication rots the guts of the consumers, but, more importantly, it reveals the cracks in the foundations of hegemonic institutions—plantations, domestic spheres, political movements, and entire communities.

Excessive drinking clarifies context in essays by Katharine A. Burnett, Ellen Lansky, and Caleb Doan and J. Gerald Kennedy. Burnett examines how white masculine privilege expressed through ubiquitous intoxication became a way to illustrate the impending ruin of the nineteenth-century Virginia plantation economy. In her reading of Richard Wright's *Native Son* (1940), Lansky shows how the tenuous social boundaries between black men and white women become dangerously permeable when both are drunk, and lowered inhibitions reframe this social "threat" as one that targets all women. Doan and Kennedy pressure Edgar Allan Poe's public disdain for the "heresy of the didactic" in their examination of how his intoxicated characters mirror ideological tension within and beyond the region. In the end, they conclude, Poe's dramatization of intemperance might be instructive after all.

Contributions by Monica C. Miller, Zackary Vernon, and David A. Davis show how expressions of intoxication signal competing theories of form. The pseudo "interleckshul" dialogue bantered about at cocktail parties became a means for Flannery O'Connor to frame a debate between metaphoric and anagogic understandings of meaning-making, according to Miller. Vernon coins the term "inebriated adaptation" to interpret the cinematic aesthetics of a big-screen adaptation of Larry Brown's *Big Bad Love* (1990). Finally, Davis argues that the oddities punctuating the drunken melee of Carson McCullers's "The Ballad of the Sad Café" (1951) point to a surrealist aesthetics that pressures popular representations of the story as Southern Gothic, and he suggests a new framework, which he terms "surregionalism." Rather than treating excessive drinking as something to be mythologized through larger-than-life figures or under the often banal rubric of storytelling, the authors in this section specify how excessive drinking works with and against prevailing narrative practices.

Iconic representations of drinking and the South often center on alcohol's illegality and the means through which it is produced and circulated despite the legislative and/or cultural prohibitions that serve as obstacles. As contraband booze transgresses literal and metaphoric lines of demarcation, its value to both producers and consumers shifts. The essays in part 3, "Alcohol's Production, Commodification, and Circulation in the South," consider alcohol as a material product, the movement and consumption of which helps critics to index evolving power structures. The high demand for contraband liquor affords those who produce and consume it a measure of social currency that often cuts against the grain of the status quo.

Jenna Grace Sciuto traces how the racial ambiguity of three of William Faulkner's most iconic bootleggers undermines plantation hierarchies. Using gender as the category undergoing conceptual revision in three on-screen representations, Jerod Hollyfield identifies a shift in the position of women bootleggers by focusing on how they forcefully and successfully respond to transnational corporate power structures that exploit the region. Comparing works about bootlegging by authors with wide-ranging regional affiliations, Christopher Rieger argues that representations of bootlegging in novels by Marjorie Kinnan Rawlings and Ernest Hemingway help root these novels in vastly different versions of Florida in the 1930s.

Perhaps no other place in the South is perceived to have such a storied and complicated cultural history of drinking as New Orleans. Robert Rea argues that surreal scene callbacks to *Gone with the Wind* (1936) in *A Confederacy of Dunces* (1980) correspond to the stereotypical versions of the South upon which midcentury Bourbon Street tourism built its foundations. Hannah Griggs notes parallels between the popularity, obscurity, and resurgence of New Orleans's Ojen Cocktail and the city's reinforcement of racist social hierarchies. *Southern Comforts* concludes with a sobering account of the "Katrina Hangover," the national phenomenon of forgetting about what *else* was lost during and after the storm, as disaster capitalism set in. In "W's Good Time," Jennie Lightweis-Goff reads post-Katrina New Orleans through the lenses of three gendered representations: the Belle, the Quadroon, and the Storyville sex worker.

Like many overdetermined cultural centers associated with the region, contemporary depictions of and affiliations with alcohol and drinking often obscure as much as they purport to reveal. As the critical discourse of this book navigates between and among these conversations—currently under way across foodways, southern studies, and publics outside of the academy—it asserts that mythologies of drinking have rarely availed themselves of rigorous critique. Alcohol is even more difficult to associate with harbingers of positive consumption, such as benevolent knowledge and community, than cornbread, barbecue, and sweet tea. Unlike food, alcohol does not even offer nourishment. For us, the material differences between food and drink offer space and opportunity to reinvigorate and reorient conversations about consumption writ large. This work is important and consequential.

Let us return, by way of example, to Nearest Green. Fawn Weaver has led the effort to recognize Green's place in the history of Jack Daniel's. Weaver re-released a 1967 biography of Daniel in 2017, in part because it locates Green as a central figure in Daniel's life. Weaver and her husband, Keith, began the Nearest Green Foundation to spread the word about Green and to "shine a light" on those "who toiled without recognition" (nearestgreen.com). The foundation has established a scholarship to send descendants of Green to college, and in February 2018 it bought out theater screenings in six cities to allow disadvantaged teenagers to see *Black Panther*. In short, the recently formed foundation was designed to draw attention to long-forgotten and often-ignored successes by African Americans in the name of one of the most successful and least acknowledged black distillers.

For their part, the Jack Daniel's brand has begun to acknowledge Green's central place in the company's history—albeit suspiciously late in the story. The labor provided by Weaver, however, pushed one of the South's (and, indeed, the world's) most famous distilleries to finally acknowledge its roots, if not the effects of obscuring those roots for so long. While this recognition may seem minimal, late, and, of course, *convenient* within critical conversations about the region, it evinces the potential of the rigorous work of scholarship.

The connections between drinking and the South that crystallize in this collection not only show the breadth of critical approaches enlivened through this focus but also point toward the potential of scholarship to meet people where they are. This collection offers an intervention into several academic discourses, and we hope it will also find a home in both public libraries and public houses. Because drinking occurs across cultures and social settings, investigations of drinking must engage and enrich a broad public's understanding of the world in which they live and the forces that have long shaped it. In spite of the fact that there are Souths that garner little attention in the eighteen essays that follow, we hope to have reinvigorated conversations that will move beyond these works.

Notes

1. Clay Risen authored two articles on the Nearest Green–Jack Daniel's story for the *New York Times*, each of which references the man seated next to Jack Daniel in the photograph. Referencing the photograph in the June 25, 2016, article, Risen writes, "In a photo of Daniel and his workers taken in the late 19th century, a black man, possibly one of Green's sons, sits at his immediate

right." Risen's second take on the Green–Daniel's story, published on August 5, 2017, hedges less on the man's identity: "The man to his right could be Nearest Green, a slave who helped teach Jack Daniel how to make whiskey, or one of Green's sons" ("When Jack Daniel's Failed"). The text accompanying the photograph on the Jack Daniel's website offers this: "The man in the photograph above, we have reason to believe, is George Green. Along with being Jack's friend, George was also the son of Nathan 'Nearest' Green."

2. Given that southern cultures are so frequently tied to mythologies, it should not be surprising that many such mythologies have fallen under critical investigation in recent years. One recent example is Anthony Szczesiul's *The Southern Hospitality Myth: Ethics, Politics, Race, and American Memory* (2017). The book unpacks how and why "hospitality"—an idea with foundations in "antebellum planters' social practices in a slave economy"—functions through erasure, covering up the very histories it would seem to index by its frequent connection to the region (2).

3. Others have explored how the myths informing consumption in the South omit representative populations. In *A Mess of Greens: Southern Gender and Southern Food* (2011), Elizabeth Engelhardt challenges the gendered stereotypes put forth in representations of moonshiners: "Women and people of color produced and distributed moonshine," though "women in moonshine have been doubly erased, first by a focus on the stereotyped male image and second by the resulting flattened approach" (25–26).

4. An article published in *Washington Post* visually illustrates the frequency of dry counties in the southeastern United States, noting that, at the time of publication, thirty-seven of seventy-five counties in Arkansas, in particular, were dry (Schwarz).

5. The answer: a coercive one, according to Scott Romine, and not a cohesive one (2). Communities, by their definition, have to exclude. Romine's *The Narrative Forms of Southern Community* challenges the very "commonality" around which communities sometimes cohere. Where communities cohere around a common set of beliefs and practices, they also tend to ignore the socially divisive function of these blindly accepted beliefs.

6. This recalls Margot Finn's observation in *Discriminating Taste* of the parallels between contemporary food culture and those of the Gilded Age (1870–1900), a name referring to "the excesses and pretensions of the newly rich" (52). She notes that "what the new trends in the Gilded Age have in common is that they were all ways of performing a certain kind of status" (51). Finn sees contemporary American food culture not as an expression of higher ideals about food reform but rather as a response to deep-seated class anxiety that manifests itself through the framework of taste.

7. Others have followed *The Bitter Southerner* in casting drinking as a somewhat uncomplicated regional practice to be continued as such. The editors of *Garden and Gun* recently published *S Is for Southern: A Guide to the South from Absinthe to Zydeco* (Harper Wave 2017), a culinary-inflected cultural tour of the region that warns in its press kit, "Tennessee whiskey may technically be bourbon, but don't let anyone in Kentucky hear you call it that." Similarly, Robert F. Moss, in *Southern Spirits: Four Hundred Years of Drinking in the American South, with Recipes* (Ten Speed 2016), "challenges the stereotypes of Southern drinking culture, including the ubiquity of bourbon and the geographic definition of the South itself, and reveals how that culture has shaped the South and America as a whole." These texts often focus on a central question—Is drinking southern?—without questioning why these sorts of affiliations are important and meaningful.

8. T. S. Arthur's best-selling *Ten Nights in a Bar-Room and What I Saw There* (1854) fictionalized the horrors of excess to promote the temperance politics of the day. See John W. Crowley's *Drunk-*

ard's Progress: Narratives of Addiction, Despair, and Recovery and Matthew J. Raphael's Bill W. and Mr. Wilson: The Legend and Life of A.A.'s Cofounder for more on how generic tropes in temperance narratives derived from the Washington Society and were later appropriated by Alcoholics Anonymous as recovery narratives. In The White Logic: Alcoholism and Gender in American Modernist Fiction, Crowley later coins the term "drunk narrative," describing it as a feature in many modernist texts that centralize drinking as "the modernist ethos of despair" (44).

Works Cited

Arthur, T. S. Ten Nights in a Bar-Room and What I Saw There. 1854. Edited by C. Hugh Holman, Odyssey Press, 1966.

Barr, Andrew. Drink: A Social History of America. Carroll and Graf, 1999.

Crowley, John W. The White Logic: Alcoholism and Gender in American Modernist Fiction. U of Massachusetts P, 1994.

——, editor. Drunkard's Progress: Narratives of Addiction, Despair, and Recovery. Johns Hopkins UP, 1999.

Dardis, Tom. The Thirsty Muse: Alcohol and the American Writer. Houghton Mifflin, 1991.

Davis, David A., and Tara Powell, editors. Writing in the Kitchen: Essays on Southern Literature and Foodways. UP of Mississippi, 2014.

Davis, Thadious M. Southscapes: Geographies of Race, Region, and Literature. U of North Carolina P, 2011.

Engelhardt, Elizabeth S. D. A Mess of Greens: Southern Gender and Southern Food. U of Georgia P, 2011.

Finn, S. Margot. Discriminating Taste: How Class Anxiety Created the American Food Revolution. Rutgers UP, 2017.

Goodwin, Donald W. Alcohol and the Writer. Penguin, 1990.

Green, Ben A. Jack Daniel's Legacy: 50th Anniversary Edition. Grant Sidney, 2017.

Hayes, Annie. "The Top 10 Best-Selling World Whisky Brands." The Spirits Business, 26 June 2017, www.thespiritsbusiness.com/2017/06/the-top-10-best-selling-world-whisky-brands/11.

Hinrichsen, Lisa, Gina Caison, and Stephanie Rountree, editors. Small-Screen Souths: Region, Identity, and the Cultural Politics of Television. Louisiana State UP, 2017.

Knepper, Steven E. "Ecology/Environment." Keywords for Southern Studies, edited by Scott Romine and Jennifer Rae Greeson, U of Georgia P, 2016, pp. 264–75.

Laing, Olivia. The Trip to Echo Spring: On Writers and Drinking. Picador, 2013.

"Nearest Green: Jack Daniel's First Master Distiller." Jack Daniel's, www.jackdaniels.com /en-us/vault/how-jack-daniel-came-make-whiskey.

Raphael, Matthew J. Bill W. and Mr. Wilson: The Legend and Life of A.A.'s Cofounder. U of Massachusetts P, 2000.

Reese, Chuck. "Why We Created the *Bitter Southerner* in the First Place." *Bitter Southerner,* 6 August 2013, bittersoutherner.com/we-are-bitter.

Risen, Clay. "Jack Daniel's Embraces Hidden Ingredient: Help from a Slave." *New York Times,* 25 June 2016.

———. "When Jack Daniel's Failed to Honor a Slave, an Author Rewrote History." *New York Times,* 15 August 2017.

Romine, Scott. *The Narrative Forms of Southern Community.* Louisiana State UP, 1999.

———. *The Real South: Southern Narrative in the Age of Cultural Reproduction.* Louisiana State UP, 2008.

Rotskoff, Lori. *Love on the Rocks: Men, Women, and Alcohol in Post–World War II America.* U of North Carolina P, 2002.

Schwarz, Hunter. "Where in the United States You Can't Purchase Alcohol." *Washington Post,* 2 September 2014.

Smith, Jon. *Finding Purple America: The South and the Future of American Cultural Studies.* U of Georgia P, 2013.

"The Story of Nearest Green," narrated by Jeffrey Wright. *nearestgreen.com,* 21 March 2019.

Szczesiul, Anthony. *The Southern Hospitality Myth: Ethics, Politics, Race, and American Memory.* U of Georgia P, 2017.

Yaeger, Patricia. *Dirt and Desire: Reconstructing Southern Women's Writing, 1930–1990.* U of Chicago P, 2000.

Zieger, Susan. *Inventing the Addict: Drugs, Race, and Sexuality in Nineteenth-Century British and American Literature.* U of Massachusetts P, 2008.

PART I

ALCOHOLISM, TEMPERANCE,
AND THE SOUTH

Mama Likes Her Gin

Black Blueswomen, Freedom, and Alcohol
in the Prohibition South

ALISON ARANT

In "Moonshine Blues," recorded in Chicago in December 1923 (Laird 433), Gertrude "Ma" Rainey belts out a confession: "I been drinkin' all night, babe, and the night before / But when I get sober, I ain't gon' drink no more / 'Cause my friend left me, standin' in my door." From there, the song, written by Rainey herself, outlines a plan to "catch the first train that's running South bound." She sings, "I'm going home, I'm going to settle down / I'm going to stop my runnin' around / Tell everybody that comes my way / I've got them moonshine blues, I say, I've got them moonshine blues" (transcribed in Davis 234).

From a contemporary standpoint, Rainey's song seems like a typical rendition of the blues, articulating lost love, travel plans, and a hangover; however, in the moment of its composition, "Moonshine Blues" challenged two major cultural movements that were under way. First, the song was recorded just three years after the Eighteenth Amendment to the United States Constitution and the Volstead Act prohibited intoxicating beverages. Thus, the song runs afoul of federal law in its description of drinking illegal liquor. Second, in the singer's fantasy of catching the first Southbound train, she imagines moving contrary to the flow of the Great Migration, which brought large numbers of African Americans from rural and southern places to urban and often northern ones in the early decades of the twentieth century.

Rainey's song isn't alone in its violation of the frameworks established by Prohibition and the Great Migration. In this essay, I show how black blueswomen articulate their relationships to alcohol and the U.S. South despite the hazards associated with both. Furthermore, I argue that, in doing so, they revise notions of racial progress, pursuing freedom through emotional catharsis rather than through middle-class respectability.

By examining the particular risks black blueswomen take in their representations of both alcohol and the U.S. South, this essay intervenes in two critical conversations, broadening one and offering a corrective to the other. First, I extend feminist scholarship that has worked since the 1980s and 1990s to recover the legacies of black blueswomen. The research of Daphne Duval Harrison and Angela Davis has demonstrated the magnitude of blueswomen's contributions to American music and the ways in which race- and gender-based prejudice erased them from popular and scholarly blues histories. In *Blues Legacies and Black Feminism,* Davis focuses on Ma Rainey, Bessie Smith, and Billie Holiday, arguing that their music gives voice to working-class freedom with regard to travel, sexuality, and entertainment, experiences that were possible in new ways after emancipation. Davis also explores the class tensions manifest in the blues, showing how celebrating these freedoms put black working-class singers at odds with black middle-class narratives of racial uplift (Davis 42–43). Davis, however, does not address what I consider a significant component of early black women's blues: the symbolically loaded idea of alcohol in the South during Prohibition. Thus, my essay reveals how the taboos associated with alcohol affected the social stakes of black women's blues.

Second, my essay corrects cultural and literary studies of alcohol that foreground and sometimes naturalize whiteness, consequently obscuring black relationships to alcohol. One example is John W. Crowley's 1994 book *The White Logic: Alcoholism and Gender in American Modernist Fiction,* which was pivotal in advancing studies of alcohol in literature. Crowley explicitly considers the links between alcoholism, masculinity, and literary modernism; however, his archive only includes white writers, which mistakenly gives the impression that these dynamics primarily concern white people. More recently, in *Love on the Rocks: Men, Women, and Alcohol in Post–World War II America* (2002), Lori Rotskoff directly addresses the racialization of alcohol. She notes that in postwar films, books, advertisements, and recovery discourse, the typical depictions of drinkers are "overwhelmingly white," though she argues that this emphasis on whiteness is "itself an artifact of the dominant culture being addressed" (10).

In contrast to these models, some scholars are moving away from cultural studies of alcohol that center whiteness. One example is Michael A. Lerner's 2007 treatment of hooch in Harlem in his study of Prohibition in New York City. Like the Harlem dynamics Lerner establishes, the black blues archive offers additional evidence of the frequency of black engagements with alcohol both before and after World War II. Studies of alcohol in contemporaneous black literature and films would further prove the point, though such work is beyond my purview here.[1] Nevertheless, this essay helps to demonstrate how the apparent whiteness of alcohol in cultural and literary studies is a function of scholarly practice and not reflective of history itself.

In order to evaluate the intersecting political valences of alcohol and the South in songs like Rainey's "Moonshine Blues," I examine four historical contexts that come to bear on the blues music of working-class black women in the 1920s and 1930s. First, I outline the discourse on racial blackness that informed white supremacist arguments for temperance in the South. Second, I show how some black temperance advocates linked abstinence from alcohol with racial uplift. Third, I establish the ways in which temperance discourse gendered alcohol as male and abstinence as female. Finally, I consider how racial uplift rhetoric at times framed the South as retrograde to black progress while also paradoxically relying on southern music for emotional catharsis. Together, these contexts enable my close reading of blues lyrics from the Prohibition era, which show how black blueswomen honestly address their complicated relationships to alcohol and the South despite the stigmas associated with both.

I argue that, in articulating their relationships to alcohol and the South amid these contexts, black blueswomen defy the repressive ideology of Jim Crow, repudiate the restrictive aspects of black middle-class aspirations, and dismantle gendered representations of alcohol. Though many blueswomen came from the South and migrated North, often to stay, they generally maintain links to the South through their songs and personas. In this way, women blues singers articulate what Mark K. Dolan might call a cathartic form of uplift (122–23), which is different from racial uplift in its ideals and relationship to freedom. Black blueswomen don't deny the drawbacks of drinking hard liquor, nor do they downplay the dangers of being black in the South; however, their emotional honesty about the benefits and the risks of both alcohol and the South evince a changing understanding of black freedom.

Prohibition and the Black Beast

The temperance movement, which began in the nineteenth century and culminated in national Prohibition from 1920–1933, had a complex relationship to racial blackness in the United States. Denise Herd traces the connections between the abolition debate and arguments for temperance throughout the nineteenth century. Though these two movements had a somewhat paradoxical relationship to each other, Herd shows that by the early twentieth century, white people in the South and in the nation as a whole cited alcohol as part of a narrative that criminalized black people, framing black freedom as a social danger. Informed by a larger discourse of white supremacy, these Prohibition advocates argued that national safety depended on controlling black access to alcohol—and other forms of freedom more generally. Herd writes, "Divergent concerns about black savagery, alcohol disinhibition, and social disorder converge in the image of the drunken black beast" (366). White people used this myth to justify lynching black people and to attempt to erase the systematic sexual violation of black people in slavery and afterward.

Melodramatic editorialists who argued for Prohibition in the South also invoked the black beast stereotype. For example, in a 1907 opinion piece titled "The Prohibition Wave in the South," John Corrigan writes, "A moment's reflection will serve to recall the terrible conditions of affairs that prevailed when swarms of negroes, many of them drunk with whisky, and all intoxicated with the delirium of new-found liberty, roamed the country at large" (329). Corrigan connects "affairs" like these to Georgia's 1907 adoption of a statewide prohibition of alcohol. He argues that Georgia's new law "directs national attention to the marvelous progress of this idea in the Southern States" (328). Here, Corrigan associates the dangers of drunkenness with a more generalized intoxication of emancipation, suggesting that both forms of freedom are too dangerous for black people and that regional and national safety depend on limits to black freedom.

The 1915 release of *The Birth of a Nation* helped to inflate the myth of the black predator emboldened by alcohol. Directed by D. W. Griffith, a Prohibition advocate, the film, viewed by more than fifty million Americans, "portrayed black people as drunken criminals and sexual beasts whose alcoholic sprees threatened to upset the social order of the entire nation" (Drowne 20). In response to this threat, the film stages national unification as the result of black subjugation. In other words, the nation is born when the North and the South realize that the drunken black rapist is what divided them all along (Morone 294). Those familiar with the film will also remember that its release caused a renewal of the Ku Klux Klan, which received a society charter from the state of Georgia in 1915, and by 1924, the Klan had more than two million national members (Drowne 21). Thus, this component of temperance discourse relied on criminalizing black consumption of alcohol.

Temperance and Racial Uplift Ideology

These strains of white temperance discourse relied heavily on racist stereotypes to further the cause of Prohibition, but black proponents supported the movement for reasons of their own. One important factor in the conversation around black support for Prohibition involved the notion of racial uplift, a nineteenth-century ideology that "refuted racist stereotypes of African Americans as biologically inferior by stressing the respectability of an African American elite and the evolutionary progress of the African American masses only a generation after slavery" (Wolcott 6). Though the values of white middle-class America informed the idea of black respectability, Victoria Wolcott argues that it took on forms that were particular to African American communities. She cites sexual restraint, cleanliness, and orderliness as elements specific to the discourse of respectability for black women (6). Within this framework, self-discipline was the likeliest way for black people to achieve freedom.

This class-based approach to black enfranchisement had divisive effects, at times engendering painful ideological rifts within black communities around questions of restraint and freedom, tensions that also inform my reading of blues music of the time. The issue of black women's support for Prohibition became a flash point in the 1928 presidential election. The rhetoric of racial uplift had largely lost traction by the early twentieth century, but black temperance women revived it in order to rally northern black voters in support of Herbert Hoover, the Republican candidate and a Prohibitionist. Though only about one-third of African Americans of voting age were living in the North, this temperance campaign focused on them because African Americans living in the South were prevented from voting despite having the legal right (Weiss xv). Because of the Republican Party's disappointing voting record on black rights, and its resistance to the involvement of black leadership, black voters, once Republican because of abolition, increasingly realigned themselves with Democrats.

In an attempt to bolster support for Hoover, black Republican women argued for a constitutional slippery slope: repealing the Eighteenth Amendment and ending Prohibition might make way for a repeal of the Reconstruction Amendments—the Thirteenth Amendment, which abolished slavery; the Fourteenth Amendment, which rooted citizenship in federal and not state jurisdiction; and the Fifteenth Amendment, which gave voting rights to black men (Materson 65). The argument was that, in fighting to gain the freedom to drink, black people might lose their constitutional right to the freedoms established in Reconstruction.

In response to arguments like these, black working-class women increasingly doubted that black middle-class women could represent their interests in national politics, and they questioned the Republican premise that alcohol was the real issue. Materson explains: "Black Republican women accused black Democrats—that is, poor black Democrats—of switching parties simply because they wanted a drink. They also insisted that Democratic voters who were willing to put their enjoyment of the vibrant leisure culture of 1920s America before the Reconstruction Amendments had betrayed the race and were in need of middle-class women's guidance" (65).

Though black Republican women argued that they were working for the good of the race, their strategy backfired. By impugning the motives of black Democratic women and framing themselves as morality bearers, middle-class Republican women reinforced the notion that the Republican Party had lost touch with the average black voter (Materson 66). In this way, the 1928 election demonstrates a widening gap between middle-class and working-class understandings of black freedom and whether its best manifestations were self-denial or self-gratification.

Gender and Alcohol

In addition to the way alcohol signified on racial blackness and class status in the Prohibition era, drinking also carried implications for gender, which come to bear on blueswomen's representations of alcohol. Throughout U.S. history, alcohol has been gendered masculine (Rotskoff 4). Statistically, men drank far more than women, and, as temperance advocates argued, men's drinking often revealed the legal, financial, and physical vulnerability of women and children in family contexts (Mattingly 14). Furthermore, temperance advocacy often converged with arguments for women's suffrage. Both the Eighteenth and Nineteenth Amendments took effect in 1920, and for organizations like the Woman's Christian Temperance Union (WCTU), as long as women had the vote, Prohibition would stand ("Protecting the Eighteenth Amendment with the Nineteenth," cited in Rose).

Additionally, alcohol itself was often personified as male. For example, the name John Barleycorn became a euphemism for grain-derived alcohol, and this figure appeared frequently in songs and literature before and during Prohibition. Jack London took *John Barleycorn* as the title of his 1913 alcoholic memoir, claiming "John Barleycorn is everywhere the connotation of manliness" (cited in Crowley 28). Associations like these contributed to the impression that alcohol itself was masculine.

In conjunction with this masculinization of alcohol, women became associated with temperance and abstinence. Becky M. Nicolaides writes, "Both through historical expression and omission, women have been portrayed as alcohol's adversaries and rarely its partakers" (1211). To show how these beliefs shaped the country's policies, Nicolaides examines laws that reinscribed the gendered binary that framed drinking as masculine and temperance as feminine. She argues that during the nineteenth century, women's consumption of alcohol was increasingly taboo because of class-based ideology that relegated women to the private sphere of the home while designating public spaces, including saloons and taverns, as the sphere of men (1213). The temperance movement further reinforced these associations, especially through figures like Frances Willard, who was president of the WCTU, or Carrie Nation, who gained national notoriety by wielding a hatchet in opposition to saloons. Such gendered notions of both drinking and abstinence shape the stakes of black women's representation of alcohol in the blues.

The South and Black Progress

Arguments over race, class, and gender shaped responses to Prohibition, and region also played a role in the discourse around progress for African Americans. As Mark K. Dolan demonstrates, many proponents of racial uplift argued that, if black people were to advance, it was necessary to leave the South and its violence behind and move North to new opportunities. However, even as large numbers of African Americans migrated from the rural South to the urban North in hopes of advancement, the blues offered a link to the South that had ongoing appeal.

Black newspapers show how such tensions played out in ads for blues albums, known at the time as "race records." In the *Chicago Defender*, the first black newspaper with a national circulation, editorials argued stridently that northern migration was essential for black enfranchisement; however, the paper also regularly featured advertisements for blues records that sometimes represented the South in nostalgic terms (Dolan 107). Thus, there was a contradiction between explicit prescriptions for southern exodus and implicit reliance on southern cultural forms. Dolan notes that references to the South appear in 148 song titles advertised in the *Defender* during the decade of the 1920s. While some of these songs rely on racial stereotyping, they simultaneously signal an effort to connect the paper's black readership to music that may have been important to them (108–9).

Though the southern attachments and fantasies embedded in blues ads were sometimes visibly at odds with the rhetoric of racial uplift, they also contained an alternative notion of freedom that offered surprising benefits. As the North failed to deliver on the promises of the Great Migration, blues records offered an emotional release through expression and recollection. Dolan writes, "The quantity and duration of the ads suggests that readers snubbed editors and seized a new uplift of their own. Their uplift captured a growing emotional freedom and self-expression, made new music, and opened a safety valve necessary for newfound city dwelling—ironically expressed in a music that had itself migrated from the South and kept the region well within its gaze" (123).

These blues ads, in other words, signal a shift in the black press, away from specific behavioral prescriptions and toward an awareness that readers should use the newspaper according to their own desires and not those of the editorial board. Though life in the South posed threats to the safety and opportunities of black people, the complex cultural relationships articulated in blues traditions offered support for those experiencing hardship, regardless of their geographic location.

The Blues' Cathartic Uplift

Some of the songs I analyze seem almost explicit in their references to the negative representations I have outlined thus far, stigmas that would frame the singers and their choices in a damning light. These songs, however, need not engage their social contexts in an overt way to register a political response to restrictive contemporaneous social forces. By singing songs that articulate complex desires that were taboo within white and black middle-class frameworks, blueswomen offer an alternative to racial uplift ideology. More specifically, in their engagements with alcohol and the South in the context of Prohibition, black women's blues perform a cathartic uplift that insists on experiences and expressions of pleasure and pain as manifestations of freedom. Though their audiences were perhaps reading the *Chicago Defender* editorials promoting northern migration and Victorian middle-class values, the paper's ads on the next page also signal the way blues songs, with their shameless treatments of sex and alcohol, mitigate the inevitable disappointments of life—North, South, or otherwise—offering pleasures of their own.

Mixed feelings about both alcohol and the South characterize "Moonshine Blues," the Ma Rainey song that framed my opening. I return to this 1923 hit in order to show how, in the contexts of Prohibition and the Great Migration, it speaks to contemporaneous anxieties about illegal drinking and the South, framing both as potentially problematic, but not in a totalizing way and not necessarily for the reasons cited by advocates of temperance or northern migration. For Rainey, moonshine is complicated—part problem, part solution:

> I been drinkin' all night, babe, and the night before
> But when I get sober, I ain't gonna drink no more
> 'Cause my friend left me, standin' in my door.

Rainey's opening lines describe a two-day alcoholic binge as her response to the abrupt departure of a lover; however, this tercet also includes her resolution to give up drinking liquor, which is possibly the reason for the speaker's relational troubles in the first place. It is unclear whether the phrase "'Cause my friend left me" explains why she has been drinking or why she now forswears alcohol, or both, but it is clear that drinking moonshine simultaneously relieves and heightens her feelings of sadness. In this song, her negative feelings stem not from the perceived loss of political standing or fear of reinforcing negative stereotypes about black women or fear of punishment for violating Prohibition, as some temperance and racial uplift proponents would suggest. Rather, her feelings stem from her individual situation, which she only partially explains to listeners. Though the song engages these broader cultural tensions, they do not overdetermine the speaker's response to her circumstances. Rather, she names both the risks and benefits of drinking moonshine in the age of Prohibition.

The song also exhibits conflicting information regarding whether the speaker considers the South to be home and whether it would be comforting to go there:

My head goes 'round and around, babe, since my daddy left town
I don't know if the river runnin' up or down
But there's one thing certain, it's mama's going to leave town

You'll find me wrigglin' and a-rockin', howlin' like a hound
Catch the first train that's running South bound

Oh, stop you'll hear me say, stop right to my brain
Oh, stop that train, so I can ride back home again

. . .

I'm going home, I'm going to settle down
I'm going to stop my running around.
(Rainey, transcribed in Davis 234)

The lyrics seem to frame the South as home and not home all at once. The speaker plans to catch a train headed South, but in the next line she mentions trying to stop the train so she can go home. Depending on the sequence of events, which is a bit unclear, it is difficult to say whether "going home" means aborting the trip South or completing it. Furthermore, while listeners could interpret the song's reference to not knowing whether the river runs up or down as evidence of the disorientation of drunkenness, it is also possible that it demonstrates a geographic dislocation that simultaneously figures home in the South and in the North without an easy or stable relationship to either. In fact, the song's suggestion that the North is a site of drunkenness and disappointment refutes the narrative that northern migration results in black uplift. Thus, while neither the South nor the North offer the hope of progress in this song, its lyrics suggest that some black blues singers still look to the South to ease their suffering through emotional recollection, if not also through literal travel.

Lovie Austin's 1923 "Barrel House Blues" does not take up the regional tensions associated with the Great Migration, but the song does engage Prohibition-era taboos regarding women and alcohol consumption:

Got the barrel house blues, feelin' awf'ly dry [Repeats]
I can't drink moonshine, 'cause I'm afraid I'd die

Papa likes his sherry, mama likes her port [Repeats]
Papa likes to shimmy, mama likes to sport

Papa likes his bourbon, mama likes her gin [Repeats]
Papa likes his outside women, mama likes her outside men.
(Transcribed in Davis 200)

The title and lyrics locate the female singer in a barrel house, a Prohibition-era term for illegal saloons. More specifically, the term refers to the makeshift way drinkers constructed a bar by laying a plank of wood across kegs of alcohol. Drowne notes that barrel houses were "overwhelmingly masculine" spaces (173), yet the woman's familiarity here disrupts the cultural narrative that drinking alcohol is for men and that women abstain from and oppose it. In Angela Davis's analysis of the song, she emphasizes its assertion of a woman's prerogative to enjoy good times and illicit sex in precisely the same way a man does (22). In doing this, the song defies middle-class notions of respectability and negative depictions of black sexuality.

However, by considering the song in the context of Prohibition, my argument complicates Davis's, showing how "Barrel House Blues" also rejects gendered representations of alcohol. In repeatedly using the possessive "her," the song emphasizes the woman's ownership of strong drinks, both port and gin. She holds her own vis-à-vis the liquor-drinking man in the song, and she refrains from drinking moonshine only out of fear of pollutants, not from fear of race- or gender-based opprobrium.

In fact, "Booze and Blues," written by J. Guy Suddoth and recorded by Ma Rainey in 1924, suggests that alcohol is so essential to the singer's sense of freedom that Prohibition is effectively worse than prison:

Went to bed last night folks, I was in my tea [Repeats]
Woke up this morning, the police was shaking me

I went to the jail house, drunk and blue as I could be [Repeats]
But the cruel old judge sent my man away from me

They carried me to the courthouse, Lordy, how I was cryin' [Repeats]
They give me sixty days in the jail and money couldn't pay my fine

Sixty days ain't long when you can spend them as you choose [Repeats]
But they seem like years in a cell where there ain't no booze

My life is all a misery when I cannot get my booze [Repeats]
I can't live without my liquor, got to have the booze to cure those blues.
(Transcribed in Davis 208)

In its reference to "tea," an ironic Prohibition-era euphemism for bootlegged alcohol, and to arrest on account of drinking, the song shows the criminalization of liquor during Prohibition. Additionally, it shows the criminalization of black alcohol consumption and the discipline of black bodies when the police show up in the singer's bedroom and the singer receives a sixty-day sentence for being drunk. Though one could argue that the song risks reinforcing the black Republican narrative that working-class black women prioritized alcohol over other rights, such as those established by the Reconstruction Amendments, the song also shows how the implementation of Prohibition damages black rights to privacy and creates black criminality. From the singer's point of view, the prospect of life without alcohol is worse than arrest, jail time, fines, or potential social censure. Here, freedom would be actualized in access to alcohol while Prohibition becomes the grounds for confinement.

From the standpoint of social respectability, black blueswomen who sang about the South and drinking moonshine risked reinforcing negative stereotypes based on race, class, gender, and region. However, in response to the potential for censure, these blueswomen were not silenced, nor did they respond by idealizing controversial subject matter or denying problems. Instead, they often vividly represent the negative aspects of both drinking and regional relocation, as Daphne Duval Harrison suggests. She cites songs like "L & N Blues" or "Gin Mill Blues," both performed by Clara Smith, as examples of songs that address Jim Crow oppression and alcoholism along with the pain caused by both. In fact, she writes, "A recitation of the list of blues lyrics that discuss drinking, its causes and effects, could become a litany" (97), one that would include descriptions of its capacity to both ameliorate and exacerbate personal and systemic problems. The same could certainly be said of blues songs that address the South, simultaneously showing its role in creating and maintaining race-based terrorism and in forging a collective consciousness that African Americans relied on as they sought greater freedom and enfranchisement in the South and the North alike.

In sum, many black blueswomen articulate their complex relationships with alcohol and with the South in expressions of freedom and in spite of the social forces that exerted pressure against such declarations. In contrast to racial uplift ideology, blues music by black women offers a cathartic uplift that takes its power from honest articulations of both desire and disappointment. These blues songs seem to assume that complicated experiences reveal the singer's humanity rather than undercutting it. However, for black blueswomen, rejecting middle-class respectability was not without its costs, as their erasure from standard blues histories goes to show. The chance to consider their work in light of unexplored intersections like those of Prohibition-era alcohol and the South suggests that we have not yet heard all that their music has to say.

Note

1. See W. J. Rorabaugh (20–21) on how alcohol consumption crossed the lines of region, race, class, and gender. Those interested in depictions of drinking in black contexts could start with Nella Larsen's *Quicksand*, Zora Neale Hurston's *Their Eyes Were Watching God*, the poetry of Langston Hughes, or the 1954 film *Carmen Jones*, famous for its all-black cast.

Works Cited

Corrigan, John. "The Prohibition Wave in the South." *The American Monthly Review of Reviews*, vol. 36, September 1907, pp. 328–34.

Crowley, John W. *The White Logic: Alcoholism and Gender in American Modernist Fiction.* U of Massachusetts P, 1994.

Davis, Angela Y. *Blues Legacies and Black Feminism.* Vintage, 1998.

Dolan, Mark K. "Extra! *Chicago Defender* Race Records Ads Show South from Afar." *Southern Cultures*, vol 13, no. 3, 2007, pp. 106–24.

Drowne, Kathleen. *Spirits of Defiance: National Prohibition and Jazz Age Literature, 1920–1933.* Ohio State UP, 2005.

Harrison, Daphne Duval. *Black Pearls: Blues Queens of the 1920s.* Rutgers UP, 1988.

Herd, Denise. "The Paradox of Temperance: Blacks and the Alcohol Question in Nineteenth-Century America." *Drinking: Behavior and Belief in Modern History*, edited by Susanna Barrows and Robin Room, U of California P, 1991, pp. 354–75.

Laird, Ross. *Moanin' Low: A Discography of Female Popular Vocal Recordings, 1920–1933.* Greenwood, 1996.

Lerner, Michael A. *Dry Manhattan: Prohibition in New York City.* Harvard UP, 2007.

Materson, Lisa G. "African American Women, Prohibition, and the 1928 Presidential Election." *Journal of Women's History*, vol. 21, no. 1, 2009, pp. 63–86.

Mattingly, Carol. *Well-Tempered Women: Nineteenth-Century Temperance Rhetoric.* Southern Illinois UP, 1998.

Morone, James. "Temperance: Crucible of Race and Class." *Hellfire Nation: The Politics of Sin in American History.* Yale UP, 2003, pp. 281–317.

Nicolaides, Becky M. "The State's 'Sharp Line Between the Sexes': Women, Alcohol, and the Law in the United States, 1850–1980." *Addiction,* vol. 91, no. 8, 1996, pp. 1211–29.

Rorabaugh, W. J. *The Alcoholic Republic: An American Tradition.* Oxford UP, 1979.

Rose, Kenneth D. *American Women and the Repeal of Prohibition.* New York UP, 1996.

Rotskoff, Lori. *Love on the Rocks: Men, Women, and Alcohol in Post–World War II America.* U of North Carolina P, 2002.

Weiss, Nancy Joan. *Farewell to the Party of Lincoln.* Princeton UP, 1983.

Wolcott, Victoria W. *Remaking Respectability: African American Women in Interwar Detroit.* U of North Carolina P, 2001.

The Spirits of Tradition

Calhoun Cocktails, Douglass Temperance, and Charles Chesnutt

JOHN STROMSKI

The opening chapters of Charles Chesnutt's novel *The Marrow of Tradition* (1902) depict a secret meeting between the town's three leading white figures, Carteret, Belmont, and McBane, otherwise known as the "Big Three." This initial meeting begins with Belmont and McBane coming to congratulate Carteret on the recent birth of his son, although they quickly move to discussing politics, as talk at the newspaper office often does. Jerry, the black porter, hears only pieces of this conversation from the other room, but nevertheless understands "that something serious was on foot, involving his own race." As readers, we are granted a complete understanding once the Big Three order Jerry to bring some alcoholic drinks, "Calhoun cocktails," with which they make racist toasts to "White Supremacy!" (37–38). The presence of alcohol in the scene grants the reader access to the conversation Jerry can only piece together.

In this scene and others throughout the novel, alcohol renders an almost Cartesian split within the town of Wellington, between the aristocratic white political leaders and the black body politic. While the white citizens of Wellington initially perceive the black political and social body as overbearing, repeated instances of drinking cause this perception to devolve into viewing black political and social autonomy as a threat. Alcohol not only emboldens the Big Three as they create their plans to assert white supremacy but also distills their white supremacist ideology into an actionable plan that will rouse the town's white citizens to action.

The ability of alcohol to bring out the worst in people was certainly not a new idea in 1902. Contemporary political and reform tracts in the early 1900s argued that drinking alcohol had a way of manifesting the weak and undesirable elements of society, and in *Marrow*, these elements have a way of nucleating around the black body. In Chesnutt's novel, when the black characters drink alcohol, they inadvertently actualize the threats that drive the Big Three's white supremacist agenda, which is itself fueled by Calhoun cocktails. Alcohol brings out the worst in the Big Three, but when the novel's black characters drink alcohol they become embodiments of the fears that drive the Big Three's racist agenda; they are murderers, rapists, thieves, and miscreants who threaten social order and norms.

Alcohol thus lubricates the political and ideological machinery that operates throughout the text, fomenting the narrative arc that culminates in the closing race riot. As the white characters drink alcohol, their white supremacist mindset is empowered and entrenched within the white political class of the town; as the black characters drink alcohol, they are reduced to stereotypes of threatening black bodies, diminishing any of the social or political capital held by the black citizenry of Wellington. Such a dynamic reflects then contemporary and long-standing discussions about black temperance. Frederick Douglass routinely advocated temperance out of concern that drinking turned the black race into the visage used by white people to establish social and political control, a conviction shared by William Wells Brown, Pauline Hopkins, and Chesnutt himself throughout the nineteenth century.[1]

Each of the novel's primary scenes of plot development anticipating the race riot involve the consumption of alcohol, particularly the drinking of Calhoun cocktails. These cocktails—and alcohol more generally—precede the materialization of racialized anxieties surrounding the consumption of alcohol and the capacity for individual autonomy, self-control, and self-governance. Whenever alcohol is involved, the characters doing the drinking are viewed as embodiments of the very characteristics that each race views as personifying the worst of the other race, and which are at the core of the novel's racial antagonism. These anxieties culminate in the scene where Sandy, after a night of drinking, believes he sees his double, who is actually Tom Delamere in blackface. Tom's crime—robbing and murdering the elderly white woman Polly Ochiltree—is blamed on Sandy and ignites the Big Three's strategy to enforce white supremacy in the town.

Throughout the novel, when characters drink, they become ideological pawns, symbols of the racial stereotypes and views that threaten to disrupt the social and political order within the town. It is not the alcohol alone that foments these ideological views but the historical and cultural legacies imbued in each of the alcoholic drinks imbibed throughout the novel, particularly the legacies of two historical figures: John Calhoun and Frederick Douglass. Alcohol takes the contemporary social and political climate of Wellington and overlays an ideological struggle between the legacies of Calhoun and Douglass.

Typically, scholars read these race relations within the context of post-Reconstruction racial views and politics in the South and the historical and imaginative operations of the white supremacist ideology that the novel depicts. Certainly, the members of the Big Three do not suddenly become white supremacists after having a cocktail. However, drawing attention to the consumption of alcohol highlights how the ideological agenda that drives racial antagonism in the novel is inherited, consumed, and absorbed into the body politic.[2]

Three Parts Racism, One Part Spirits

When the Big Three first order General Belmont's "special mixture," Calhoun cocktails, the drink is described as a "nectar of the gods," "originally compounded," Belmont touts, "by no less a person than the great John C. Calhoun himself" (38). Accompanying the first time the Big Three meet to discuss their plans to assert white supremacy in Wellington, the three toast to "White Supremacy everywhere!," and Carteret, "inspired" by the conversation and the drink alike, pens an editorial that eventually pushes the town's white citizens into the frenzy that precipitates the race riot. The Calhoun cocktails coalesce each of the Big Three's respective anxieties over statesmanship, Democratic politics, and white supremacy into one digestible object, which, once taken into the body, portends the racist agenda each member desires to advance.

It is only through a communion of the new white political vanguard with the political body of the old aristocrats (Calhoun, in this case) that political action comes about. Calhoun, former leader of the southern Democratic Party, became a cultural icon within the South toward the end of the nineteenth century, exemplifying southern ideals and often invoked as a model of statesmanship. The legacy of Calhoun was significant not only to the Democratic Party but also to the South more broadly, particularly within the Carolinas.[3]

A memorial created for Calhoun in Charleston, South Carolina, just a short time before Chesnutt began working on the novel, speaks to the ways Calhoun would be invoked to critique contemporary politics. On April 26, 1887, a large statue of Calhoun was "presented to the city of Charleston by a committee of Southern women" ("Fine Arts" 449). The statue's presentation reinforces the role of the southern statesmen—and of Calhoun in particular—as protector of southern women. Democratic senator Lucius Quintus Cincinnatus Lamar furthered this note in his invited speech to honor Calhoun at the monument's unveiling: "It is well that this monumental statue on South Carolina's soil has been reared through the instrumentality of her own fair daughters. His [Calhoun's] life was one uninterrupted homage to women" (Lamar 47). Within Lamar's numerous praises of Calhoun's career, he also comments on Calhoun's position as a slaveholder, noting how Calhoun had certain amiable "qualities which enabled him to take a race of untamed savages, with habits that could only inspire disgust, with no arts, no single tradition of civilization, and out of such a people to make the finest body of agricultural and domestic laborers that the world has ever seen; and, indeed, to elevate them in the scale of rational existence to such a height as to cause them to be deemed fit for admission into the charmed circle of American freedom, and to be clothed with the rights and duties of American citizenship" (4).

Lamar's telling of Calhoun's stance toward the black race shows his view of the importance of white supremacy, in order to "elevate [African Americans] in the scale of rational existence" and to clothe them with "the rights and duties of American citizenship." Yet Lamar also relates this particular mind-set to the ideals of the contemporary Democratic Party. Lamar goes on to criticize contemporary politics, invoking Calhoun's stance toward party voting and the election process to ask of the present administration, "Can any one who will duly reflect on these things venture to say that all is sound and that our government is not undergoing a great and fatal change? Let us not deceive ourselves" (38). Lamar's invocation of Calhoun not only further solidifies Calhoun's position as a Democratic figurehead but also demonstrates the importance to the contemporary party of honoring Calhoun's legacy.

Calhoun's importance to the Democratic Party would continue to be idealized, frequently embodying ideals the Democratic Party was thought to be missing or prevented from achieving. In 1902, Clarence H. Poe (editor of the *Progressive Farmer* in Raleigh, North Carolina) would argue that creating an atmosphere of white supremacy was necessary to further create great statesman like Calhoun. During the era of Reconstruction, Poe argued, "the South lost prestige in national affairs with both political parties, because she no longer considered questions on their merits, but judged them solely by their relation to the incubus [slavery] with which she struggled. Such a condition was fatal to statesmanship. In all this period, the South produced no Washington or Jefferson or Marshall or Calhoun or Clay. Such men could not grow in an atmosphere poisoned by such influences, or among a people whose judgment and intellect were kept in subjection by the presence of a negro problem" (534). Poe's remarks demonstrate how, for the Democratic Party, particularly in Wilmington, North Carolina, Calhoun's ideals needed to be reabsorbed by party officials for the good of both the party and the white race.

It is within this context of the Democratic Party's desire to reclaim the political and racial ideals of Calhoun that the Democratic members of Wellington, the Big Three, secretly meet. The second time they do, to discuss the printing of the anti-lynching article in the local black newspaper, the group again sends Jerry to fetch Calhoun cocktails. This time, the gentlemen do not make a toast but, upon receiving the drinks, they quickly "exchanged compliments and imbibed—McBane at a gulp, Carteret with more deliberation, leaving about half the contents of his glass" (Chesnutt 89). Belmont, though, is more reflective upon the actual drink, and he "drank slowly, with every sign of appreciation. 'If the illustrious statesman,' he observed, 'whose name this mixture bears, had done nothing more than invent it, his fame would still deserve to go thundering down the endless ages'" (89). Belmont's appreciation of the drink echoes his respect for and appreciation of Calhoun.

What is most significant about alcohol in this chapter, though, is not the usage of it by the Big Three but the drinking of it by Jerry, after he takes the glasses away. Carteret's glass being nearly half full, Jerry seizes the opportunity and "swallowed the remaining contents" (90). In Jerry's following monologue, he comes to claim "I'm gwine ter look at dat newspaper dey be'n talkin' 'bout, an' 'less'n my min' changes might'ly, I 'm gwine ter keep my mouf shet an' stan' in wid de Angry-Saxon race,—ez dey calls deyse'ves nowadays,—an' keep on de right side er my bread an' meat'" (90). The legacy of John Calhoun is so strong that not only are the Big Three motivated and compelled, through the imbibing of Calhoun cocktails, to forward their white supremacist ideology but also Jerry's thinking is altered; he will now view the article in question so as to more favorably align his views with the Big Three.

The ideals of white supremacy are passed down not solely through party affiliation—Jerry is not a Democrat—but also through the absorption of Calhoun's legacy. Through his consumption of alcohol, Jerry falls victim to what temperance advocates like Douglass, Brown, Hopkins, and Chesnutt feared:

he becomes a stereotyped image of the black race that the members of the Big Three use to support their racist agenda. Jerry's attempt at self-preservation, hitching himself to the "Angry-Saxon race," puts on display what Douglass warned was alcohol's false promise of individual empowerment.

In the Spirit of Frederick Douglass

The political context of the Wilmington race riot, scholars note, was largely a matter of the predominantly white Democratic Party against the black-supported Republican Party and the Fusion Party, which rose out of that. Just as the Democrat Calhoun is invoked through the consumption of alcohol, so, too, is Republican statesman Frederick Douglass invoked through the act of drinking, by the novel's black characters. Although Calhoun is only mentioned in small details and Douglass is not mentioned at all in the novel—though Chesnutt was very familiar with Douglass's life and politics, having written his biography in 1899—the ideological legacies of both these political and cultural figureheads permeate and are central to a complete understanding of *The Marrow of Tradition*. The legacies of Calhoun and Douglass become codified within the alcoholic drinks the characters imbibe throughout the novel. While the issue of temperance would be taken up by various activist groups throughout the nineteenth century, and notably by Douglass, the issue would often become racialized—especially in the South—and alcohol would be seen at some times as a form of racial control and at others as a form of racial antagonism.

Douglass had long supported temperance and throughout his career had spoken prominently about the subject, notably in 1846, during his address in Scotland titled "Intemperance Viewed in Connection with Slavery," where he claimed, "This intemperance enslaves—this intemperance paralyses—this intemperance binds with bonds stronger than iron, and makes man the willing subject of its brutal control" (Douglass, "Intemperance," 167). But this was not a viewpoint that Douglass had always held, and in his speeches, as here, he often would tell modified versions of how, when he had drunk liquor, it induced in him a feeling "like a president": "I used to love to drink—That's a fact. . . . I found in me all those characteristics leading to drunkenness. . . . One of my principal inducements was the independent and lofty character which I seemed to possess when I got a little drop . . . I felt like a president" (170).

In close proximity to these remarks, Douglass frequently would tell the story of a black man who got so drunk that he crawled into a pigsty and attempted to bring the animals to order. Although this story seems mainly intended for comedic effect (and was often interrupted or followed by laughter or applause from the audience), during this Glasgow speech, Douglass equates the empowerment the drunken black man in the pigsty felt to matters of statesmanship and civic authority, saying that when "he got a drop he felt as if he was the moderator, or judge, or chairman of a society—or as one who had the responsibility of keeping good order" (170). While trying to instill order upon a group of pigs is comical for its futility, alcohol reduces the ideas of a black man's self-assertion and political prowess into farce. This speech occurred fifty-two years before the Wilmington race riot, but it underscores the perceived threat of liquor allowing black men to assert themselves or to have imagined feelings of equality and political prowess—the very same concepts that are so threatening to the Big Three at the outset of Chesnutt's novel.

It was not just that alcohol created delusions of grandeur, Douglass argued, but that alcohol was used to disillusion the slave about the value of freedom. Douglass often would tell variations of the story about how the white master would keep the black slave oppressed through the consumption of alcohol: "On each Saturday night it is quite common in the State of Maryland . . . for masters to give their slaves a considerable quantity of whiskey to keep them during the Sabbath in a state of stupidity. At the time when they would be apt to think—at a time when they would be apt to devise means for their freedom—their masters give them of the stupefying draught which paralyzes their intellect, and in this way prevents their seeking emancipation. . . . They do this for the purpose of disgusting the slave with his freedom" (166).

Throughout his public speaking career, and even as late as 1889, Douglass often would draw correlations between temperance and slavery, arguing that progress toward one would bring progress toward eliminating the other. A similar line of thinking was shared by a number of other black temperance advocates. In her prize-winning 1880 essay advocating temperance, "The Evils of Intemperance and Their Remedies," written for Charles Chesnutt's magazine, Pauline Hopkins associates drinking with economic and moral depravity. Such a linkage can be traced back throughout the nineteenth century, and Robert Levine highlights how William Wells Brown's beliefs that temperance will bring about the black man's "economic, social, and moral elevation" influenced his writings (Levine 107). The very things that influenced Douglass, Brown, Hopkins, and Chesnutt to advocate for temperance in the first place—fears of economic, social, and moral degradation—were used by white people on the other side of the conversation as evidence of the vices inherent to the black race, waiting only to be drawn out and make themselves known. On both sides of this discussion, alcohol is viewed not merely for its effects on the individual but also for its effects upon the broader community and race.

In Douglass's 1883 address in Louisville, "Parties Were Made for Men, not Men for Parties," he goes beyond merely commenting upon and condemning the crimes and problems associated with intemperance to equating the ideology that makes such moral outrages possible with the legacy of John Calhoun. Douglass provides an example of Calhoun's legacy being materialized in a literal way: "A grandson of John C. Calhoun, an Arkansas land owner, testifying the other day before the Senate Committee of Labor and Education, says the 'negroes are so indolent that they fail to take advantage of the opportunities offered them; that they will only devote so much of their time to work as will enable them to procure the necessities of life; that there is danger of a war of races.'

"His testimony," Douglass continues, "proclaims him the grandson of the man whose name he bears. The blame which belongs to his own class he shifts from them to the shoulders of labor. It becomes us to test the truth of that assertion by the light of reason, and by appeals to indisputable facts" (Douglass, "Parties" 97–98). The story of Calhoun's progeny demonstrates how his presence and legacy is still heavily involved not only in southern thought but also within the state government, and how the effects of that occlude "reason" and "indisputable facts." Later, in an 1889 address in Washington, DC, Douglass says, "This old slave-holding Calhoun and McDuffy doctrine, which we long ago thought dead and buried, is revived in unexpected quarters, and confronts us to-day as sternly as it did forty years ago. Then it was employed as the sure defense of slavery. Now it is employed as a justification of the fraud and violence by which colored men are divested of their citizenship, and robbed of their constitutional rights in the solid South" ("Nation's" 406).

In 1889, Douglass traces the contemporary ideology of white supremacy and black oppression "in the solid South" to the "Calhoun and McDuffy doctrine," which, for Douglass, is the source of contemporary oppressive racial thinking. Throughout his public speaking career, Calhoun often represented, for Douglass, the source of racial oppression within the government and the legal system, and he demonstrated how that oppression becomes legitimated through popular and prominent statesmen. In *Marrow*, Chesnutt shows what happens when these legacies and traditions materialize, by framing the Calhoun cocktail as both the manifestation and facilitator of such legacies.

Seeing Double

Apart from the political overtones and undertones within the novel, the drinking of alcohol reflects larger social practices and concerns within the nineteenth century, particularly with regard to race. Racialized feelings and perceptions toward alcohol would continue throughout the Reconstruction era and into the early twentieth century. In *Alcohol: How it Affects the Individual, the Community and the Race* (1909), Henry Smith Williams describes how "the argument for alcohol as a means of eliminating the weakly and undesirable elements of society would ill accord with the modern conception of public polity. For precisely the same argument might with equal logic be applied in favor, for example, of contagious diseases. Only the weaker tenth of humanity, it might be said, succumb to tuberculosis; ergo, tuberculosis is an excellent agency for the strengthening of the race" (100–101).

Although he refutes it, Williams notes an argument in the early twentieth century that alcohol was "a means of eliminating the weakly and undesirable elements of society." Though Williams is invoking eugenics to make his argument, the same line of logic undergirds the Big Three's actions in *Marrow*. Through Polly Ochiltree's murder, with the attendant fears of crime and miscegenation, the Big Three are emboldened to take matters into their own hands and eliminate what they see as undesirable elements in society via the race riot. Within the race riot started by the Big Three, alcohol plays a more active role in what they claim to be the improvement of society: the removal of the black race.

Although the racist ideology absorbed by the Big Three on a regular basis is powerful enough to affect Jerry's constitution, Jerry is not the only black man to drink alcohol in the novel. Indeed, alcohol gets Sandy into a considerable amount of trouble when "in his loneliness Sandy accepted an invitation to go with Josh and have a drink,—a single drink." The next paragraph details Sandy's walk home from his "single drink" with Josh Green: "Sandy was going home about eleven o'clock, three sheets in the wind, such was the potent effect of the single drink and those which had followed it" (Chesnutt 166–67).

Although the "single drink" seems to be again brought up and emphasized largely for comedic effect, it resonates more strongly with Douglass's temperance views and his emphasis that the effects of this "single drink" work to keep the black race enslaved. Indeed, as late as 1889, Douglass would continue preaching his pro-temperance message, saying "But these old slave-holders have their allies, and one is strong drink. Whiskey makes the negro drunk, and drunkenness makes him a criminal as well as a pauper, and when he is made both a pauper and criminal the law steps in for satisfaction" ("Nation's" 420). Soon after Sandy's "single drink," the law—or at least the law of the Big Three—does demand satisfaction.

After Sandy leaves Josh Green's, "he was scared almost into soberness by a remarkable apparition. . . . Possibly the muddled condition of Sandy's intellect had so affected his judgment as to vitiate any conclusion he might draw, but Sandy was quite sober enough to perceive that the figure ahead of him wore his best clothes and looked exactly like him" (Chesnutt 167). Although Sandy blames this "apparition" on "the bad liquor he had drunk," as "bad liquor often made people see double" (167), Sandy's out-of-body experience here reflects larger contemporary thoughts about alcohol and race. The drinking of alcohol allows Sandy to momentarily view the qualities brought about by alcohol that temperance advocates wanted to eliminate, much as Williams wrote how there was an "argument for alcohol as a means of eliminating the weakly and undesirable elements of society" (Williams 100). Indeed, through Sandy's existential moment, the alcohol allows him to see the thieving black criminal that the white southerners (as well as both the Democratic Party and various pro-temperance leagues) want to destroy. In addition, it is Sandy's drunkenness that fuels the fire for the white supremacists in their murder and rape allegations against Sandy.

Once Sandy returns home and confronts Tom, the actual thief and murderer, they have the following conversation:

> "Mistuh Tom," inquired Sandy anxiously, "would you 'low dat I'd be'n drinkin' too much?"
>
> "No, Sandy, I should say you were sober enough, though of course you may have had a few drinks. Perhaps you'd like another? I've got something good here."
>
> "No, suh, Mistuh Tom, no, suh! No mo' liquor fer me, suh, never! When

liquor kin make a man see his own ha'nt, it 's 'bout time fer dat man ter quit drinkin', it sho' is!" (Chesnutt 168)

This exchange between Sandy and Tom echoes the dynamic between master and slave in regards to alcohol that Douglass had earlier vilified in his pro-temperance speeches, where he would simultaneously equate the problems of slavery and black suppression with intemperance.

Tom, much like the slave master that Douglass had described, offers Sandy more drink in an effort to keep him "in a state of stupidity," diminishing any possible suspicion that could be placed upon Tom as the perpetrator of the crime. Tom's motivation in proffering the drink is not just to further disguise his own commission of the crime—beyond having dressed up in Sandy's clothes and blackening his face. It is also intended to "paralyze" Sandy's intellect, to prevent him from figuring out the events that actually occurred. Eventually, it is the remembrance of this scene that becomes crucial to proving Sandy's innocence and freedom, and, as Douglass had previously remarked, "In the Southern States, masters induce their slaves to drink whiskey, in order to keep them from devising ways and means by which to obtain their freedom. In order to make a man a slave, it is necessary to silence or drown his mind" ("Temperance" 207). Though Sandy easily figures out the truth, his state of drunkenness—combined with his status as a black man—prevent him from definitively arguing his case to obtain his freedom. Indeed, the fact that Sandy was drunk permeates the white citizens' minds in imagining Sandy's criminal acts.

By the end of *The Marrow of Tradition*, when "crowds of white men and half-grown boys, drunk with whiskey or with license, raged through the streets, beating, chasing, or killing any negro so unfortunate as to fall into their hands" (Chesnutt 298), the "license" the mob gets to do so is granted by their being "drunk with whiskey." The contemporary views of alcohol that warranted for white supremacists the oppression of the black race to protect white citizens is granted license through the whiskey. By being drunk with whiskey, the white mob can simultaneously demonstrate its superior position and its social supremacy—by being able to freely drink alcohol and to freely terrorize the black citizens of the community. This white supremacist ideology, in combination with the legacy of Calhoun's oppressive racial policies, becomes crystallized within the alcohol, giving the consumers free range to carry out their murderous riot.

It is important to note, though, that the mob is drunk on whiskey, not on Calhoun cocktails. The Calhoun cocktails are the drinks of the statesmen, the leaders—Carteret and Belmont—who attempt to orchestrate the riot without action. Whiskey, however, is the drink of McBane, and the mob's drinking of it parallels the opening meeting of the Big Three, when McBane orders three whiskies and toasts to "No nigger domination" (37).

The final race riot renders another Cartesian split, this time of white supremacist thought. Unable to control the angry mob, Carteret abandons the scene, leaving the anger of the riot to "burn itself out" (305) and absolving himself of further responsibility. The political and supremacist ideals that Carteret had advocated now, through the accompaniment of alcohol, give way to the brute force of the white body politic, the angry mob that, drunk with power, is granted license through its drinking to commit whatever crimes it sees fit. The ideological desire for white superiority, represented by Carteret and Belmont and their Calhoun cocktails, eventually cedes to the sheer force and racism of McBane and his whiskey, emphasizing that, whatever the political or ideological motivations and factors behind the race riot—in both Wellington and Wilmington—in the end it all boils down to both their racist and their whiskey base.

Notes

1. Frederick Douglass had abandoned his commitment to temperance in the 1890s.

2. Often, scholarship focuses on the economic and political disenfranchisement of both Wellington's and Wilmington's African American citizens. For more on the economic and political disenfranchisement of the towns' African American citizens, see McGowan and Sundquist. For more on the discussion of the ideological violence that informs the novel, see Roe.

3. For an example of what John Calhoun's legacy meant in South Carolina in the late nineteenth century, see Cunningham.

Works Cited

Chesnutt, Charles. *Frederick Douglass*. 2nd ed. Small, Maynard, 1899.

———.*The Marrow of Tradition*. Edited by Eric J. Sundquist, Penguin, 1993.

Cunningham, Clarence, editor. *A History of the Calhoun Monument*. Lucas, Richardson, 1888.

Douglass, Frederick. "Intemperance Viewed in Connection with Slavery: An Address Delivered in Glasgow, Scotland, on 18 February 1846." *The Frederick Douglass Papers*.

Series One: Speeches, Debates, and Interviews, vol. 1, edited by John W. Blassingame, Yale UP, 1979, 165–70.

———. "The Nation's Problem: An Address Delivered in Washington, DC, on 16 April 1889." *The Frederick Douglass Papers. Series One: Speeches, Debates, and Interviews,* vol. 5, edited by John W. Blassingame and John R. McKivigan, Yale UP, 1992, 403–26.

———. "Parties Were Made for Men, not Men for Parties: An Address Delivered in Louisville, Kentucky, on 25 September 1883." *The Frederick Douglass Papers. Series One: Speeches, Debates, and Interviews,* vol. 5, edited by John W. Blassingame and John R. McKivigan, Yale UP, 1992, 85–110.

———. "Temperance and Anti-Slavery: An Address Delivered in Paisley, Scotland, on 30 March 1846." *The Frederick Douglass Papers. Series One: Speeches, Debates, and Interviews,* vol. 1, edited by John W. Blassingame, Yale UP, 1979, 205–9.

"The Fine Arts: The Calhoun Statue." *The Critic,* 20 June 1896.

Lamar, Lucius Quintus Cincinnatus. *Oration on the Life, Character and Public Services of the Hon. John C. Calhoun, Delivered Before the Ladies' Calhoun Monument Association, and the Public, at Charleston, South Carolina.* Lucas, Richardson, 1888.

Levine, Robert S. "'Whiskey, Blacking, and All': Temperance and Race in William Wells Brown's *Clotel.*" *The Serpent in the Cup: Temperance in American Literature,* edited by David S. Reynolds and Debra J. Rosenthal, U of Massachusetts P, 1997, pp. 93–114.

McGowan, Todd. "Acting Without the Father: Charles Chesnutt's New Aristocrat." *American Literary Realism, 1870–1910,* vol. 30, no. 1 (Fall 1997), pp. 59–74.

Poe, Clarence H. "Suffrage Restriction in the South; Its Causes and Consequences." *North American Review,* October 1902, p. 175.

Roe, Jae E. "Keeping an 'Old Wound' Alive: *The Marrow of Tradition* and the Legacy of Wilmington." *African American Review,* vol. 33, no. 2 (Summer 1999), pp. 231–43.

Sundquist, Eric. *To Wake the Nations: Race in the Making of American Literature.* Belknap, 1993.

Williams, Henry Smith. *Alcohol: How it Affects the Individual, the Community and the Race.* Century, 1909.

The Last Black Temperance Activist

Frances Harper and the Black Public Sphere

SUSAN ZIEGER

Almost thirty years after historian Donald Yacovone observed it, the black temperance movement remains undeservedly forgotten from history (281). Temperance, whether as a moral reform exhorting individuals to drink less or no alcohol or as a political program leading to the regulation or prohibition of alcoholic beverages, often seems dwarfed by other nineteenth-century black political goals. Less urgent than responding to the crises of the Fugitive Slave Act in the 1850s or lynching beginning in the 1880s, black temperance was also clearly less ambitious and impactful than abolition and suffragism, the movements with which it allied.

Drunkenness was not a notable problem in free black communities, but black temperance reflected aspirations to dignity, social control, and respect for those communities (Pease and Pease 124). As part of an uplift program, temperance seems to have appeased the racist social order by accepting its own segregated status and by validating chimerical white anxieties about black drunkenness. Aiming to reshape individual choices and customs to conform to the existing social order rather than pushing for systemic changes, it can seem quiescent and even complicit in the long institutional history of U.S. racism.

Yet temperance played a key role in black communities since at least 1788, when the Free African Society of Philadelphia denied membership to those who drank (Quarles 93). Temperance featured centrally in Frederick Douglass's thinking about social transformation; he lectured on the subject in the United States and Britain and wrote about it frequently in the *North Star* and *Frederick Douglass' Paper*. Martin Delany called on people of color to adopt total abstinence. W. E. B. Du Bois supported temperance in the 1880s and researched black drinking habits for *The Philadelphia Negro* (1899). Thousands of less famous activists organized societies, assisted the intemperate—who often were also poor and unlettered—and wrote and spoke out against the use of alcohol. At the height of racial turmoil within the Woman's Christian Temperance Union (WCTU), between 1880 and 1920, more than six thousand black women joined the organization (Herd, "We Cannot Stagger" 158). Why?

The division of black thought and politics into polarized camps of assimilation and nationalism has obscured the nuanced ethical and political questions that black activists confronted (Dossett 3). The renunciation of alcohol formed the core of their ideals of Enlightenment perfectibility, uplift, and respectability, shaping a vision that, though framed by white racism, performed the crucial work of fostering and expanding a national black public sphere.

Temperance principles remained central to the long career of Frances Ellen Watkins Harper, the black activist, novelist, poet, and orator, and they throw into relief the present-day challenge of understanding her oeuvre in its full political and cultural context. Scholars remember and study Harper chiefly for her authorship of the novel *Iola Leroy, or, Shadows Uplifted* (1892), with its fraught plot of passing, but her other novels, poetry, speeches, letters, and travels reveal the animating force of temperance in black and U.S. political and social histories.

Harper, grounded in Christian ideology and unchanging in her commitment to temperance from 1850 to her death in 1911, can sometimes seem to have been unequipped to respond to urgent issues such as lynching and to accommodate racism in her work with the WCTU.[1] Houston Baker has referred to her "soothing mulatto utopianism" and "bright Victorian morality in whiteface" (Baker 33). More recent work, such as Brittney C. Cooper's *Beyond Respectability* (2017), has tried to recover the politics of Harper's clubwomen colleagues such as Julia Cooper.

Yet, far from being oblivious to the uncomfortable ironies of advocating for black temperance in a racist context, Harper deemed them less important than working toward her long-term vision of an enlightened, just black public sphere as a model for the flawed white one. Harper's conceptualization of the public sphere most nearly matches Jürgen Habermas's rational, deliberative model that leaves little room for affect or identification. As Lauren Berlant has demonstrated, in her reading of the "anti-passional logic" of *Iola Leroy*, "the desire to become national seems to call for a *release* from sensuality—this is the cost, indeed the promise, of citizenship" for people of color (239). Temperance figured crucially in this vision, and its characteristic tension, resulting from rationalizing sensuality and emotion, dominates Harper's instructive, exemplary writing and speeches. Temperance sought to purify mind and body of the corrosive pleasures stoked by the profit motive, producing an ideal community of healthy bodies and orderly minds.

Temperance rationalism governs Harper's vision of a national black public sphere in which the South strives to rebuild after slavery and military defeat and the North attempts to rectify its own racism. The national aspirations of Harper's vision are everywhere apparent, notwithstanding recent readings of her poetry that emphasize its transnational and diasporic dimensions, and in spite of the critical disagreement over whether to classify her as a northern or a southern writer.[2]

Harper, born in Baltimore in 1825, became politicized after the passage of the Fugitive Slave Act effectively exiled her from her home state (Dietzel 166). She lived briefly in Maine, Massachusetts, and Ohio, but made her base in Philadelphia for many years. Crucially, she undertook lecture tours to almost every state in the South after the Civil War, staying among freed people and writing poems about them, collected in *Sketches of Southern Life* (1872). In her letters to her fellow Underground Railroad activist William Still, these travels have the benevolent air of missionary trips. The black public sphere she envisioned required the two regions' interdependence, and though the method for bringing it about inscribed a quasi-colonial mode of instruction, Harper's status as a black woman lecturer was likely instructive to southern whites and inspiring to freed people. Harper made sure to balance her missionizing in the South with criticizing northern racism in employment practices; the force of Enlightenment perfectibility meant that each region could always do better.

Yet her vision—and the ideals of black temperance—confronted insurmountable obstacles in the 1890s, when the WCTU pursued national influence by courting racist southern whites. Though she was not literally the last black temperance activist, Harper, whose ideals of voluntarism, self-mastery, and renunciation of pleasure were formed during the antebellum period, was out of sync with the political realities driving temperance at the turn of the twentieth century.

Ironies of the Black Temperance Movement

The black temperance movement expresses a painful paradox at the heart of black antebellum activism: making rational demonstrations of black sobriety—

and thus, worthiness for freedom—activists confronted the irrational domination of white racism and slave mastery. Yet northern black activists throughout the period avidly pursued temperance and its strategy of uplift, forming organizations, meeting at conventions, and publishing periodicals. In 1840, in Cincinnati, more than one-quarter of the black population belonged to the adult and youth temperance society; societies also flourished in New York, Pennsylvania, and Connecticut (Quarles 95–96). As R. U. Cheagle demonstrates, temperance featured in publications such as the *Northern Star and Freeman's Advocate,* the *Liberator,* the *Lily,* the *Pennsylvania Freeman,* the *Colored American,* and others. Nonetheless, black temperance groups operated within a depressingly familiar dialectic of segregation: formed in exclusion from white organizations, they in turn barred women.

Black temperance also was a northern phenomenon, especially beginning in the 1830s, when it aligned with abolitionism and renewed free people of color's commitment to the enslaved. Many turned from moderation to total abstinence as drinking alcohol came to symbolize complicity with slavery (Yacovone 288). In the southern states, slaveholders were largely forbidden to give their slaves alcohol, and many only did so on special holidays, as Douglass recounts in his *Narrative,* to neutralize potential insurrection (Sellers 29). Purposely getting their slaves drunk, masters cheated them "with a dose of vicious dissipation, artfully labeled with the name of liberty. The most of us used to drink it down, and the result was just what might be supposed. . . . We felt, and very properly too, that we had almost as well be slaves to man as to rum" (Douglass 115–16). A related, racialized irony emerges here. As Herd describes the paradox, white southerners saw alcohol as a goad to slave rebellion, whereas Douglass and other black abolitionists viewed it as a technique of white domination. Thus, both attacked drunkenness, but for radically incompatible reasons.

Temperance activity of all kinds came to a halt during the Civil War, resuming during Reconstruction. In the post-Reconstruction period, it turned more decisively from a moral reform of individual behavior to a political push toward prohibition legislation. The 1851 passage of the Maine Law eliminating the sale of alcohol for ordinary consumption, and the "crusades," women's hatchet attacks on saloons in the 1870s, foretold this turn. By the 1880s, temperance shifted from reform to politics, became ideologically aligned with racism, and alienated its black activists.

Temperance was integral to abolition's uplift strand, but a further irony bedeviled it. This took the shape of an unfortunate comparison between the literal intemperance caused by overconsumption of alcohol and the metaphoric intemperance of slave mastery. Mistaken as it may now seem, the idea that the drunkard's "enslavement" to alcohol was worse than chattel slavery was commonly found in temperance speeches by black activists such as William Whipper, Douglass, and Harper.[3] In a speech reprinted in the *A.M.E. Church Review* in 1891, Harper put it this way: "If mind is more than matter, if the destiny of the human soul reaches out into the eternities, and as we sow so must we reap, then bad as was American slavery, the slavery of intemperance is worse. Slavery was the enemy of one section, the oppressor of one race, but intemperance is the curse of every land and the deadly foe of every kindred, tribe and race which falls beneath its influence" ("Symposium" 373).

Writing after Reconstruction, Harper's wide, almost universal view retrospectively blunts the critical force and urgency of the abolitionist message. During slavery, temperance rhetoric exhorted the putatively free black person to avoid drinking, but the slave, suffering under extreme domination, lacked the same personal resources to make such choices. When Douglass, in *My Bondage and My Freedom,* and Harriet Beecher Stowe, in *Uncle Tom's Cabin* (1851), implied that slaves could choose to further degrade themselves by drinking, or remain sober and dignified in spite of their captivity, they lessened critical pressure on the system of slavery and the culpability of white masters.

Levine reveals this paradox in Douglass's writing, which suggests that slaves can remain temperate and nonviolent in the model of uplift while also enacting the revolutionary violence required to overthrow the slave system (Levine 127–28). The dilemma stems from the temperance model's overreliance on rationalism, which posits a mind that is free from its body and always able to control it. Constrained by the paradox of advocating voluntarism in the context of slavery, the black temperance movement nonetheless pursued a public sphere grounded in self-mastery, and Harper was one of its most active proponents.

North and South in Harper's Vision of a Black Public Sphere

Temperance is presented as the ground of reason and organized community in Harper's novels *Sowing and Reaping* (1877), *Trial and Triumph* (1889), and *Iola Leroy* (1892). In *Trial and Triumph,* the inhabitants of Tennis Court, "under the besotting influence of beer and even stronger drinks," indulge in "gossiping, news-carrying and tattling . . . which often resulted in quarrels and contentions . . . [and] sadly lowered the tone of social life." When one of the drunken gossipers sends the young Annette Harcourt to the saloon for beer, Annette's grandmother lectures her, and the offender eventually becomes "a good temperance woman herself" (197). Patricia Sehulster observes that Harper avoids the sensationalism of white temperance because she wishes to show the collective rather than the individual results of drinking (1144).

Though she eschews the melodrama and gore of Washingtonian-style temperance narratives, Harper's temperance fiction is similarly beset by the fundamental narrative dilemma of the genre: in order to heighten the stakes of the individual's choice to drink or to abstain, the pleasure of drinking must be attractively described, generating an aesthetic excess that undermines the text's didacticism.[4] For example, in *Sowing and Reaping*, John Anderson opens a saloon, "a magnificent palace of sin" in which "sparkling champagne, or ruby-tinted wine [was] served in beautiful and costly glasses" (107). In prose richly laden with detail that departs from her typically spare style, Harper describes the saloon's upholstery, its female patrons, and their fashionable dress.

She sensualizes and eroticizes alcohol again when the beacon of reason, Anna Lasette, recalls her youthful renunciation of Frank Miller, a proprietor of yet another lavish saloon. When Frank presses Anna's hand during a dance, she experiences sexual pleasure and reacts to it by removing and burning her glove, defiant acts that dampen the party atmosphere. As she later recalls the incident, she had resolved she would never lay the foundations of her happiness "over the reeling brain of a drunkard" (262).

In spite of literary lapses into representations of pleasure, for Harper's heroic characters, the mind always wins out over the body and, by analogy, as Michael Stancliff shows, moral regulation wins out over the laissez-faire capitalism that supports the liquor trade (95). The renunciation of bodily and erotic desire, and of the conviviality that alcohol facilitates, secures elements of a rational, regulated black public sphere such as Mrs. Lasette's salon and the security of Tennis Court in *Trial and Triumph* or Belle Gordon and Paul Clifford's marriage, family, and efforts to bring about Eden and paradise on earth in *Sowing and Reaping*.

While some scholars contend that Harper's fiction "deracializes" its characters, it nonetheless consolidates a black public sphere drawn from the actually existing ones in Philadelphia and other northern cities. DoVeanna Fulton cites the indeterminate racial identities of the characters in *Sowing and Reaping* as examples of Harper's appeal to white and black audiences and as a reflection of black ambivalence about espousing temperance in a racist context (Fulton 210–11; see also Rosenthal 153–64). Yet this tendency in *Sowing and Reaping*—as well as in Harper's first temperance short story, "The Two Offers" (1859)—is balanced by *Trial and Triumph* and *Iola Leroy,* in which black characters such as Grandmother Harcourt, Mrs. Lasette, Robert Johnson, and Iola espouse temperance principles. Moreover, the serialized stories appeared in black publications. The *Anglo-African Magazine* published "The Two Offers," and *Sowing and Reaping* and *Trial and Triumph* unfolded in the pages of the *A.M.E. Church Review;* the latter, as Jaime Osterman Alves has shown, intervened in black education debates.[5] *Trial and Triumph's* protagonist, Annette, is explicitly identified as aspiring to "the upper tens"—a phrase W. E. B. Du Bois would reformulate as "the talented tenth."

Harper drew her messages of uplift from her observations of black community activism and reform within Philadelphia, coded as the fictional town of "A.P." in the short novels. The labeling of her fiction as "deracialized discourse" has thus obscured its cultural role in strengthening an already existing black public sphere, and its effort to expand it to the South. That expansion is the model outcome of both *Trial and Triumph* and *Iola Leroy*: Annette and Iola each travel to the South to perform educational work. Annette, having received the education of the black leadership class, was "doing what she could to teach, help and befriend those on whose chains the rust of ages had gathered" (*Trial* 284). Iola becomes a Sunday school teacher who attempts to rescue the poor from "dens of vice [that] are spreading their snares for the feet of the tempted and inexperienced"—in other words, grogshops, taverns, and saloons (*Iola* 278). Harper fictionalized the temperance work fostered by the northern black public sphere, imagining its replication in the South.

Iola Leroy represents temperance as part of the reform of the South, while complicating a straightforward North–South colonial relationship. The topic pops up in several different plotlines; the two most notable being when Robert Johnson rediscovers his Aunt Linda and mother in North Carolina. Here, temperance emerges as the modern reform of old Southern ways, when Robert and Iola reject Aunt Linda's superb homemade wine.

> "I reckon Robby's right," said his mother, setting down her glass and leaving the wine unfinished. "You young folks knows a heap more dan we ole folks."

"Well," declared Aunt Linda, "you all is temp'rence to de backbone. But what could I do wid my wine ef we didn't drink it?"

"Let it turn to vinegar, and sign the temperance pledge," replied Robert. (185)

The family has reunited, but its old customs are subject to modern rationality, which permits them to enjoy only Aunt Linda's flaky biscuits and amber jelly. Though the older generation submits to the new ideas, Harper allows Aunt Linda to voice her own knowledge of how she and other freed people could best be helped. Linda complains that temperance workers reach out only at election time, "an' keeps dem at a proper distance wen de 'lection's ober. Some ob dem say dere's a trick behine it, an' don't want to tech it" (160).

A more heartfelt and sustained reform, rooted in the community, would help temperance succeed. Harper has Aunt Linda voice a call for reform rather than politics: "We might be a people ef it warn't for dat mizzable drink. . . . I wants some libe [library] man to come down yere an' splain things ter dese people. I don't mean a politic man, but a man who'll larn dese people how to bring up dere chillen, to keep our gals straight, an' our boys from runnin' in de saloons an' gamblin' dens" (160). Such instructive reform plainly calls for cultural colonization. In her black vernacular wisdom, Aunt Linda identifies temperance, taught by a northern male instructor, as the condition of black peoplehood. In Harper's vision, this option appears a more successful and humane alternative to the fleeting interest of temperance politicians.

Annette's and Iola's service resembles Harper's own. Harper's early biographer, William Still, extolled the range and depth of her involvement with freed southerners: "I know of no other woman, white or colored, anywhere, who has come so intimately in contact with the colored people in the South as Mrs. Harper. . . . She has found a vast field and open doors to teach and speak on the themes of education, temperance, and good home building, industry, morality, and the like" ("Introduction" 1–2). Still's description casts Harper as a missionary or ethnographer, making contact with the "natives," attaining their trust, and generally edifying them. Her own accounts of her work, quoted liberally in Still's chapter about her in *The Underground Railroad* (1872), evoke both an optimism in continued progress and the extreme poverty she encountered. In Greenville, Georgia, which she describes as "heathen ground," she finds no window glass in a schoolroom; in Montgomery, Alabama, a woman gives birth in the cabin where Harper is staying, so she moves to a teacher's home lit only by large holes that also let in the cold (Still, *Underground* 772–73).

Harper's lectures in the South included standard temperance advice: men should not get drunk and beat their wives; mothers should eliminate the influence of alcohol in their children's lives. As a black woman lecturer in the South during Reconstruction, Harper found herself in risky situations. On trains, she observes, conversations became heated: "I got in a conversation with a former slave dealer, and we had rather an exciting time. I was traveling alone, but it is not worthwhile to show any signs of fear." She spoke in Darlington, South Carolina, where "about two years ago, a girl was hung for making a childish and indiscreet speech" (Still, *Underground* 768).

Harper's vulnerability enacts her concept of public service as inherently precarious, a logic that Katherine Henry says rejects the common white, liberal understanding of citizenship as protection from the social body. Harper exposed herself to danger to make the platform safe for black women public intellectuals (Cooper 23). She raised awareness, defeating white audience members' suspicions that she was too expert a communicator to be either black or a woman. As she wrote to Still, "I don't know but that you would laugh if you were to hear some of the remarks which my lectures call forth: 'She is a man,' again 'She is not colored, she is painted'" (Still, *Underground* 772). Thus, though Harper's southern travels resemble a familiar northern colonial or missionary attitude toward the South and its inhabitants, her lectures also performed a raced and gendered vulnerability that underscored black temperance's voluntarist drive.

Harper often interspersed her lectures with readings of her poems. Her *Sketches of Southern Life* (1872) carries forward her temperance reform program in a poetic mode. "Save the Boys," "Nothing and Something," "Wanderer's Return," "Fishers of Men," and "Signing the Pledge" all reflect a temperance message. Though they have drawn less critical attention than the "Aunt Chloe" poems, the southern context of the volume reframes their timeworn lessons, matching them to their moment and place. For those attempting to locate family members after slavery, the temperance idea that eschewing alcohol binds families together would have been apt. For example, in "Wanderer's Return," the speaker rejoices that her son has returned home: "The streets were not safe for my darling child; / Where sin and evil attractions smiled. / But his wandering feet have ceased to roam, / And to-night my wayward boy is at home—" (Harper, *Complete Poems* 143). "Signing the Pledge" is voiced by a drunkard turning a new leaf: "Do you see this pledge I've signed to-night? / My mother, wife, and boy / Shall read my purpose on that pledge / And smile through tears of joy" (146).

Likewise, Harper's poems that touch on electoral sobriety—those exhorting freed people not to sell their votes for drinks—offered lessons for those transitioning to citizenship, who urgently needed real civic representation. "Save the Boys" calls on free blacks to vote for temperance: "Oh! freemen, from these foul decoys / Arise, and vote to save the boys" (140). "Nothing and Something" presents a voter to whom "it is nothing" to vote for the liquor trade but to whom "it was something" later on, "When his daughter became a drunkard's wife" (142).

Melba Joyce Boyd notes that Harper's temperance poems have been dismissed for their sentimentality yet are valuable for witnessing the tragedy of alcoholism (76). Harper's unornamented, allegorical style plainly illustrates to readers how the self-mastery required by temperance reshapes chaos into organized families and an orderly public sphere. While the volume might have served as ethnography for black and white northern readers, for freed people it might have operated more as instruction and support during postwar tumult. Performed between exhortatory passages of lecturing, the poems made temperance accessible to hearers by giving them simple models of identification.

Though her own reform activism may resemble a kind of temperance colonization, Harper, in the tradition of black temperance, held anticolonization sentiments. In the antebellum period, black activists resisted efforts to send free people of color to Africa. The U.S. government purchased Liberia in 1822 for this project, and the American Colonization Society, founded in 1816, undertook it. Many free people of color quickly rejected colonization because they astutely saw it as a strategy to protect slavery (Cheagle 54–55).[6] Their commitment to the enslaved kept them in the United States, motivating their abolitionist activism. They enlisted temperance in their anticolonial cause: if they could maintain sobriety in the United States, they would prove colonization schemes unnecessary (Herd, "We Cannot Stagger" 151).

Harper, lecturing in the early 1860s, denounced Abraham Lincoln's colonization plan as political expediency, arguing for the value of uncoerced labor to the United States and for the right of freed slaves to the U.S. soil they had enriched through their labor (Peterson 135). Harper extends this vision in *Trial and Triumph,* when Annette's former schoolteacher, Mr. Thomas, describes to the white merchant Hastings his vision of national unity: "Can men corrupt and intimidate voters in the South without a reflex influence being felt in the North? Is not the depression of labor in the South a matter of interest to the North?" (222). Hastings responds, "I should be sorry to know that by our Southern supineness we were thoughtlessly helping create a black Ireland in our Gulf States" (225).

For Harper, the two regions' economic and political ties required racial amity to forge national unity, rather than an imperial relationship such as that between Britain and Ireland. Freed people possessed manual labor skills that could generate value, if racist northern whites could be persuaded to hire them. Otherwise, the habitual racism of the white middle class would create and maintain the South as a desultory colony. More broadly, temperance, which fought against the corrupting influence of drink on voters and workers, black and white alike, was for Harper a basic component of modern industrial and democratic performance. Her missions to the South figuratively enact colonialism as an effect of temperance's urgent drive to consolidate the black public sphere; its consistent emphasis on perfectibility always required a "supine" body to raise up.

The Woman's Christian Temperance Union and the End of Reform

Bureaucratic debates within the WCTU show how, as temperance shifted from the moral reform of individual behavior to the legislative politics of Prohibition, white southerners cast off the metaphoric colonial relationship with the North, transferring it more squarely to people of color. The WCTU was founded in Ohio, in 1873, to focus middle-class women's Christian principles on temperance, suffragism, and other reforms related to public health and equality. It had special departments of Southern Work and of Work Among Colored People; Harper served as superintendent of the latter.

In 1889, the southern chapters protested this organizational structure, claiming, "It is painful to be reported as a missionary field, as are the colored and Foreign work" (quoted in Mattingly 85). The WCTU accordingly abolished that department—yet retained the one missionizing people of color. As WCTU president Frances Willard began enlisting southern white women to extend the organization's political reach and influence on the national level, she made such concessions to their racism.

Harper expressed her frustrations with a different aspect of the WCTU's structural racism: the separate-but-equal black and white local chapters. Harper felt that self-organized black chapters should be allowed but should be recognized as equal to the white ones at the national level (Mattingly 87–88). When the white chapter of the Louisville, Kentucky, WCTU insisted that the black chapter be titled "colored," the black women who had formed it disbanded; a black North Carolina chapter refused to be called "colored" and adopted instead the title "WCTU no. 2" (Blum 203). Harper challenged racism within the WCTU in an essay published in the *A.M.E. Church Review,* in 1888, claiming that conflict within the organization "is not the contest of a social club, but a moral warfare for an imperiled civilization. Whether or not the members of the farther South will subordinate the spirit of caste to the spirit of Christ, time will show" ("Woman's Christian Temperance Union" 284). Consistent with her lifelong commitment to a rational, moral black public sphere, Harper tried to convey the universal stakes of temperance—its transcendence of racial, social, and class difference. But her protest produced no action.

Race relations within the WCTU further deteriorated. The well-known imbroglio over the WCTU's position on lynching, in which Ida B. Wells challenged Willard's racism, reveals the crisis of black temperance and its idealized public sphere, and Harper's awkward appearance at the scene of their demise. To validate southern whites' racist violence, Willard recirculated the false specter of drunken black masculine violence: "The colored race multiplies like the locusts of Egypt. The grog shop is its centre of power. The safety of women, of childhood, of the home, is menaced in a thousand localities at this moment" (quoted in Blum 202). The trope of the drunken, crazed black man looking to rape white women and wreak mayhem would soon morph into the even more tragically absurd notion that cocaine-fortified black male bodies could resist police bullets (Musto 7).

In reality, southern people of color were largely temperate. After Reconstruction, they tended to vote Republican or "dry" on local measures, and yet they were scapegoated for tensions between wet and dry whites (Herd, "We Cannot Stagger" 166). Harper's public statements were inadequate to the situation. If the crazed drunken trope were true, she suggested, "then I hold that the deeper the degradation of the people the louder is their call for redemption." She also said, "I do not believe lynchings of negroes who assault girls are brought about alone by the color of the criminals" (quoted in Mattingly 190–91).

Especially compared to Wells, Harper underperformed in her response to Willard's racist hijacking of temperance. In a symposium on temperance in 1891, Harper acknowledged the brutality of lynching but also implied that its pretexts might be real: "Men of my race, do not think when colored men are still murdered, lynched, and even burned for real or supposed crimes that our work is done. . . . With clear brains and earnest hearts . . . help to create . . . a great and glorious first party . . . wearing sobriety as a crown, and righteousness in the girdle of its loins" ("Symposium" 375). Harper's formulation "real or supposed crimes" was an equivocation. Moreover, she called her listeners to moral power by urging them not to drink—just when black sobriety had become spectacularly irrelevant. Her comments failed to identify, analyze, and counteract her own organization's complicity in lynching. These were exactly the problems that Wells's speech identified, as she explained how, because whites lost no opportunity to take advantage of people of color, their intemperance would only worsen their situation and "give judges and juries the excuse for filling the convict camps of Georgia" (380). Where Harper spoke allegorically of crowns, Wells gave pragmatic suggestions for linking black temperance efforts to a critique of racial injustice, in the press, churches, and schools.

In *Iola Leroy*, Aunt Linda called for northern instruction rather than politicians to help build freed southern communities; in "Symposium—Temperance," Harper similarly construed black temperance politics vaguely, as a kind of fantasy. A second 1891 essay by Harper, "Temperance," further advocated political withdrawal. Calling on her readers to acknowledge the "community of interests" between whites and people of color in the United States, she characteristically proposes uplift—the development of "self-reliance, self-control, and self-respect"—as superior to politics in providing solutions to black crises (reprinted in Boyd 200). Alluding to the most urgent of these crises, lynching, she writes that if the government will not protect people of color, then "let the colored man abate somewhat of his political zeal, and do all he can to shame the nation into a higher regard for human rights, and human life, than it now possesses" (200).

Harper framed her exhortation to temporarily abandon politics as a response to the realities of black poverty and powerlessness, which rendered political support for either party too weak to count. Addressing temperance at the end of the speech, Harper claims that the liquor trade, so powerful it can "awe one [party] into silence and entice the other into alliance" was "too strong and dangerous for us to give it aid or countenance" (201). Harper's plan was based on the unfortunate miscalculation that the U.S. government, or white voters, might be shamed into moral action. Responding to the failures of Reconstruction, Harper felt that more time and preparation were needed to ready people of color for robust participation in a racist public sphere. At a moment when southern states were enacting laws to disenfranchise black voters, withdrawal was a risky strategy, and elsewhere Harper urged whites, "Instead of taking the ballot from [the African American's] hands, teach him how to use it" (Harper, "Black Woman," 357).

Even here, she focused on long-term solutions. Her much-desired national black public sphere remained an ideal on the horizon—as the voluntarist, antipolitical, reform model of temperance had always seen it. In its ideology, perfection might never come, though it was the object of constant striving. Forever rising above the imperfections of politics, it could drift into the sphere of fantasy and myth. Michael Warner illustrates the centrality of this fantastic vision to temperance discourse in his interpretation of the conclusion of Walt Whitman's *Franklin Evans* (1842), when a crowd identifies and celebrates the very last drunkard to become sober. The novel's "voluntarist utopia" was also Harper's (Warner 275).

By the 1890s, the new political realities brought about by her own organization had rendered Harper's ideas and style outmoded. The WCTU's campaign, encapsulated in its slogan "No North, No South, No Sectionalism in Politics, No Sex in Citizenship," forged a vision of a white-dominated public sphere that eclipsed Harper's hopes for an exemplary black one and for an integrated national one (Blum 194). The idea of black exemplarity and white shame as political strategies may never have been efficacious, but they now were clearly exposed as vulnerable to racist misrepresentation and ignorance. Freed people's abstemiousness could not prevent their portrayal as intemperate and chaotic or rescue them from homicidal racist violence. Likewise, Harper's specific policy recommendations, such as for educational voting requirements, were born in an earlier, more idealistic era. She wanted to eradicate white voters' racism through education, and to thus design a more perfect citizenry, but southern racists also endorsed education as a way to disenfranchise people of color—a tactic more attuned to political urgencies.

Frederick Douglass had disavowed his earlier commitment to temperance in the 1880s, and W. E. B. Du Bois also dropped temperance from his political portfolio. Once the WCTU programmed its racism, black intellectuals and activists found temperance impossible to endorse and fell silent on the topic (Herd, "Paradox" 369). The antebellum alliance of temperance, abolition, and suffrage was gone, its influence dissipated. Additionally, Harper's characteristic rational-ization of the emotions and denial of sensuality as a ground for political subjec-tivity was falling out of style. When the Great Migration brought people of color to urban centers, music, drink, and dancing created a new, modernist culture that privileged physical pleasure and featured alcohol, particularly during Prohi-bition (Herd, "We Cannot Stagger" 178). The antebellum black temperance bar-gain, of requesting citizenship and civil rights by renouncing sensuality, faded; with it went the rigidly rational, unreachably perfect model of the black public sphere.

Unrealistic as its hyperrationalism may now seem, the public sphere that black temperance imagined should not remain a footnote in history. Black temperance held that reason could exist within politics, which would straight-forwardly reflect the noble characters of its actors. In a prepolitical time and space, education and uplift, the techniques of reform, would prepare them, one at a time, to enter the public sphere together. Though it was a naive political theory, reform accomplished much in the nineteenth century and afterwards. Black women joined the WCTU in spite of its racism, because it offered ways for them to strengthen their communities through a national organization at a time when not many would include them and when few government programs could help. In the WCTU, they could perform "social purity work, work with prisoners, kitchen gardens, flower missions, [and] work among fallen women" (Dublin and Scheuerer).

Such ideals and activities continued to inform and inspire subsequent gen-erations of black women activists and community builders, most immediately in the National Association of Colored Women, the International Council of Women of the Darker Races, and the Young Women's Christian Association.[7] The success of the voluntarism and idealism that fueled reform movements such as black temperance may best be judged by their broad legacies; after all, such voluntary institutions and their descendants became political forces in their own right, their relevance enduring to this day.

Notes

1. Frances Harper's cousin William J. Watkins, a colleague of Frederick Douglass's who crit-icized white abolitionists, supported the Free Soil Party, and advocated for Haitian emigration, never collaborated with her, perhaps because her politics were too right wing. See Peterson 133.

2. On Harper's transnational poetry, see Callahan 57–58. On Harper as a southern writer, see Dietzel 164–68. On her northernness, see Carby 62–94.

3. For an extended discussion of the metaphor of intemperance as self-enslavement, see Zieger chapter 2.

4. On gore in Washingtonian narratives, see Reynolds 68.

5. On education in the novel, see also Robbins 81–89. On education and class in Harper's novels, see Williams.

6. R. U. Cheagle also describes the American Colonization Society's temperance program, including the Liberia Temperance Society. Despite official statements, the testimony of an ex-colonist suggests it was not a success (56–62). For an account of Amanda Berry Smith's temperance missions to Liberia in the 1880s, see Dublin and Scheuerer.

7. On the National Association of Colored Women, the International Council of Women of the Darker Races, and the Young Women's Christian Association, see Dossett 15–65.

Works Cited

Alves, Jaime Osterman. *Fictions of Female Education in the Nineteenth Century.* Routledge, 2009.

Baker, Houston A., Jr. *Workings of the Spirit: The Poetics of Afro-American Women's Writing.* U of Chicago P, 1991.

Berlant, Lauren. *The Queen of America Goes to Washington City: Essays on Sex and Citizenship.* Duke UP, 2007.

Blum, Edward J. *Reforging the White Republic: Race, Religion, and American Nationalism 1865–1898.* Louisiana State UP, 2005.

Boyd, Melba Joyce. *Discarded Legacy: Politics and Poetics in the Life of Frances E. W. Harper, 1825–1911.* Wayne State UP, 1994.

Callahan, Monique-Adelle. *Between the Lines: Literary Transnationalism and African American Poetics.* Oxford UP, 2011.

Carby, Hazel V. *Reconstructing Womanhood: The Emergence of the Afro-American Woman Novelist.* Oxford UP, 1987.

Cheagle, R. U. *The Colored Temperance Movement.* Master's thesis, Howard University, 1969.

Cooper, Brittney C. *Beyond Respectability: The Intellectual Thought of Race Women.* Urbana: U of Illinois P, 2017.

Dietzel, Susanne B. "Frances Ellen Watkins Harper." *The History of Southern Women's Literature,* edited by Carolyn Perry and Mary Louise Weaks, Louisiana State UP, 2002, pp. 164–75.

Dossett, Kate. *Bridging Race Divides: Black Nationalism, Feminism, and Integration in the United States, 1896–1935.* UP of Florida, 2008.

Douglass, Fredrick. *Narrative of the Life of Frederick Douglass, an American Slave.* 1845. Edited by Houston A. Baker Jr., Penguin, 1982, pp. 115–16.

Du Bois, W. E. B. "The Talented Tenth." *The Negro Problem,* edited by Booker T. Washington, James Pott, 1903. pp. 31–76.

Dublin, Thomas, and Angela Scheuerer, eds. Introduction. *Why Did African-American Women Join the Woman's Christian Temperance Union, 1880 to 1900?* State University of New York at Binghamton, 2000.

Fulton, DoVeanna. "Sowing Seeds in an Untilled Field: Temperance and Race, Indeterminacy and Recovery, in Frances Harper's *Sowing and Reaping." Legacy,* vol. 24, no. 2 (2007), pp. 207–24.

Habermas, Jürgen. *The Structural Transformation of the Public Sphere: An Inquiry into a Category of Bourgeois Society.* 1962. Translated by Thomas Burger and Frederick Lawrence, MIT Press, 1991.

Harper, Frances. "A Black Woman Appeals to White Women for Justice for Her Race." *The Female Experience: An American Documentary,* edited by Gerda Lerner, Bobbs-Merrill, 1977, pp. 354–57.

———. *Complete Poems of Frances E. W. Harper.* Edited by Maryemma Graham, Oxford UP, 1988.

———. *Iola Leroy, or, Shadows Uplifted.* 1892. Oxford UP, 1988.

———. "Symposium—Temperance." *A.M.E. Church Review,* vol. 7, no. 4 (April 1891), pp. 372–81.

———. *Trial and Triumph.* 1889. Minnie's Sacrifice, Sowing and Reaping, Trial and Triumph: *Three Rediscovered Novels,* edited by Frances Foster Smith, Beacon, 1994, pp. 179–286.

———. "The Woman's Christian Temperance Union and the Colored Woman." 1888. *A Brighter Coming Day: A Frances Ellen Watkins Harper Reader,* edited by Frances Smith Foster, Feminist Press at the City University of New York, 1990.

Henry, Katherine. *Liberalism and the Culture of Security: The Nineteenth-Century Rhetoric of Reform.* U of Alabama P, 2011.

Herd, Denise. "The Paradox of Temperance: Blacks and the Alcohol Question in Nineteenth-Century America." *Drinking: Behavior and Belief in Modern History,* edited by Susanna Barrows and Robin Room, U of California P, 1991, pp. 354–75.

———. "We Cannot Stagger to Freedom." *The Yearbook of Substance Use and Abuse,* vol. 3 (1985), 141–86.

Levine, Robert S. *Martin Delany, Frederick Douglass, and the Politics of Representative Identity.* U of North Carolina P, 1997.

Mattingly, Carol. *Well-Tempered Women: Nineteenth-Century Temperance Rhetoric.* Southern Illinois UP, 1998.

Musto, David. *The American Disease: Origins of Narcotic Control.* 3rd ed. Oxford UP, 199.

Pease, Jane H., and William H. Pease. *They Who Would Be Free: Blacks' Search for Freedom, 1830–1861.* Atheneum, 1974.

Peterson, Carla L. *"Doers of the Word": African-American Women Speakers and Writers in the North (1830–1880)*. Oxford UP, 1995.

Quarles, Benjamin. *Black Abolitionists*. Oxford UP, 1969.

Reynolds, David S. *Beneath the American Renaissance: The Subversive Imagination in the Age of Emerson and Melville*. Oxford UP, 1988.

Robbins, Sarah. "Gendering the Debate over African Americans' Education in the 1880s: Frances Harper's Reconfiguration of Atticus Haygood's Philanthropic Model." *Legacy*, vol. 19, no. 1 (2002), 81–89.

Rosenthal, Debra J. "Deracialized Discourse: Temperance and Racial Ambiguity in Harper's 'The Two Offers' and *Sowing and Reaping*." *The Serpent in the Cup: Temperance in American Literature*, edited by David S. Reynolds and Debra J. Rosenthal, U of Massachusetts P, 1997, 153–64.

Sehulster, Patricia J. "Frances Harper's Religion of Responsibility in *Sowing and Reaping*." *Journal of Black Studies*, vol. 40, no. 6 (July 2010), 1136–52.

Sellers, James Benson. *The Prohibition Movement in Alabama, 1702–1943*. U of North Carolina P, 1943.

Stancliff, Michael. *Frances Ellen Watkins Harper: African American Reform Rhetoric and the Rise of the Modern Nation State*. Routledge, 2011.

Still, William. Introduction. *Iola Leroy: or, Shadows Uplifted*, by Frances Harper, Oxford UP, 1988, pp. 1–3.

———. *The Underground Railroad: A Record*. Porter and Coates, 1872, pp. 755–850.

Warner, Michael. *Publics and Counterpublics*. Zone, 2002.

Williams, Andreá N. *Dividing Lines: Class Anxiety and Postbellum Black Fiction*. U of Michigan P, 2013.

Yacovone, Donald. "The Transformation of the Black Temperance Movement, 1827–1854: An Interpretation." *Journal of the Early Republic*, vol. 8, no. 3 (Autumn 1988), 281–97.

Zieger, Susan. *Inventing the Addict: Drugs, Race, and Sexuality in Nineteenth-Century British and American Literature*. U of Massachusetts P, 2008.

"It's Either the Candy or the Hooch"

Unlawful Appetites in Orson Welles's Border Noir Touch of Evil

CARA KOEHLER

> The plot [of film noir] is murky, like a nightmare
> or the ramblings of a drunkard.
> —GEORGES SADOUL (in Borde and Chaumeton, "Definition" 24)

> The personal element in the film is the hatred I feel
> for the way police abuse their power.
> —ORSON WELLES (in Bazin et al. 50)

It is easier now than it would have been in 1958 to imagine that a major studio film would unabashedly address racist law enforcement and border policy corruption. Even more provocatively for the time, some of *Touch of Evil*'s well-known actors were staged in brownface makeup, under the direction of cinema's wunderkind (and subsequent enfant terrible) Orson Welles, in order to lampoon corrupt policing.[1] The film not only is recognized as the wildly boisterous, brutish nightcap for the so-called classical noir epoch but also is acknowledged as a meta noir, a highly self-aware product eager to comment on its own constructedness (Auerbach 102). Welles achieves this effect by engaging with real-life border politics of both past and present.

About forty years prior to the film's release, the Eighteenth Amendment was passed, and Prohibition "gave rise to a lucrative and violent smuggling enterprise that set law enforcement, smugglers and civilians on a collision course" that, according to Miguel Antonio Levario, "would not be settled until the repeal of the amendment in 1933" (95). The problem with Levario's claim, however—that clashes between Mexicans and U.S. law enforcement were "settled" after 1933—is apparent in the political struggles of the Eisenhower presi-

66

dency at the time *Touch of Evil* (1958) was being filmed. During this period, as Donald Pease has noted, the United States came face-to-face with new issues such as migrant laborers, undocumented migrants, and border policing jurisdictions. But the subversive political unconscious of the film that Pease describes didn't capture scholarly attention until the 1970s, which suggests that, while this film proffers an important imaginary of the U.S. South, it possibly wouldn't have registered with 1958 audiences as "southern" because it appeared at a time when television and film were circling other imaginaries, such as those in Tennessee Williams's stories and their filmic adaptations or in southern chain gang tales of black/white race relations, such as *The Defiant Ones* (1958), released the same year as *Touch of Evil*.

There is no doubt that, although it was perhaps less manifest than the on-screen African American civil rights struggle in the South, the theme of border tensions between Hispanics and Americans in *Touch of Evil* nevertheless carries relevance and renewed importance in light of present-day border politics in the United States, notably the ongoing war on drugs, the "illegal" immigrant crisis, and, most recently, President Donald Trump's proposed border wall. The question that scholars of film and culture have yet to explore, however, is why *Touch of Evil* relies so heavily on the aesthetic of substance abuse and indulgent behavior to communicate moral and cultural corruption, especially racism, in law enforcement. And what does the entwinement of national borders and borderless delirium suggest about the southern specificity of noir as a genre that returns, with Welles's late masterpiece, to its inebriated roots?

Welles leans on the dynamic of alcohol abuse to communicate moral and cultural corruption because addiction perfectly satirizes crooked law enforcement practices by evoking the abject. (It is no coincidence that "bad," "pig," and "dirty" are among the most common collocations associated with police.) Carnal, illicit desire was thematically nothing new in southern-set films of the 1950s; in fact, two of the most commercially popular Tennessee Williams adaptations, *A Streetcar Named Desire* (1951) and *Baby Doll* (1956), both directed by Elia Kazan, ooze a humid, titillating quality. Both were dubbed morally indecent, though *Streetcar* introduced what critic Roger Ebert calls a "smelly" hero who "smokes and drinks in a greedy way."

This hero was embodied by Marlon Brando, and his muscular torso stands in stark contrast to the far more abject drinker portrayed in *Touch of Evil*, where the midcentury South provides fertile ground for a type of noir that doesn't negotiate the contrast between decadent cities and the pastoral heartland but, rather more interestingly, the border between the purportedly lawful white America and lawless incursions from criminal Latin America. As Peter Stally-brass and Allon White write in *The Politics and Poetics of Transgression* (1986), the "most powerful symbolic repertoires" of bourgeois societies are situated at their "borders, margins and edges, rather than at the accepted centres" (20, quoted in Lott). Like Welles's mash-up of the high (A-list actors and a studio-backed production) with the low (garish brownface makeup and flaunty cli-chés), symbolic polarities work in unison to signify the political.[2]

Julian Murphet rightly claims that "any reference (no matter how veiled) to blackness in U.S. culture instantly evokes the entire history of race relations in U.S. politics and everyday life" (22). The South was, of course, the epicenter of racial conflict in America. Yet Murphet simply conflates race with blackness. He goes on to say that "blackness" constitutes the "political unconscious" of the noir cycle, since African Americans do not appear in these postwar noir films (22, 28).

By and large, Murphet is correct: black figures, let alone black and white racial tensions, are almost wholly absent from classical American film noir. Eric Lott's essential essay "The Whiteness of Film Noir" (1997) goes further, noting how "at a [historical] moment when bold new forms of black, Chicano, and Asian activism and visibility confronted resurgent white revanchism and vig-ilantism," film noir turned its "moral focus on the rotten souls of white folks" (543). *Touch of Evil* tapped into equally pressing racial conflicts of its time: those between white and Hispanic communities. In the following sections, I explain how unchecked appetites, whether the dogged pursuit of justice or the excessive consumption of alcohol, stand in for the larger insecurities of the nation at that time, and how the tropes of addiction and race resonate with this narrative of borderless America and with each other.

From Noir to a New Southern Imaginary in 1950s Cinema

The paradoxically parched setting of *Touch of Evil*—the fictional border town of Los Robles—is critical in conveying an alcoholic vibe. Perhaps nowhere else in the noir universe is the importance of geographic setting more prominent and yet more nebulous than in *Touch of Evil*. Set on the southern border between the United States and Mexico, the plot pivots on the question of jurisdiction: a car bomb planted on the Mexican side of town blows up on the American side, and two law enforcement heads, well-respected figures on each side of the border, struggle for control and for an affirmation of their integrity.

The issue of border town jurisdiction, however, is not limited here to the *who, what,* and *where* of seeking justice for a crime in an ambiguous precinct. In *Touch of Evil,* jurisdiction and border ambiguity also befoul the act of *self-policing;* the audience is asked to consider how officers of the law decide on the appropriate code of conduct when straddling the line of their sanctioned enforcement zones. Considering the visual log of evidence in Welles's film, the answer becomes fuzzy, and this legal gray zone is approximated not only by bizarre camera angles and the constant crossing of literal and symbolic borders but also by the centrality of alcohol abuse to the plot. The film envelops the decidedly derelict border town of Los Robles in an aura of contamination, a taboo filth that concretizes myriad plagues on society: alcohol, drug abuse, criminal deceit, and racial contempt.

This abject imagery is inextricably tied to its location (the U.S.–Mexican border) and to the tension between the "locals" (Mexicans) and the "law" (cops and detectives). The two figures of the law—Detective Hank Quinlan and Miguel "Mike" Vargas—are the protagonists of this essay. I probe how the added element of racial difference in film noir steers or alters the aesthetic of addiction—how, in other words, the sense of disorder triggered by racial difference ties in with noir's uncontrolled pleasures of consumption. The setting at the periphery of the American South, a place already marked as historically hostile to its nonwhite "citizens," adds another layer of dread to this narrative of power and substance abuse.[3]

This peripheral South in *Touch of Evil* complicated for audiences more recognizable southern imaginaries: the agrarian South, the Civil War and civil rights South, and, more and more, the Southern Gothic. The "new" understanding of the South that Welles put forth emerged when noir moved away from its urban roots to the border/periphery of rural America. *Touch of Evil* not only is one of the final films in the classical noir period but also stands out as a distinct turn away from urban to wilderness, and this happened under the influence of the Southern Gothic. While Gothic noir reigned as a compelling hybrid in the 1940s, with films like Alfred Hitchcock's *Rebecca* (1940) or André De Toth's *Dark Waters* (1944), southern noir had yet to emerge as its own filmic fusion.

An early indication of the shift from Gothic noir to southern noir would be Jacques Tourneur's *Nightfall* (1957) and most certainly Charles Laughton's *The*

Night of the Hunter (1955), both set in rural, liminal, but imprecise southern spaces. Noir's turn, during the 1950s, from its classically urban California aesthetic to the wilderness/rural, I suspect, occurred under the influence of the Southern Gothic, especially given the uptick in Southern Gothic adaptations in 1950s American cinema (such as *Baby Doll, Cat on a Hot Tin Roof,* and *Long Hot Summer*). The border town feature of this new southern turf, like the one in *Touch of Evil,* is nevertheless still very representative of California, where noir has its roots. The motel (a strong motif in the film) could even be called the epitome of nonurban space in the California context.

Director Orson Welles was very much aware of the fraught California–Mexico border politics and the migrant worker exploitation of the era, as evinced in Donald Pease's essay. Taking echoes from slavery's role in the Southern Gothic, Welles takes border politics into new territory in *Touch of Evil* with the Mexican immigration issue. Thus, the film updates the Southern Gothic by shifting the focus to another racially maligned community—Mexicans—while maintaining focus on Gothic tropes such as evil (much in the tradition of Flannery O'Connor), porosity (in its liminal figures and landscapes), and decay (through the image of Quinlan's rottenness and bloatedness, and most famously in the final scene of his death in an oily swamp). Incidentally, the swamp is possibly the ultimate trope of the southern wilderness as a site of resistance for liminal individuals that society cannot integrate.

Southern Drinking in 1950s Cinema
and *Touch of Evil*

One southern trope that would have been immediately recognizable to those who had read or seen the filmic adaptations of *Cat on a Hot Tin Roof* or *A Streetcar Named Desire* is excessive alcohol consumption. It not only is a common thread within American film noir but also is a vital aesthetic and narrative device through which corrupt law enforcement is satirized in *Touch of Evil.* The unique role alcohol plays in southern border politics is best understood through the prism of race. Midway through the film, American police captain Hank Quinlan downs a few rounds of bourbon in a Mexican bar and professes to his partner, Menzies, "I never drink on my own beat." "Beat" refers to a policeman's patrol shift and, more importantly here, his or her territory. And when Menzies laments, a few lines earlier, that he's been in every bar in town looking for

Quinlan, the latter replies, "Yeah, I've been in half of them, only here on the wrong side of the border."

If Eric M. Krueger is right to note that border towns "bring out the worst in countries" and are perhaps "metaphors for what those countries really are," one could, in fairness, apply this same logic to Welles's film. Border towns bring out the worst in individual people, which is evident in the criminal activity in the early moments of the film—the planting of a car bomb—but also in law enforcement. With the explosion of the car bomb comes the scattering of "all that lies repressed in the mother country thriv[ing] on the surface in the border town" (58).[4] Two of these latent desires are sex and inebriation, signs of which appear in almost every frame in the film's opening sequence, in the form of neon letters spelling out "Liquor" and "Girls." Also repressed, however, are the emotions of American cop Hank Quinlan, namely his prejudice against Mexicans, which cannot even be quelled by sobriety.

Prejudice and alcohol, as it turns out, are important parts of the southern border backstory. Prohibition was a key moment in the exacerbation of fraught relations between U.S. law enforcement and Mexico after the Mexican Revolution, as contraband spirits flowed in through border towns like El Paso, and "violence that often erupted between [law enforcement] and the [Mexican alcohol] smugglers complicated matters even more by reinforcing the idea of the Mexican as criminal" (Levario 112). Once Quinlan hits the hooch, he reveals his own "backstory wound," to borrow a term from Michaela Krützen—namely, that his wife was murdered by a "half-breed." I agree with James Naremore's point that this supposed explanation of Quinlan's character comes across rather feebly. Quinlan is not just a token white, racist cop. His character ranges from psychopathic to pathetic, from charming to sentimental—even to, as Naremore also aptly remarks, that of a child (151–52).

The border town breeds hybrid people looking for firm ground amid criminal, escapist temptations. The role of alcohol cannot be divorced from southern law enforcement on the U.S.–Mexico border, and the American film industry has historically figured these borderlands as "unsafe (racialized) spaces" in need of intense policing as far back as the Progressive Era (Brégent-Heald 14). The sum of the aforementioned temptations—whether candy or hooch, women or gambling—created a border subculture in 1950s America that posed unique challenges to authorities and affected the racial and cultural imaginary of this new South, protruding like a belly under the belt of the United States.

The Southern Hispanic Imaginary in *Touch of Evil*

In her chapter "Latin," from *Keywords for Southern Studies* (2016), Claudia Milian points out Latin America's protuberant, split geography—"to the west of
the U.S. Southeast and to the south of the U.S. South"—which makes it geographically distinguishable from the U.S. national imaginary but, in terms of
culture and "life practices," has been kept at a close distance to the United
States. Milian also draws attention to how "Latin significations" possess the
power to widen the paradigmatic black–white binary that "has historically omitted a brownness-cum-blackness as well as varying shades between black and
white" (182–83). I would argue that, in *Touch of Evil,* this notion of darkness
takes on more nuance. The shadowy, chiaroscuro trademark look of film noir
is complicated by the symbolic tones of, for example, white American actor
Charlton Heston and Armenian actor Akim Tamiroff wearing makeup to appear
more Latino. The layering effect of "dark" and white citizenship, a self-aware
practice, teases out the contrived manufacturedness of any film before it that
used browning makeup on white actors to pit the alien Other against the—
often—white hero.[5]

Welles's capstone to the film noir period, which obsessively expanded notions of the black/white binary, seemed also to unmask another "shade" of troubled U.S. citizenship in the vast and evolving southern regions. The border between the United States and Mexico was, for the director, not an arbitrary but a
very deliberate setting for his noir drama of police injustice. I am not the first to
stress the border setting and its loaded significance within the cultural context
of 1958 America.[6] Naremore invokes a series of historical facts that align *Touch
of Evil* with a southern racial social-commentary thematic: the Supreme Court
ruling on segregation had taken place just four years prior to 1958, the civil
rights movement was in full swing, and the 1957 National Guard operation at
Little Rock Central High School was still fresh in the minds of audiences (148).
By making the victims of police power abuse not African American but Mexican, Welles mirrors the plight of one disenfranchised community in the U.S.
South with that of another.

Donald Pease reads this film even more specifically against the backdrop
of 1950s Mexican–American relations, an era marked by border policing and
mass deportations.[7] It is within this state-of-emergency period that Pease locates the film's absent cause, or an element that "does not appear in the field
[of the film's] effects" but is latent in its mise-en-scène as what the film desires

to represent (Copjec xii). Looking for the same invisible effects, I find that the physical markers in *Touch of Evil*'s southern landscape and those of the main characters (their actual bodies) signal changing attitudes about addictive behavior, leisurely consumption, and racial stereotypes.

The Mexican law enforcement officer Vargas (Heston) navigates the film as the amorphous head of an "emergency state" and is thereby lawfully absolved of the same "police state tactics" he employs to sabotage American police captain Quinlan (Pease 84). Vargas's specific assignment in the film—as Pease also duly notes—is to work under the Pan-America Narcotics Commission to prosecute drug traffickers. Whereas Vargas flashes his carte blanche to fight "the perceived threat that illegal substances . . . pose to the public's moral health," Quinlan's attempt to frame a young Mexican man for the murder of a rich white man and his female escort reveals a parallel resistance against the threat that "'illegal aliens' were reputed to pose to the public's moral health" (93). Pease's rhetoric registers the harm of excesses by calling to mind a surfeit of power, the indulgent enforcement of law on both sides of the line. Quinlan's alcoholic body, fattened with power, evokes this excessive hegemonic lust, which itself is an addiction to control that leads to a symbolic poisoning of the cultural contact zones Quinlan navigates, as evinced by the drunken, "used" landscape of Los Robles.

Although Welles's thriller-cum-social satire brings to a crescendo many of the trademark tropes running through the classical noir period (approximately 1941–1958), such as labyrinthine landscapes, oblique filming angles, moody lighting, crime, and existential crisis, Anthony Mann's 1949 *Border Incident* was perhaps the first noir to deal explicitly with U.S.–Mexico's charged border control relations and what critic Jonathan Auerbach cleverly calls "noir citizenship."[8] To Auerbach, noir citizenship describes the telltale existential condition of the noir figure, a "condition of statelessness or nonexistence that sheds light on the psychological contours of *film noir* as well as the anxieties of a nation-state at midcentury intent on policing itself against uninvited outsiders" (102–3). Correctly invoking the political climate of midcentury America, and certainly of the Cold War, Auerbach goes on to show how the geographic setting of film noir on a border sensitized audiences to the United States' own fear of border infiltration during the second Red Scare. Extrapolating from Auerbach, I consider noir's geography to shed light on the "brown scare"—a term I use to describe the power struggles along the racially diverse U.S. South–Mexican border. And where Auerbach and *Border Incident* draw our attention to a "condition of statelessness," I argue that the condition of "power inebriation" denotes a hegemonic high that successfully allegorizes the United States' power profligacy in the late mid-twentieth century.

The Southern Male Drinker

The toxic effects of corrupt policing are conveyed through the symbolic figure of megalomaniacal American cop Quinlan, who is unable to cope with his waning influence and efficacy in law enforcement. By interrupting his detective work to get drunk, and thus coming under the influence of alcohol's mock power, Quinlan ironically relinquishes control to a Mexican drug lord, who coerces him into using excess force and uncouth methods to throw his competition, Mike Vargas, off the trail of Quinlan's own corrupt practices.

With a plot of this caliber, it's no wonder *Touch of Evil* throws the audience off its guard. Until now, the discussion has focused on *Touch of Evil's* imagined territories and shades of southern citizenship, and the way in which they signal troubled attitudes about addictive behavior and racial stereotypes. In the remainder of the essay, I want to argue that this southern borderland geography squares with a narrative of overindulgent consumption of both the alcoholic and authoritative kind. Doing so will answer a question I raised at the outset of this essay: What does the entwinement of borderlessness and loss of control suggest about the southern specificity of noir as a genre?

For a cycle of films grounded by rather fixed aesthetic conventions (dark, expressionistic) and mood (bleak), noir's geography was nonetheless far more flexible. Vast, rural borderlands operate here just as menacingly as the unfeeling urban jungle or the torpid southern United States. I will first consider the importance of geographic setting in popular cinema, specifically with regard to framing a particular brand of (white) masculinity. Then I shift the focus to popular film framings of the prototypical southern white male whose (fraught) masculinity is by and large characterized by alcohol abuse, a tool employed widely throughout American cinema to index a loss of agency or latent, taboo desires. I consider specifically the tormented, powerless male figures that appear in 1940s and 1950s Hollywood noir productions and who are often "the masochistic type, [their] own executioner" (Borde and Chaumeton, *Panorama* 9).

An archetypal film tactic used to highlight a compromised male authority with waning agency is to make that figure an alcoholic, given alcohol's notorious impairment of both libido and decision-making abilities. Films released contemporaneously to Welles's 1958 border noir likewise employed the setting of the U.S. South to scrutinize troubled male drinkers, most notably the melodramas of Douglas Sirk—*Written on the Wind* (1956)—and Richard Brooks—*Cat on a Hot Tin Roof* (1958). In these films, set in big oil Texas and on an old Mississippi plantation, respectively, the southern imaginary is evoked inside the walls of sumptuous mansions housing the spoiled, damaged children of wealthy industrialist families whose antics and drinking habits threaten the family legacy. In the years following *Touch of Evil,* southern drinking narratives were one-upped by transporting the tales to the Southwest. Two blockbusters starring John Wayne, *Rio Bravo* (1959) and *True Grit* (1969), featured a boozed and bruised law enforcement figure who somehow prevailed as a flawed but "good" man among "evil" or "bad" men.

I see *Touch of Evil*'s male antihero as more closely aligned with the emasculated white law enforcement of the late 1950s and 1960s Westerns than with the southern alcoholics of the classic melodramas, who drank primarily to veil sexual impotence and, occasionally, to repress homosexual desires.[9] Nevertheless, melodrama, like noir, also negotiated topical subjects such as "afflictions and injustices of the modern, post-Enlightenment world" (Williams 53). The gap between the melodrama and Western genres that *Touch of Evil* bridges is important, most of all because it makes use of the noir aesthetic— widely recognized for its ability to camouflage illicit, politically charged themes in its style—in order to escape censorship by the infamous Hays Code union, much as the so-called sensation scenes in melodramas functioned to "put forth a moral truth in gesture and picture that could not be fully spoken in words" (Williams 52).[10] The cinematographer Russell Metty, who had worked on Sirk's melodrama *Written on the Wind* (and would go on to photograph John Huston's melancholy Western *The Misfits*) joined forces with Orson Welles for *Touch of Evil* to stage yet another whirlwind, "baroque" tale of loose-grip alcoholic men whose power is melting away in the hot southern landscape.

Excessive Consumption and Power Abuse

In its disorderly aesthetics and camerawork, as well as in the transgressive reversal of racial prejudices, *Touch of Evil* exposes hitherto offensive "border cinema" conventions of color-coded stereotypes frequently seen in the Western genre. Its obsession with grime and the grotesque challenges and parodies American culture's own preconceived notions about race, power, addiction, and the abject connotations they evoke. Not only do so-called border films speckle the canvas of classical noir but also the period as a whole, from *The Maltese Falcon* up through *Touch of Evil*, "seemed uncomfortable with borders" (Reft).

Captain Quinlan embodies this discomfort, and he pays with his life for his hyperbolic hatred of Mexicans. He resents not only external borders but also limits in general, especially those that draw out the investigations he undertakes. *Touch of Evil* undermines white male authority by discrediting the figure of the Law both visually and narratively—Quinlan eats and drinks like he does detective work: without limits or scruples.

The fat cop is an interesting trope to consider in light of Quinlan's hyper-caloric embodiment.[11] The fat villain figure may have been recognizable to the trained noir eye, for it harked back to Casper "the Fat Man" Gutman in both Dashiell Hammett's 1930 hard-boiled novel *The Maltese Falcon* and John Huston's proto-noir film adaptation of Hammett's book in 1941.[12] This figure no doubt stands for excess and unscrupulous drives, no matter the ethics or cost, in both the early noir and in Welles's *Touch of Evil*. This is yet another example of the central claim I am making, that noir's subtle subtexts were perfectly employed to conflate excessive oral consumption with a broader condition of lawlessness among U.S. law enforcement agents at a time when both studio heads and committees like the House Un-American Activities Committee kept a close watch on Hollywood directors.

Alcohol abuse was always a loaded practice in film noir, but *Touch of Evil* stretched the limits of the metaphor. In early iterations of the white male detective in film noir, such as Sam Spade (*The Maltese Falcon*) or Phillip Marlowe (*The Big Sleep*), an air of witty, dry-humored charm and unflappability characterized their approach to crime solving. It was not uncommon for them to chain-smoke and sip scotch with clients, or even alone in their darkly latticed offices. As the noir period progressed, a decline in social acceptability of white male drinking becomes evident, as the very look of the figures who themselves are supposed to embody social stability and the Law shifts from cool (Bogart) to corpulent (Welles). Welles's decision to caricature the white male figure of the Law as an obese alcoholic marked one of the first truly creative provocations of Hollywood's stereotyped portrayals of degenerate "ethnic" peoples, whether African American, Native American, or Mexican (see Pease 85–86).

Additional visual elements convey a muddled, inebriated consciousness and further align the film with discourses on illegal substances, an observation that Pease, in his analysis of the film, makes only briefly (93). While the central plot involves Quinlan's seemingly back-burner struggle with alcohol addiction, the symbolic importance of temptation and indulgence increases over the course of the film. Welles's aesthetic immediately strikes viewers as erratic; the behavior of the figures seems disorderly and compulsive. Between multi-accented shouting, nervous mumbling, and breathy whispers, not to mention the numerous disorienting camera angles, it is no accident that *Touch of Evil* sends the audience into a private state of stupor, in turn approximating the sensation of toxicomania and the queasiness of a mind trying to resist the lure of drug indulgence. Quinlan's famously grunted lines function as a border language in their own right, a niche dialect of spoken riddles aimed to further bewilder the nonnationals and make them wary of the drunkard-like dispositions of American law enforcement. Alongside the excellent script, the visuals in *Touch of Evil* evoke an even greater state of toxicity.

Within minutes of the film's opening, American audiences would have recognized that the handsome actor in brownface playing Miguel Vargas, the Mexican narcotics cop, was Charlton Heston and that the man wearing the fat suit and scarfing chocolate candy bars between mumbled lines was the director himself, Orson Welles.[13] What viewers also learn early in the film is that Hank Quinlan is a recovering alcoholic known to rely on—in perfect Wellesian irony—his *gut* feeling to catch the perpetrators.[14]

While Welles employs carefully calculated stereotypes, at no time do the representations slip into mere objective representations of reality. In fact, alcohol plays an important role in the rejection of the objective lens: from the moment Quinlan takes his first shot (that is, of bourbon), the entire narrative trajectory and film aesthetic slip into an even more intemperate stupefaction, distorting reality for the viewer. Welles and his art direction provide ample road signs for a loss of agency that accompanies heavy drinking. For example, Quinlan is always forgetting his cane—an allusion to his unsteady legs and frame of mind—and in one scene he plucks a tiny bird's egg from a nest, only to accidently smash it between his maladroit hands. Incidentally, he has just come from the bar in this scene. The loss of agency and the audience's disbelief at Welles's stark physical transformation are mirrored most eloquently, however, in an early dialogue between Quinlan and his former lover, Tanya, who fails to recognize him when he walks into her brothel. Trash blows across a field of oil derricks just before Quinlan passes through the arched doorway to Tanya's:[15]

(*Pianola music plays throughout in the background*)

QUINLAN: Have you forgotten your old friend, hmm?

TANYA: I told you we were closed.

QUINLAN: I'm Hank Quinlan.

TANYA: I didn't recognize you. You should lay off those candy bars.

QUINLAN: It's either the candy or the hooch. I must say, I wish it was your chili I was getting fat on. Anyway, you're sure lookin' good.

TANYA: You're a mess, honey.

QUINLAN: Yeah. That pianola sure brings back memories.

TANYA: The customers go for it. So old it's new.

In this abbreviated but loaded dialogue, the audience comes to understand that Quinlan used to enjoy the simpler southern comforts of making love and eating chili (the latter perhaps even a euphemism for the former), and even the company of a Mexican woman, but that he has become unrecognizable thanks to a former drinking habit and, recently, his obesity. The final line of the dialogue borders on nostalgia, the mention of the pianola a nod to the Western genre in which it was a saloon mainstay. Here, however, on the dust-blown and seedy border between the United States and Mexico, the comment seems an acknowledgment of that troubled southern notion of the "good ol' days before the war." Like the ex-Confederate soldier found in countless American Western films, who lives out his ethnic cleansing fantasies on the American frontier, Captain Quinlan, in this bad cop/border noir hybrid, uses the badge as a smoke screen for his racist philosophy of law.

Even more intriguing in these lines is the mention of "the candy or the hooch," the actual brown consumables Quinlan devours—chili and chocolate—mirroring his penchant for chewing up and spitting out the Mexican criminals of the border town. The unchecked appetite of the white male authority figure treats the brown body as a consumable, and, along the lines of Kyla Wazana Tompkins's thinking in *Racial Indigestion*, "encod[es] all the ambivalence and terrible violence of American racial politics" along with it (90).

The pianola scene in Tanya's brothel is paralleled by another critical moment, later in the film, when Quinlan's chocolate bar is cast aside for yet another brown-hued consumable: bourbon. While Quinlan is making a deal with a Mexican drug ring leader, Grandi, the same song that was coming from Tanya's pianola begins playing in the background, though this time from a modern jukebox. Nostalgia hits Hank as he gazes off frame, apparently remembering something, distracted. The music underlines the narrative refrain, but it also reminds the viewer of Quinlan's confession to Tanya that he needs candy bars so he doesn't slip back into alcoholism.

Despite all his brilliant observations in *The Magic World of Orson Welles* about Quinlan's childlike qualities mixed with his "viciousness" (152), Naremore misses one more symbol embedded in the scene set in the Los Robles bar: Quinlan's childishness is no doubt linked both to his love of chocolate bars and to a bottle fetish, an emblem of infantilism. These props suggest "at one and the same time Quinlan's self-delusion and his idealism. . . . [They are] a pathetic attempt to return to preadolescence" (153). The shot glasses framed in close-up at a low angle in in the bar scene—one empty, one in Quinlan's hand—likewise dramatize his self-deluded attempts to "get straight," in the sense of both sobering up and cleaning up his integrity. Quinlan robotically sets down the shot glass in the scene just following, an action that bespeaks reflex more than contentment.

Aside from food and drink, imagery of dirt, trash, and oil abound in this film. Jonathan Auerbach observes how imagery of blood and soil (107) dominate the allegorical aesthetic of *Border Incident*, a film about the illegal smuggling of Mexican laborers across the U.S. border. In *Touch of Evil*, the Mexican–American border is similarly figured as "mucky," but instead of soil as the dominant element, we're offered a series of heady, liquid imagery, from a stagnant river to perspiration to alcohol, which figures the southern milieu as one in which the "evil" acts of injustice committed on the border cannot be neatly absorbed back into the land. The evil stagnates at the surface and manifests itself as toxic elements—the sweat that excretes from a human's pores; the ooze of crude oil that is pumped from the land in the background and pools into a river of sludge, again evoking the abject imagery of the swampy Southern Gothic. Much like the loaded term "evil" in the film's title, the two -isms that plague Hank Quinlan's existence—racism and alcoholism—are only vaguely "touched" upon yet are unmistakably present, thanks to the palpability of the visual metaphors.

The conflation of alcoholic excess and filth has been a submerged part of the cultural imaginary ever since the temperance movement (Berk), and in film noir it becomes a highly effective visual device, evoking both moral and physical disgust. Quinlan's belligerent attempts to frame Vargas and other Mexicans, as Eric Lott rightly argues, "only cements our sense of Vargas's moral purity and exposes the processes of projection and abjection that would pin white criminal activities on dark bodies and deploy them as racial metaphors for white crimes" (563). The American symbol of the Law (Quinlan) atones with his life for his transgressions and falls into the murky river of sewage and oil. Vargas, on the other hand, flees with his American bride, across the border and into the darkness, to remove her from the "filth" and to keep her "name clean"—sentiments he repeats several times throughout the film.

The film's inky gasoline landscapes reveal a dark side of overconsumption that links directly with southern ecology. Unlike the traditional agrarian South, evocative of plantation-based commerce and consumption, the South figured in *Touch of Evil* is permeated with industrial machinery, specifically the facilities and tools of the petroleum industry.[16] The frame is often infiltrated by blowing trash and ciphers of crude consumables, such as the oil derricks dotting the landscape and creating a sense of foreboding.

The skeletons of these crude industries looming in the dusty background draw an interesting parallel with the other major consumer industry between Mexico and the U.S. South: tourism. Beginning around the time of Prohibition and running throughout World War II and into the 1950s, border tourism boomed, growing "twenty-fourfold between 1935 and 1970" (Lorey 102). Tourism on the Mexican side of the border centered around indulging appetites for food, drink, and entertainment, all of which is apparent in the opening minutes of *Touch of Evil*, during which brightly lit advertisements lure with the promise of girls and alcohol and locals with street carts hawk their goods. These visual elements convey a muddled, inebriated consciousness of border towns, but they also realign the film with the history of illegal trade and resource extraction. These histories fuel the prejudice and power struggles that still define a border remarkable for its refusal, despite all efforts of policing and control, to be closed.

Conclusion

This 1958 film corroborates what remains a topical issue in the United States with regard to police bias and brutality against nonwhite Americans. In one particularly powerful line, Vargas tells Quinlan that "a policeman's job is only easy in a police state." As signs of a U.S. police state loom darkly into view at the dawn of a new so-called American Greatness, two fraught issues addressed in the film have dominated American politics and public culture: police brutality and border politics. *Touch of Evil* feels ripe for reexamination, as it powerfully dramatizes a bloated, belly-up body politic and an "evil" that cannot be washed away or absorbed into the earth, as Quinlan's body floating among plastics and trash vividly implies. Welles managed to convey a truly unique understanding of borders by compelling audiences to visualize binational tensions that both reinforced (through narrative) *and* undermined (through camp) popular images of the threshold border zones. They are just as constructed, skewed, and sharply angled as the film.

Michael Denning reminds us, in *The Cultural Front*, that Orson Welles's "narratives of race and racism were central to his anti-fascist aesthetic," a sentiment that possesses an especially eerie ring in the Trump era (395).[17] That *Touch of Evil* emplots a parable of fascism and racism is undeniable, but it can also be understood as a catalyst for an array of "dirty cop" films that would come to an aesthetic peak in 1992 with Abel Ferrara's infamously drug- and booze-infused *Bad Lieutenant*. In 1958, Orson Welles helped pop the proverbial cork on "bad cop noir," and proof of the genre's longevity is found in a series of emulators, from *Dirty Harry* (1971) to both Ferrara's film and Werner Herzog's 2009 reimagining of *Bad Lieutenant*. In the latter cult classic and in the recent television drama *True Detective* (2014–), addiction and corrupt law enforcement are figured side by side on a southern landscape still imbued with an allegorical noir that translates power addictions of the body into unrestrained vices of the body politic.

Notes

1. The effect of this brownface is best (if not somewhat problematically) described by James Naremore as a film "peopled with celebrity friends as if dressed for a Halloween party" (146).

2. See Lott (562–63) for an eloquent reading of the high–low, white–brown border crossings as represented by Charlton Heston in *Touch of Evil*.

3. Much like Vivian Sobchack's concept of the "chronotope" of film noir, the U.S. South becomes another backdrop in noir's obsession with the "inversion of intimacy and domesticity and . . . a space symptomatic of the upheavals and insecurities of the time" (Gustafsson 52). Noir links, in this sense, quite naturally to the Southern Gothic literary mode. Southern fiction giant William Faulkner cowrote the screenplay to Howard Hawks's noir *The Big Sleep* (1946).

4. James Naremore also views Los Robles as "a kind of subconscious for Northerners, a night world just outside their own boundaries," but also as "a zone where latent corruption . . . [and] economic exploitation of one country by another becomes more obvious" (158–59).

5. This practice was most widely used in the Western genre, in which white actors would wear "redface" to portray Native Americans.

6. See Pease, Denning, Bazin, and Naremore, among others.

7. One can even draw parallels here to the 1943 Zoot Suit Riots, which occurred in Los Angeles and were the result of racist anti-Mexican sentiments, primarily on the part of sailors and soldiers (members of the then racially segregated military).

8. Anthony Mann's work may also offer clues to the link between the border-crossing cop figure in noir and the Southern Gothic cinema of the 1940s and 1950s: his (uncredited) noir classic with director Alfred Werker, *He Walked by Night* (1948), features a Hispanic cop. Mann likewise filmed a heady adaptation of Erskine Caldwell's 1933 novel *God's Little Acre*, which was released in the same year as *Touch of Evil* (1958) and seems comparable in its bizarre, sexualized, and jarring performances and narrative.

9. Film theorist Linda Williams says of 1950s melodrama that its critics "delighted in the way the repressed emotions of characters seemed to be 'siphoned off' onto the . . . general hysteria of the mise-en-scène" (44), while Thomas Elsaesser notes that melodrama's "mechanisms of frustration and over-compensation" are outed through characters who abuse alcohol (86). He specifically names *Written in the Wind* (1956) as a film that best explores the "metaphoric possibilities of alcohol (liquidity, potency, the phallic shape of bottles)" and the oil derrick trope that would appear in *Touch of Evil* (87). Both of these claims make it clear that homosexuality made only oblique appearances to an audience bold enough to read the queer subtext. Peter Bradshaw, revisiting *Cat on a Hot Tin Roof* (1958) in a 2012 article for the *Guardian*, does not mince words about the film's repressed homosexual hero.

10. As Michael Billington, along with countless critics of the adaptation have noted, homosexual overtones in Tennessee Williams's *Cat on a Hot Tin Roof* were stamped out by the Hays Code for the Hollywood adaptation.

11. Before noir, the stereotype of the fat sheriff was embodied most iconically by actor Roscoe "Fatty" Arbuckle and the Keystone Kops in silent movies such as *The Sheriff* (1918) and *The Round-Up* (1920). After noir came the fat police chief Gillespie from the five-time Academy Award–winning *In the Heat of the Night* (1967), which was also concerned with race relations, and Louisiana sheriff J. W. Pepper, who appears in two James Bond movies, *Live and Let Die* (1973) and *The*

Man with the Golden Gun (1974). Orson Welles's Hank Quinlan is an interesting link between them: physically depraved like the early Fatty but also morally dysfunctional like the racist cops who would replace Arbuckle in the 1960s and 1970s.

12. The atomic bomb dropped on Nagasaki at the end of World War II was nicknamed "Fat Man" by Manhattan Project physicist Robert Serber, who was inspired by actor Sydney Greenstreet's performance as the Fat Man.

13. Jonathan Munby, in *Public Enemies, Public Heroes: Screening the Gangster from Little Caesar to Touch of Evil*, points out that Heston insisted that Welles direct the film, even though the studios regarded Welles as vexatious and he was under investigation by the FBI for his "dubious political affiliation" (223).

14. See Gilman, "How Fat Detectives Think" for a fascinating history of the truth behind "gut feelings," fatness, and rationality.

15. This shot recalls yet again the Western genre, namely the iconic final scene of *The Searchers* (1956), in which the male figure of the Law (also an unabashed racist, played by John Wayne), captured in silhouette, pauses under the door frame of a home before deciding he shall not enter.

16. In 1921, more than 25 percent of the world's oil came from the Mexican border state of Tamaulipas (Lorey 42), and natural gas discovered in the 1940s and 1950s provided additional wealth (102).

17. Welles's numerous contributions to the political left and his activism for the disenfranchised, from public broadcasts on the radio to films, are detailed in Denning.

Works Cited

A Streetcar Named Desire. Directed by Elia Kazan, performances by Vivien Leigh and Marlon Brando, Warner Bros., 1951.

Auerbach, Jonathan. "Noir Citizenship: Anthony Mann's 'Border Incident.'" *Cinema Journal*, vol. 47, no. 4 (Summer 2008), pp. 102–120, www.jstor.org/stable/20484414.

Baby Doll. Directed by Elia Kazan, performances by Karl Malden and Carroll Baker, Warner Bros., 1956.

Bad Lieutenant. Directed by Abel Ferrara, performances by Harvey Keitel and Brian McElroy, Aries Films, 2009.

Bad Lieutenant: Port of Call New Orleans. Directed by Werner Herzog, performances by Nicolas Cage, Eva Mendes, and Val Kilmer, First Look, 2009.

Bazin, André, et al. "Interview with Orson Welles (II)." 1958. *Orson Welles: Interviews*, edited by Mark W. Estrin, UP of Mississippi, 2002.

Berk, Leah Rae. "Temperance and Prohibition Era Propaganda: A Study in Rhetoric." Brown University Library Center for Digital Scholarship, www.library.brown.edu /cds/temperance/essay.html.

The Big Sleep. Directed by Howard Hawks, performances by Humphrey Bogart and Lauren Bacall, Warner Bros., 1946.

Billington, Michael. "Cat on a Hot Tin Roof: Tennessee Williams's Southern Discomfort." *Guardian*, 30 September 2012, theguardian.com/stage/2012/sep/30/cat-on-a-hot-tin-roof.

Borde, Raymond, and Etienne Chaumeton. *A Panorama of American Film Noir: 1941–1953*. 1955. Translated by Paul Hammond, City Lights, 2002.

———. "Towards a Definition of Film Noir." *Film Noir Reader*, translated by Alain Silver, edited by Alain Silver and James Ursini, Limelight, 1996, pp. 17–25.

Border Incident. Directed by Anthony Mann, performances by Ricardo Montalban, George Murphy, and Howard Da Silva, Warner Brothers Pictures, 1949.

Bradshaw, Peter. "The Cat on a Hit [*sic*] Tin Roof Film May Be Censored—but in Some Ways it's Superior." *Guardian*, 17 October 2012, www.theguardian.com/stage/2012/oct/17/cat-hot-tin-roof-film-censored.

Brégent-Heald, Dominique. *Borderland Films: American Cinema, Mexico, and Canada During the Progressive Era*. U of Nebraska P, 2015.

Caldwell, Erskine. *God's Little Acre*. Grosset and Dunlap, 1933.

Cat on a Hot Tin Roof. Directed by Richard Brooks, performances by Elizabeth Taylor, Paul Newman, and Burl Ives, MGM, 1958.

Copjec, Joan, editor. *Shades of Noir: A Reader*. London and Verso, 1993.

Dark Waters. Directed by Andre De Toth, performances by Merle Oberon and Franchot Tone, United Artists, 1944.

Denning, Michael. *The Cultural Front: The Laboring of American Culture in the Twentieth Century*. 1997. Verso, 1998.

Dirty Harry. Directed by Don Siegel, performances by Clint Eastwood and Harry Guardino, Warner Bros., 1971.

Ebert, Roger. "*A Streetcar Named Desire*." Rogerebert.com, 12 November 1993, www.rogerebert.com/reviews/a-streetcar-named-desire-1993.

Elsaesser, Thomas. "Tales of Sound and Fury: Observations on the Family Melodrama." *Imitations of Life: A Reader on Film and Television Melodrama*, edited by Marcia Landy, Wayne State UP, 1991, pp. 68–92.

Gilman, Sander L. "How Fat Detectives Think." *Cultures of the Abdomen: Diet, Digestion, and Fat in the Modern World*, edited by Christopher E. Forth and Ana Carden-Coyne, Palgrave Macmillan, 2005, pp. 221–37.

Gustafsson, Henrik. "A Wet Emptiness: The Phenomenology of Film Noir." *A Companion to Film Noir*, edited by Andrew Spicer and Helen Hanson, Wiley-Blackwell, 2013, 50–66.

He Walked By Night. Directed by Alfred Werker and Anthony Mann, performances by Richard Basehart and Scott Brady, Eagle-Lion, 1948.

In the Heat of the Night. Directed by Norman Jewison, performances by Sydney Poitier and Rod Steiger, MGM, 1967.

Krueger, Eric M. "*Touch of Evil*: Style Expressing Content." *Cinema Journal*, vol. 12, no. 1 (Autumn 1972), pp. 57–63.

Krützen, Michaela. *Dramaturgie des Films: Wie Hollywood erzählt.* Fischer Taschenbuch, 2004.

Levario, Miguel Antonio. *Militarizing the Border: When Mexicans Became the Enemy.* Texas A&M UP, 2012.

Live and Let Die. Directed by Guy Hamilton, performances by Roger Moore, Yaphet Kotto, and Clifton James, MGM, 1973.

The Long, Hot Summer. Directed by Martin Ritt, performances by Orson Welles, Paul Newman, and Joanne Woodward, Twentieth Century Fox, 1958.

Lorey, David E. *The U.S.–Mexican Border in the Twentieth Century.* SR Books, 1999.

Lott, Eric. "The Whiteness of Film Noir." *American Literary History,* vol. 9, no. 3 (Autumn 1997), pp. 542–66.

The Maltese Falcon. Directed by John Huston, performances by Humphrey Bogart and Mary Astor, Warner Bros., 1941.

The Man with the Golden Gun. Directed by Guy Hamilton, performances by Roger Moore, Christopher Lee, and Clifton James, MGM, 1974.

The Misfits. Directed by John Huston, performances by Montgomery Cliff, Clark Gable, and Marilyn Monroe, United Artists, 1961.

Milian, Claudia. "Latin." *Keywords for Southern Studies,* edited by Scott Romine and Jennifer Rae Greeson, U of Georgia P, 2016, pp. 179–88.

Munby, Jonathan. *Public Enemies, Public Heroes: Screening the Gangster from Little Caesar to Touch of Evil.* U of Chicago P, 1999.

Murphet, Julian. "Film Noir and the Racial Unconscious." *Screen,* vol. 39, no. 1 (Spring 1998), pp. 22–35.

Naremore, James. *The Magic World of Orson Welles.* 1978. Southern Methodist UP, 1989.

The Night of the Hunter. Directed by Charles Laughton, performances by Robert Mitchum and Shelley Winters, United Artists, 1955.

Nightfall. Directed by Jacques Tourneur, performances by Aldo Ray and Anne Bancroft, Columbia, 1957.

Pease, Donald E. "Borderline Justice/States of Emergency: Orson Welles' *Touch of Evil.*" *New Centennial Review,* vol. 1, no. 1 (2001), pp. 75–105.

Rebecca. Directed by Alfred Hitchcock, performances by Joan Fontaine and Laurence Olivier, United Artists, 1940.

Reft, Ryan. "Living on Noir Borders: Race, Sexuality, and Law Enforcement in *Touch of Evil* and *Crimson Kimono.*" *Tropics of Meta,* 8 October 2013, www.tropicsofmeta.word press.com/2013/10/08/living-on-noir-borders-race-sexuality-and-law-enforcement -in-touch-of-evil-and-crimson-kimono.

Rio Bravo. Directed by Howard Hawks, performances by John Wayne, Dean Martin, and Ricky Nelson, Xenon, 1959.

The Round-Up. Directed by George Melford, performances by Roscoe Arbuckle and Buster Keaton, Famous Players-Lasky, 1920.

The Searchers. Directed by John Ford, performances by John Wayne and Jeffrey Hunter, Warner Bros., 1956.

The Sheriff. Directed by Roscoe Arbuckle, performances by Roscoe Arbuckle and Betty Compson, Comique Film, 1918.

Sobchack, Vivian. "Lounge Time: Postwar Crises and the Chronotope of Film Noir." *Refiguring American Film Genres: History and Theory,* edited by Nick Browne, U of California P, 1998, pp. 129–70.

Stallybrass, Peter, and Allon White. *The Politics and Poetics of Transgression.* Methuen, 1986.

Tompkins, Kyla Wazana. *Racial Indigestion: Eating Bodies in the Nineteenth Century.* New York UP, 2012.

Touch of Evil. Directed by Orson Welles, performances by Orson Welles, Charlton Heston, and Janet Leigh, Universal, 1958.

True Detective. Directed by Cary Joji Fukunaga, performances by Matthew McConaughey and Woody Harrelson, HBO Studios, 2014.

True Grit. Directed by Henry Hathaway, performances by John Wayne, Glen Campbell, and Kim Darby, Paramount, 1969.

Williams, Linda. "Melodrama Revised." *Refiguring American Film Genres,* edited by Nick Browne, U of California P, 1998, pp. 42–88.

Written on the Wind. Directed by Douglas Sirk, performances by Rock Hudson, Lauren Bacall, Robert Stack, and Dorothy Malone, Universal, 1957.

The Tennessee Two-Step

Narrating Recovery in Country Music Autobiography

MATTHEW D. SUTTON

Country music and alcohol share a well-established connection, from 1920s recordings of Appalachian moonshiner songs like "Take a Drink on Me" to the beer-soaked clichés of today's "bro-country." However, country musicians' internalization of the South's historical ambivalence toward secular, institutionalized treatments for alcoholism is less obvious and far less discussed. Numerous performers—disproportionally male—have attested to bouts of problem drinking, many of them within craftily plotted, coauthored autobiographies. In analyzing the autobiographies of two complementary country stars—Johnny Cash (in *Man in Black*, published in 1975, and *Cash*, from 1997) and George Jones (*I Lived to Tell It All*, 1996)—we find an unresolved tension between the dual self-portrayal of the southern hell-raiser and the more reflective and repentant recovering alcoholic. Both narratives selectively employ the disease model and the "recovery-speak" emanating from Alcoholics Anonymous's Twelve Steps, yet they spurn the collectivism and nonspecific spirituality of AA. In short, each man represents inebriety and sobriety as two successive, discrete phases that resolve neatly with a reaffirmation of domesticity and faith, rather than as stages in an ongoing process, like the Twelve Steps. As autobiographical subjects, both Cash and Jones perform for their readers an interpretive dance of sorts, which might be termed the Tennessee Two-Step, to simultaneously make a claim for recovery and affirm the normative values of country music and the South.

Occasional tour mates and longtime friends, Cash and Jones had life stories familiar to even casual fans. As a contemporary of Elvis Presley and Jerry Lee Lewis on Memphis's Sun Records, Cash pioneered a signature sound grounded in his deep baritone voice and stripped-down instrumentation. In classics like "I Walk the Line" (1955) and "Folsom Prison Blues" (1955), Cash contained multitudes, expressing both devotion and transgression. Uniquely able to transcend the cultural divisions of his day, the singer became a popular draw on tour and on television, capable of advocating for Native Americans and drug addicts and, with equal sincerity, performing at the Nixon White House and on Billy Graham Crusades. Overcoming both an addiction to pills in the 1960s and a stint in rehab in the 1980s, Cash found stability in his marriage to June Carter and his born-again Christianity. While maintaining a loyal fan base that traversed genre boundaries, his music reached a new audience with *American Recordings* (1994) and subsequent volumes, called simply *American* (1996–2006), and the posthumous biographical film *Walk the Line* (2005).

As Leigh H. Edwards has noted, Cash's enduring popularity rests in large part on his embrace of unresolved contradiction. As a traditionalist who found favor with both the 1960s counterculture and the 1990s alternative rock audience, a devout Christian and an admitted addict, and an interpreter of songs alternately tenderhearted and tough-minded, Cash embodied both authority and rebelliousness. By grounding much of his style in a folk ballad tradition, Cash avoided many of the lyrical clichés of honky-tonk country, particularly the fixation on alcohol. Although honky-tonk music equates sociality (particularly homosociality) with inebriation, Cash projected a somber, stoic persona—the semimythical "Man in Black"—even in songs like "Sunday Morning Coming Down" that refer to intoxication.

In contrast to Cash, Jones's public identity was virtually shaped by his associations with drinking. Top ten country hits like "White Lightning" (1959), "If Drinkin' Don't Kill Me (Her Memory Will)" (1981), and "Tennessee Whiskey" (1983) embedded an image of Jones as an Everyman turning to liquor either as fuel for a "hell-raisin'" good time or as solace for a broken heart. Even classic Jones numbers without explicit references to alcohol, like "The Grand Tour" (1974), "Choices" (1999), and his acknowledged masterpiece "He Stopped Loving Her Today" (1980) resound with the hungover melancholy of the remorseful problem drinker. The publicity surrounding his turbulent marriages (most publicly to his fellow country superstar and duet partner, Tammy Wynette), his financial troubles, his habit of missing concerts without warning, and his arrests on alcohol-related charges reinforced the tone of loss, regret, and commiseration found in many of his best-loved songs.

Enhancing his image is an oft-told story of Jones stubbornly driving his riding lawn mower eight miles to the nearest liquor store after his wife confiscated his car keys, which became a staple of Nashville lore (Jones 112–13). Allegedly, producers carefully calibrated Jones's alcohol intake during recording sessions so he would be "loose" in the studio but still intelligible (Kienzle 86). According to one biographer, Jones was held in such esteem among industry veterans that they credited him as a success story for sobriety years before it actually happened, in the process enabling his excessive drinking and concurrent cocaine use (Kienzle 178). As Barbara Ching notes, even as country music proclaims normative values and an ideal of "frugality, hard work, and moderation, Jones . . . stands for bankruptcy, extravagance, and addiction," becoming an unlikely hero in the process (126). Aside from an unsuccessful detour into rockabilly during the mid-1950s, Jones's music resisted fashion, a trait especially apparent during Nashville's periodic drifts toward the mainstream, and remained a touchstone of country's notion of stylistic authenticity.

During the most celebrated periods of their careers, Cash and Jones embodied the stereotype of hard-drinking, contentious southern masculinity that Ted Ownby, following W. J. Cash, terms the "helluvafella." Helluvafellas characteristically acted out when intoxicated, using liquor as the fuel to, in W. J. Cash's colorful description, "stand on his head in a bar, to toss down raw whisky at a gulp, to fiddle and dance all night, to bite off the nose of a favorite enemy, to fight harder and love harder than the next man" (50). The associations W. J. Cash draws between heavy drinking, barroom brawling, and down-home music making are not incidental. The southern imaginary exalts helluvafellas, larger-than-life figures, not only for their capacity for drink but also for their related recklessness and independent streaks, which resist the introspection and relationality that most therapeutic culture endorses. The trajectory of country music's most mythologized star, Hank Williams Sr., who underwent a brutal cycle of abstinence, drinking binges, and stays in hospitals and sanitariums during the 1950s yet turned his pain into unpretentious art before dying at twenty-nine, illustrates both the tragedy and allure of the hard-living helluvafella image. Williams's contemporary Faron Young (famed for his honky-tonk anthem "Live Fast, Love Hard, Die Young") summarized the male country star's typical headstrong resistance to therapeutic understanding when he boasted, "I'm not an alcoholic . . . I'm a drunk" (Carlin 444).

The streamlining of the country music industry and its lucrative turn toward a more affluent suburban audience made rebellious figures like Williams and Young nearly obsolete, while Cash and Jones suffered career declines as a new generation of stars found favor. The artist–fan relationship once bolstered by personal appearances became mediated through music videos and concerts with spectacular lighting and special effects. Paradoxically, the more popular country became, the more fans were kept at arm's length (Malone 81).

The publication of *Cash* and *I Lived to Tell It All* coincided with the 1990s' turn toward "civility and self-effacement" within mainstream Nashville, a campaign of upward mobility, mass acceptance, and conspicuous piety exemplified and monetized by Garth Brooks (Cox 123). Beer and whiskey shots remained lyrical staples, but radio playlists and sanitized media coverage of well-groomed country stars featured little realistic depiction of alcohol or alcoholism; traces of the hard-drinking excesses of Williams and Young were more likely to be found in anti-Nashville "outlaw" country and southern rock.

To certify their double-edged status as "legacy artists" (as opposed to current hit makers), Cash and Jones made their own peace with Music City USA by collaborating with seasoned country music journalists in their memoirs, who kept their subjects' candor well within unwritten industry bounds. Resigned to looking back rather than forward, Cash and Jones, like many in their generational cohort who helmed "as told to" autobiographies, addressed readers as longtime friends and devised a discursive style that privileged colorful, informal storytelling over strict veracity.

Perhaps due in part to this incongruence with the "crossover" ambitions of popular country, life stories by industry veterans often draw upon antiquated confessional forms. By their own descriptions, Cash and Jones model drinking behaviors in terms that predate the common use of the term "alcoholic." Consistently in his two autobiographies, Cash exhibits habits that nineteenth-century reformers called "intemperance," or an indulgence in drinking, where intoxication is not always the result or goal. Jones, on the other hand, resembles the problem drinker once labeled an "inebriate," the social outcast who represented the scourge of the temperance movement (Crowley 4). Likewise, many of the personal accounts collected over seventy-five years and appearing in Alcoholics Anonymous's foundational text, commonly known as the Big Book, adhere to a structure taken from the pages of the pre-Prohibition "drunkard narrative." In such cautionary tales, a young man of great potential falls in with a group of imbibing peers and begins to lose self-control after his first drink. A slow, sad decline follows, in which the protagonist loses all or nearly all he has, until a beneficent outside influence leads him to sobriety (Parsons 11).

For all their differences, Cash's and Jones's recountings of their past drinking share this familiar, melodramatic narrative structure. Both were born during Prohibition, and the two men's reminiscences focus on their childhoods in the "dry" South—Cash in rural Arkansas, Jones in Beaumont, Texas. Although Cash identifies his father as a problem drinker and Jones's father made moonshine, strong mothers and the church compensate as stabilizing influences. Brought up as Baptist teetotalers—Cash as a Church of God member, Jones as a Pentecostal—they shun alcohol as youths largely in deference to their faith and their abstemious maternal influences.

Their intemperance begins in earnest when they leave the South to join the armed forces and encounter hard-drinking northerners who lead them astray from the commandments of God and mother. After a "fatal first drink," further iniquity ensues. Initially content to play gospel music on his guitar while his Air Force buddies carouse, the innocent young Cash soon capitulates. "From beer I graduated to German cognac and having more wild times," Cash recalled in *Man in Black*. "The booze and the profanity began launching me into all kinds of other habits which soon became second nature" (67). Likewise, Jones recalls of his stint in the Marines, "What I didn't know about drinking before I went into the service I had learned by the time I got out" (36). The anachronistically judgmental manner in which they describe their impressionable younger selves, their past excesses, and their breaks with their fundamentalist upbringing suggests that their stories of their first encounters with intoxicants are more iterative than personal, and mindful of an audience segment unreceptive to drinking tales that lack a moral.

Addressing another, more secular readership in their autobiographies, however, both performers revel in the retelling of their wild days among other helluvafellas on the 1950s and 1960s country music touring circuit. Adding to the litany of tall tales related in earlier Cash biographies, such as Christopher S. Wren's *Winners Got Scars Too*, the singer recounts experiences on the road with alcohol, drugs, weapons, wrecked cars, fire, antagonistic law enforcement, and other essentials of the helluvafella mythos. Similarly, Jones, feigning abashment, retells vivid yarns of liquor and cocaine benders (some of which he admits he has no firsthand memory of), fights with girlfriends and wives, arrests, onstage meltdowns, and a series of cruel, booze-fueled pranks at other singers' expense.

Outside of the Nashville "bubble," many analysts of similar alcoholic narratives find such self-mythology a defense mechanism against wounded male pride and note that predominately male AA meetings occasionally take a turn toward escalating exchanges of macho drinking tales, called "drunkalogues" (Rotskoff 140–41; Halloran 70). In this way, they carry on the common trope that Bill C. Malone and others have identified in country music legend, in which performers indulge in outrageous acts of destructive male bonding on the road before being pulled back centripetally into the intertwined safety nets of domesticity, traditionalist-minded Nashville, and Jesus.

In collaboration with their respective coauthors, Cash and Jones credit their recovery from alcohol abuse to such a combination of personal, industry, and religious inspirations. Largely abandoning alcohol by the mid-1960s in favor of amphetamines and barbiturates, Cash returns to his roots through the intervention of his future wife, June Carter, and the Carter family, descendants of the "first family of country music."

"June and her mother and father formed a circle of faith around me, caring for me and insulating me from the outside world," Cash writes (*Cash* 172). Following a drug relapse in the 1980s, Cash agrees to a stay in the Betty Ford Center after an intervention by June and his children. Though admitting in the mid-1990s that the process remains "an ongoing struggle," he ascribes the end of his addiction in equal measure to the intercession of a loving family, the "tough love" of the clinic, and a renewed devotion to God.

By comparison, Jones's emergence from addiction is less clear cut. Whereas Cash underwent an orderly transformation as a result of intervention and his treatment program, Jones describes drying out, just as Hank Williams (and William Faulkner) experienced it, as a harrowing succession of psychiatric hospitals and rehabilitation facilities. Though surmising that drinking was the gateway to his cocaine addiction and the root of his personal and financial woes, Jones ultimately declares his independence from any recovery group, announcing in his preface, "I haven't been saved by Alcoholics Anonymous . . . I think that AA has been wonderful for a lot of folks, and I respect the life-changing improvements others have had through spirituality" (vii). Implying that AA's fundamental Twelve Step process and its related method of nondenominational spirituality work only for "others," Jones holds firm to a belief in personal salvation without outside interference or group affiliation.[1]

Remarkably, Jones suggests that he regards his drinking problem as more of an inherent character flaw (specifically a defect in his manliness) than a treatable disease, which is opposite of the model of recovery promoted by AA (162).

As in Cash's story, that flaw can only be resolved by the care and devotion of a woman—in Jones's case, his fourth wife, Nancy Sepulvado. Just as the prototype inebriate's tale blames young men and rowdy homosocial culture for leading a well-meaning man to drink, only a self-sacrificing woman can return him to the fold of domesticity and reassert his patriarchal privilege.

Autobiographies by female country performers reinforce this "guardian angel" persona. Typically, women in country music claim only a relational knowledge of alcoholism via fathers, uncles, brothers, and husbands, and they act in predictably enabling roles. In Loretta Lynn's immensely popular *Coal Miner's Daughter* (1976), the singer's experiences with alcohol are mostly secondhand, as she must balance her career with her caretaking of her helluvafella husband. "I've learned to live with it," she writes, "but it hurts me when he drinks too much" (134).

In this vein, the autobiographies by Tammy Wynette and June Carter Cash complement their husbands' recollections, emphasizing their own sacrifice. Though talented performers in their own right, both subsume their public personas in deference to the needs of their husbands. As Pamela Fox summarizes, "Country discourse [has] equated women's gender authenticity with nurturing domesticity" (127).

As nondrinkers, both women employ standard rhetorical approaches to contextualize their respective husbands' struggles. In *Stand by Your Man* (1979), Wynette's narrative characterizes Jones in broad strokes as an inebriate Jekyll-and-Hyde figure in the mold of a nineteenth-century temperance novel. Wynette comes face-to-face with Jones's alcoholic "demons," in classic Gothic fashion, only after they have married and settled in a mansion (which Jones demolishes in a drunken rage). Even after Jones pulls a rifle on her during a bender, Wynette characterizes his drinking sympathetically as a relational issue, marked not only by his spells of excess and sobriety but also by her incomprehension and worry that her "nagging" exacerbates his problem (151). June Carter Cash's testimony arrives at a similar conclusion but adopts a more clinical tone, as she labels herself a "codependent," suffering sympathetic anguish with her husband as he seeks treatment at the Betty Ford Center.

Only in the 1990s, in memoirs by performers like Reba McEntire and Tanya Tucker, did women in country music regularly break away from the temperance model and address their own social drinking without shame. However, such accounts took pains to stress that the love of the honky-tonk culture did not interfere with one's responsibilities as a wife, mother, and caretaker, in unspoken accord with AA's tradition of prioritizing men's stories of change and reform. Similar to the way southern conversion accounts portray wives as the gentle yet forceful persuasion behind their husbands' renewed devotion to the church, women in many AA-inspired programs are tasked to fulfill instrumental roles for recovering alcoholics, a gender bias still evident in the language of the Big Book (Amende 136–41). In their own books, Tammy Wynette and June Carter Cash do not question this division of labor, criticize their husbands' more lurid drunkalogues, or challenge the wisdom and efficacy of their husbands claiming recovery outside of the Twelve Step model. Therefore, they become willing partners in the recovery dance.

Just as Wynette and Cash naturally fall into AA-prescribed roles for female caretakers, AA's permeation of the larger culture can be gauged by the number of therapeutic phrases that have entered the common lexicon, such as "One day at a time," "Sick and tired of being sick and tired," and the Serenity Prayer ("God grant me the serenity to accept the things I cannot change . . ."). Although AA prides itself on its international reach, inflections of U.S. regionalism have persisted in the group's central writings. From the beginning, AA's confounders, Bill Wilson ("Bill W.") and Dr. Robert Smith ("Dr. Bob"), both native Vermonters, established within the organization a discourse of "blunt and deflationary pragmatism" (Crowley 157). The founders' use of "we" and "our" in the Twelve Steps and the first sections of the Big Book, and the exhortations to the reader delivered in second-person voice, presume a sense of egalitarian community to ease one's individual struggles. In turn, the first-person narratives by followers of AA, in the second half of the Big Book, contain few digressions, idiosyncratic turns of phrase, or other storytelling quirks. Unsentimental stories by men and women recounting estranged family relationships, work failures, and financial ruin undercut any hint of braggadocio or posturing.

As histories of Alcoholics Anonymous attest, much of the success of the first group chapter in Akron, Ohio, can be traced to such plainspoken personal stories, some of which have remained in the Big Book since its initial publication in 1939. Much of the Big Book's discourse still betrays its humble Midwest origins. In defense of its lack of overt evangelizing, the Big Book demurs in nonconfrontational fashion: "Of necessity there will have to be discussion of matters medical, psychiatric, social, and religious. We are aware that these matters are, from their very nature, controversial. Nothing would please us so much as to write a book which would contain no basis for contention or argument" (*Alcoholics Anonymous* 19). Though Bill W. formulated the notion of a personally defined "Higher Power" as a compromise between Christians and nonbelievers in early AA, remnants of the preferred pre–Twelve Step method of recovery through religious conversion remain (Hartigan 121–24).

Somewhat incongruously, the current Big Book retains from the original 1939 edition the first-person testimony of a southern man's struggles with "John Barleycorn," under the patronizing title "Our Southern Friend." Following the script of the drunkard narrative, the author of "Our Southern Friend" defies his mother and his faith when he leaves the farm and takes up drinking after leaving the region to work as a traveling salesman. After accepting his power-lessness over alcohol, the transplanted southerner accuses himself of "playing God" by intervening prematurely in others' recovery, shortcutting the Twelve Step process (*Alcoholics Anonymous* 217). Such presumptions enable members to potentially move directly from admitting a problem to claiming sobriety, an abridgement of the program that some in AA circles deride as "two-stepping" (see Djos 159). The narrator ultimately finds redemption and balance through both AA and the church, implying that, in its early stages, the secularly oriented program accepted overt evangelism from its southern members, in deference to regional mores.

Revisions in the subsequent editions of the Big Book—in 1955, 1976, and 2001—have typically eschewed regional and cultural distinctions in favor of more universal descriptions of problem drinking; most recent vignettes in AA literature are set in nameless suburbia, narrated by members of the professional managerial class. Though American membership in AA hovers around two million, exact numbers of AA membership in the South are difficult to verify. (In addition to member anonymity, the organization keeps no official roll.) However, there are quantifiable indications that AA holds less influence in the region.[2] According to aa.org, Georgia (with a U.S. Census–estimated population of 10.3 million in 2016), hosts eight central chapters, while Tennessee (with a population around 6.6 million) contains seven. By comparison, Michigan, with a 2016 population of more than 9.9 million, has twenty-seven AA centers and Massachusetts's nine chapters within a small geographic area serve more than 6.8 million residents. Some of this variation can be ascribed to demographics, yet the South's traditions of conspicuously condemning liquor from the pulpit and imbibing in private cannot be discounted in considering why AA meeting places are relatively scarce below the Mason–Dixon line. The rigid abstentionist position of Baptist sects, combined with the pockets of prohibition that remain in the South, hinders the openness and "sharing" that AA encourages among recovering alcoholics.

Additionally, the epiphany that accompanies conversion or being "born again" through baptism encourages subjects to hew to a simplistic, before-and-after, retrospective narrative that is incongruent with AA principles. In the model of recovery advocated by Bill W., sobriety is intended to be a lengthy, self-reflective process, not an instant rebirth (Hartigan 89). By contrast, Johnny Cash represents the intervention of God, his wife, and his family as the impetus for his sudden change in habits, and he craftily refers to his treatment at the Betty Ford Center as "basically a concentrated twelve-step program" (*Cash* 182).[3] Instead of quitting cold turkey, George Jones commits only to slowing down his drinking following the end of his cocaine addiction, adopting a harm-reduction model rather than the abstinence required of AA members (see Laing 32).

Both men characterize alcohol as a demon, but they employ the metaphor in a simple good versus evil dyad to explain how their faith has been tested (*Cash* 141; Jones 127). In their renditions of the Tennessee Two-Step narrative, Jones and Cash further legitimize these accounts of sobriety and redemption by co-opting the language of AA, such as by crediting their emergence from alcohol and drug dependence to "taking one day at a time" (Jones 243), through an act of "surrender" (*Cash* 124). Their easy adoption of recovery jargon to confirm their renewed commitment to family, faith, and career verifies their sincerity to the reader while seeming to support the criticism that AA primarily serves white men whose alcohol consumption has taken them off the path of middle-class conventionality and paternalist family life.

Admittedly, the "anonymous" part of Alcoholics Anonymous testimonials is impossible to pull off completely within the medium of celebrity autobiography. Still, both Cash and Jones give lip service to the AA program, regarding it as an adjunct to self-help and personal faith rather than as an all-encompassing system built around group support. While their autobiographies allude to and quote AA literature, neither Cash nor Jones committedly follows or endorses AA's required Twelve Steps to recovery, suggesting that the two steps bookending the program are sufficient. Their narratives essentially pick and choose the prescribed actions between Step 1 (admitting a problem with alcohol) and Step 12 (acknowledging a "spiritual awakening" and carrying the message to others).

As Lori Rotskoff observes, "Only two of the steps actually mention alcohol or alcoholics: the first, in which one admits that one is 'powerless over alcohol' and that life has 'become unmanageable,' and the twelfth, in which one pledges to carry the AA message to other alcoholics" (106). The intervening ten steps call on the individual to take systematic actions to assume humility under a higher power ("God as we understand him," in AA parlance), to take a "moral inventory," and to ask forgiveness from others for past transgressions.

As biographer Steve Turner recapitulates, Cash had little trouble reconciling this program of introspection and atonement with his faith, but he did not substitute AA tenets for his born-again beliefs (173–74). In the aftermath of his intervention, under the care of medical staff and counselors, the singer admits his weaknesses and humbles himself before God, generally following Step 4 through Step 7. Cash utilizes his first autobiography to openly make amends with several of his country music contemporaries (and uses his second book to expose other, less remorseful drinkers), reaffirming his place in Nashville's star system in the process. While such gestures fall within the parameters of Step 8 and Step 9, Cash makes it clear that they grow out of his own personal concern and sense of integrity, not out of obligation to any group.

Jones, however, omits Step 2 through Step 11 entirely but frames key anecdotes in his autobiography with direct quotes from Alcoholics Anonymous. Immediately after denying any overt influence from AA, Jones unapologetically explains in his preface, "I quit drinking and using drugs because I got sick and tired of being sick and tired" (vii). Recalling his initial exposure to alcohol counseling, Jones repeats AA's injunction to "live life one day at a time" (243). Summarizing his decision to kick his habits for good, Jones takes verbatim from AA the saying "An alcoholic will either sober up or he'll wind up locked up or covered up" (298). In these and other examples, Jones recasts AA's language into homilies for self-aggrandizing purposes.

Significantly, neither Cash nor Jones adopt the most revealing words in Alcoholics Anonymous's vernacular: "My name is . . . and I'm an alcoholic." In *Cash,* the singer owns up to his longtime addiction to pills yet describes his past drinking as "the equivalent of what alcoholics call a 'binge drinker,'" implicitly excluding himself from the category of chronic alcohol abuser (142). Characteristically, Jones speaks more bluntly. Echoing the lyrics he cowrote in his 1976 song "A Drunk Can't Be a Man," he expresses contempt for the "drunk" who, in time-honored inebriate fashion, disregards his family and fails in the public sphere because of liquor. However, in his book, Jones registers uncertainty about the disease model of alcoholism, declining to self-identify as alcoholic, concluding, "I'm not ready to take a stance either way. Maybe some folks are alcoholics and others are just voluntary drunks" (162). The suggestion that Jones considers himself a "voluntary drunk" in the Faron Young mold (as opposed to succumbing to the disease of alcoholism) and continues to partake in "moderate" drinking underscores the stubborn individualistic streak he is obligated to perpetuate in the name of traditional country and his complex performance persona.

The differentiation between "alcoholic" and "drunk" becomes especially charged when a person with an admitted problem uses the language of recovery to make such a value judgment. Jones's belligerence and self-pity have precedent in similar recovery texts in which, in Matts G. Djos's analysis, "confession, anger, and misanthropy may serve as a defense from feelings of inferiority and loneliness," traits that many in recovery associate with "dry drunks" (2). Cash's and Jones's two-step rejection of the "alcoholic" label and diffidence toward any sustained involvement in AA resemble what some members call "playing group," or repeating the language of recovery without full commitment to the Twelve Steps (Laing 237). Tellingly, neither star's self-declared break from alcohol dependence involves the support jobs many AA adherents undertake, such as sponsoring other recovering alcoholics or volunteering in AA administration. Such labors would likely blur the line that the narratives draw between reformed problem drinker and recovering alcoholic.

In contrast to stories in the Big Book that end provisionally, describing sobriety as a never-ending, never-closed process, Cash's and Jones's final chapters have relatively clear conclusions, summarizing the personal and professional plateaus each man has reached and promising a renewed commitment to their fans. In each book's photo section, rough snapshots of the respective performers at "rock bottom" give way to pictures of older, wiser men at peace, a paratextual companion to the narrative. Through word and image, their memoirs deftly two-step to reinforce an artificial binary between the problem drinker before Step 1, unwilling to face alcohol dependence, and after Step 12, following his "spiritual awakening."[4]

As a distinctively southern form of therapeutic culture, country music autobiography, with its reliance on melodrama, regionally influenced evangelism, and clear narrative resolution, reads inharmoniously with AA's more rational, "northern," open-ended discourse. Cash, Jones, their cowriters, and their wives attest to the fact that the domestic sphere and the Baptist church have effectively dominated the institutional therapeutic role of addressing alcohol abuse in the South. To acknowledge these influences, these autobiographies credit family and faith for their role in assisting a two-stage recovery/conversion, rather than the systematic process, fellowship among former drinkers, and less doctrinaire spirituality offered by the Twelve Step program.

Nonetheless, Cash and Jones borrow the cultural capital of AA to win sympathy from readers and to attest to their sobriety in familiar terms. In contrast to the Big Book's explanation that alcoholics' reflective stories ideally reveal "what we used to be like, what happened, and what we are like now," Nashville-approved autobiographies like Cash's and Jones's freely rewrite AA's conception of the ever-recovering alcoholic to reinforce the twinned personae of the reformed drinker and the helluvafella. In the realm of country music recovery narratives, with anonymity an impossibility, the impulse to exalt a down-home public image conflicts with AA's admonition to surrender the ego and "work the Steps." Ultimately, in memoirs like *Cash* and *I Lived to Tell It All*, the desire to reinforce a public image and leave behind recurrent troubles with alcohol results in a type of narrative dance made up of two simple yet highly choreographed steps.

Notes

1. The complete Twelve Steps are listed on the website of Alcoholics Anonymous: www.aa.org /assets/en_US/smf-121_en.pdf.

2. In keeping with its privacy policy, AA has no official attendance requirement or membership structure. AA's Tradition 3 states, "The only requirement for AA membership is a desire to stop drinking" (*Twelve* 139). Additionally, the total number of AA chapters is inexact, because only about one-third of groups listed as "Alcoholics Anonymous" are registered with AA's General Service Office (Travis 3–4).

3. The Betty Ford Center follows the inpatient treatment method known as the Minnesota Model, which promotes abstinence from drinking and a twelve-step program but has no official affiliation with Alcoholics Anonymous.

4. The performers' respective museums, adjacent to Nashville's tourist strip, reflect their divergent legacies of drinking. The George Jones Museum makes light of the singer's travails; a riding lawn mower similar to the one an intoxicated Jones drove to a liquor store is encased in a Plexiglas display, with an accompanying painting and descriptive signage illustrating the incident as a harmless farce. Whereas the Johnny Cash Museum features an upscale coffee bar with tasteful lighting and appropriate monochromatic decor, the George Jones Museum boasts a well-stocked neon-lit bar that is open during museum hours, in addition to an after-hours rooftop party space. The Cash

Museum's souvenir shop deemphasizes barware, discreetly selling more utilitarian pint glasses and Mason jars amid T-shirts, videos, and CDs, whereas the Jones Museum hawks an impressive array of commemorative stemware, shot glasses, flasks, and beer cozies.

Works Cited

Alcoholics Anonymous: The Story of How Many Thousands of Men and Women Have Recovered from Alcoholism. 4th ed. Alcoholics Anonymous World Services, 2001.

Amende, Kathaleen E. *Desire and the Divine: Feminine Identity in White Southern Women's Writing.* Louisiana State UP 2013.

Carlin, Richard. "Faron Young." *Country Music: A Biographical Dictionary,* Routledge, 2003.

Cash, Johnny. *Man in Black.* Zondervan, 1975.

Cash, Johnny, with Patrick Carr. *Cash: The Autobiography.* Harper, 1997.

Cash, June Carter. *From the Heart.* Prentice Hall, 1987.

Cash, W. J. *The Mind of the South.* 1941. Vintage, 1991.

Ching, Barbara. *Wrong's What I Do Best: Hard Country Music and Contemporary Culture.* Oxford UP, 2001.

Cox, Patsi Bale. *The Garth Factor: The Career Behind Country's Big Boom.* Center Street, 2009.

Crowley, John W. *The White Logic: Alcoholism and Gender in American Modernist Fiction.* U of Massachusetts P, 1994.

Djos, Matts G. *Writing Under the Influence: Alcoholism and the Alcoholic Perception from Hemingway to Berryman.* Palgrave Macmillan, 2010.

Edwards, Leigh H. *Johnny Cash and the Paradox of American Identity.* Indiana UP, 2009.

Fox, Pamela. *Natural Acts: Gender, Race, and Rusticity in Country Music.* Ann Arbor: U of Michigan P, 2009.

Hartigan, Francis. *Bill W.: A Biography of Alcoholics Anonymous Cofounder Bill Wilson.* St. Martin's, 2000.

Jones, George, with Tom Carter. *I Lived to Tell It All.* Villard, 1996.

Kienzle, Rich. *The Grand Tour: The Life and Music of George Jones.* Dey Street, 2016.

Laing, Olivia. *The Trip to Echo Spring: On Writers and Drinking.* Picador, 2013.

Lynn, Loretta, with George Vecsey. *Coal Miner's Daughter.* 1976. Da Capo, 2001.

Malone, Bill C. *Don't Get above Your Raisin': Country Music and the Southern Working Class.* U of Illinois P, 2002.

O'Halloran, Seán. *Talking Oneself Sober: The Discourse of Alcoholics Anonymous.* Cambria, 2008.

Ownby, Ted. "Freedom, Manhood, and White Male Tradition in 1970s Southern Rock Music." *Haunted Bodies: Gender and Southern Texts,* edited by Anne Goodwyn Jones and Susan V. Donaldson, UP of Virginia, 1997, pp. 369–88.

Parsons, Elaine Frantz. *Manhood Lost: Fallen Drunkards and Redeeming Women in the Nineteenth-Century United States.* Johns Hopkins UP, 2003.

Rotskoff, Lori. *Love on the Rocks: Men, Women, and Alcohol in Post–World War II America.* U of North Carolina P, 2002.

Travis, Trysh. *The Language of the Heart: A Cultural History of the Recovery Movement from Alcoholics Anonymous to Oprah Winfrey.* U of North Carolina P, 2009.

Twelve Steps and Twelve Traditions. Alcoholics Anonymous World Services, 1997.

Wren, Christopher S. *Winners Got Scars Too: The Life of Johnny Cash.* Ballantine, 1971.

Wynette, Tammy, with Joan Dew. *Stand by Your Man: An Autobiography.* Simon and Schuster, 1979.

PART II

REVISING NARRATIVE THROUGH
INTOXICATION

Drink, Doubling, and Perverseness in Poe's Fiction

CALEB DOAN AND J. GERALD KENNEDY

The somewhat misleading image of Edgar Poe as a chronic drunk has long dogged his literary reputation. But the truth is more complicated, and so is his fictional representation of drinking. Poe penned several shocking tales about intemperance and the "moral insanity" it was then thought to produce. Some of these tales dramatize clashes between counterparts that lead to sadistic or gruesome murders. In one, Poe links insobriety to the "spirit of perverseness," or radical self-destructiveness, that resides (so his narrator claims) in every human soul.

The legend of Poe's drinking, which dates from his year at the University of Virginia, has nevertheless generated wild misinformation, and readers should be wary of facile biographical readings of his tales. But the *Poe Log* (Thomas and Jackson) also documents multiple occasions when the author's public insobriety damaged him socially and professionally.[1] His career unfolded as temperance reformers deplored the alcoholic excess that accompanied nation building in antebellum America.[2] To Poe's chagrin, he became the target, in the early 1840s, of antidrinking satire, and yet he continued to write horrifying narratives hinging on drunken cruelty.

After considering how drink figures in a few lesser-known tales, we will investigate four major stories—"William Wilson," "The Black Cat," "The Cask of Amontillado," and "Hop-Frog"—that associate alcohol with acts of monstrous inhumanity. In the first three, doubling and perverseness produce a fatal struggle with a dissolute self. Examining Poe's narratives in the context of temperance reform, we will consider the possibility that Poe, despite his scorn for "the heresy of the didactic" and moralizing fiction, produced drinking narratives not to subvert the sensational temperance tale but, with a kind of double perverseness, to inscribe a darker moral pedagogy.[3]

A sober look at Poe's infamous career at the University of Virginia, from February to December 1826, reveals potential insights into his relationship to alcohol. With its "established system of minimal rules and maximum self-governance," Thomas Jefferson's university bred student inebriation, gambling, and violence (Silverman 31). In letters to his guardian, John Allan, Poe detailed brawls, likely inflamed by drunkenness, in which students regularly drew pistols.[4] These incidents not only frightened Poe—as when he told of a young Kentuckian who bit another student from "the shoulder to the elbow" so severely that large, morbid "pieces of flesh" required removal (Poe, *Collected Letters* 1: 9) —but also instructed him about perverse impulses that led to monstrous acts. Alcohol reduced self-regulating inhibitions and allowed hidden brutalities to emerge. Poe himself likely turned to drink to blend in socially, after Allan's refusal to provide adequate financial support left the Richmond youth "regarded in the light of a beggar" by wealthy fellow students, sons of planters, who were attended at school by personal slaves (1: 59).

Still, Poe strove to find acceptance: he acquired what a classmate described as a "marked" and "peculiar" "passion for strong drink" that involved "seiz[ing] a full glass without water or sugar, and send[ing] it home at a single gulp." "This," Thomas Goode Tucker explained, "frequently used him up; but if not, he rarely returned to the charge" (Thomas and Jackson 70). Poe's habit of downing his undiluted drink in a single gulp arguably betrayed a desperate need to belong, the bitter effect of rejection as the never-adopted foster son of a childless couple. Years later, while editing the *Southern Literary Messenger,* Poe sometimes took on a southern affect when opining on matters of sectional debate, and he sought liquid conviviality often enough that his employer thought him "rather dissipated" (167). Resisting an uncritical autobiographical approach, one can nevertheless see analogies between Poe's drinking in Virginia and the self-ruin of fictional characters from William Wilson to Hop-Frog.

Poe's career as a "magazinist" in the 1830s and 1840s coincided with both the rapid proliferation of newspapers and periodicals and the rise of the temperance movement. According to Michael Warner, temperance became a "full-scale, mass-mediated social movement" because of its symbiotic relationship with the "early national entrepreneurial press"; indeed, Warner claims that "temperance and the mass press planted each other on the national scene."

Reform tracts and newspapers "achieved mass circulation in exactly the same years that saw the first penny daily newspapers" (30–31). But in an increasingly competitive literary marketplace, temperance ideology also began to splinter: zealous advocates began calling for total abstinence rather than moderation, but the mostly working-class Washingtonians (who organized in 1840) extended sympathy and urged drinkers to pledge to reform themselves. Like abolitionism, temperance reform originated in New England and the Mid-Atlantic states; the South largely resisted cultural change, and temperance militated against southern hospitality.

Certain authors nevertheless exploited temperance readers' desires for lurid material. Debra Rosenthal and David Reynolds have described this as a shift from "evangelical" or "conventional" discourse to "Washingtonian" or "sensational" (4). Whereas authors of conventional tracts sermonized on the after-effects of insobriety in lieu of detailing the misdeeds of drinkers, fearing "that vivid descriptions of evil, even if motivated by reform, tended to make evil attractive" (Reynolds 24), the new tracts reveled in the depravity of drunkenness with tantalizing accounts of sex and violence. No longer did stories end with "a moralistic affirmation of social reintegration" (24). Instead, authors outlined fatalistic examples of self-ruin. Because stories and tracts showed how the dissolution of alcoholics affected families and friends, Warner provocatively concludes that "the temperance movement *invented* addiction" (32, emphasis in original).

Many of Poe's early, often satirical tales of the Folio Club, however, ridiculed conventional temperance values. An introduction from 1833 describes a cohort of eleven oddly named storytellers, said to be "a mere Junto of Dunderheadism," who produce monthly tales, discussing them "over a glass of wine" (Poe, *Collected Works* 2: 203). The Folio Club tales range from romanticized accounts of desperate excess to extravaganzas featuring comical tipplers, with Poe thumbing his nose at the movement's admonitions. Yet one striking tale, "The Assignation" (a contribution attributed to "Convolvulus Gondola"), portrays a shocking double suicide with poisoned wine, insinuating a connection between drinking, thwarted dreams, and death.[5] The Byronic protagonist and the Marchesa Aphrodite (the wife of a nobleman) have agreed to signify their love with an act as absolute as their devotion. The era sentimentalized a Romantic union in death, and, to that end, the poet-visionary gestures to a portrait of the marchesa and then swallows "several goblets of the wine" that hasten his end (165–66).

Other Folio Club tales allude humorously to drink. In "Bon-Bon," the narrator-restaurateur, a self-styled philosopher, imbibes wine incessantly because he takes the concept of "in vino veritas" literally and believes "there are few men of extraordinary profundity who are found wanting in an inclination for the bottle" (Poe, *Collected Works* 2: 98). While conversing with the devil, Bon-Bon consumes five bottles of wine, offending even the devil by his "disgusting and ungentlemanly situation" (114). "King Pest" portrays medieval London during the Black Death, and two drunken sailors discover intoxicated plague victims ensconced in an alehouse, each claiming royal titles and bearing surnames including the word "pest." "Lionizing," a spoof of British salon culture, offers more oddly named characters, including one Bibulus O'Bumper, who talks only about wines and liqueurs.

These early tales reveal a smirking—though not necessarily southern—preoccupation with drink; Poe flouts temperance concerns while flaunting his knowledge of wines and spirits. But, beneath the forced levity, one discerns a recurrent association of drinking with death. That idea informs "Metzengerstein," a Folio Club tale discussed by Matthew Warner Osborn as a story of "self-destructive compulsion" involving an "intemperate rider" and a supernatural black horse (179). Osborn emphasizes Poe's use of fantastic phenomena—like the spectral horse or the vortex in "A Descent into the Maelström"—to metaphorize the power of drink.[6]

Poe's only novel, *The Narrative of Arthur Gordon Pym* (1838), gestures toward a more probing exploration of self-ruin. In the novel's opening scene, first published in the *Southern Literary Messenger,* Poe crafted a sensational story typical of later Washingtonian literature.[7] After a bout of drinking, Pym's friend Augustus can't sleep and persuades Pym to go sailing. Far "out of the lee of the land," Pym realizes that Augustus is "drunk—beastly drunk" (Poe, *Imaginary Voyages* 59).[8] Poe appeals to a mass audience fascinated by brazen excess and repelled by sermonizing. The episode hints, however, at a psychic insight behind the sensationalism. When, in the darkness, a much larger ship smashes the sailboat, Pym's account reveals his drunken alienation from himself: "The body of a man was seen to be affixed in the most singular manner to the smooth bottom [of the larger ship] . . . and beating violently against it with every movement of the hull. After several ineffectual efforts . . . I was finally disengaged from my perilous situation and taken on board—for the body proved to be my own" (62). Pym's awkward shift in point of view and the ultimate disclosure betray the self-estrangement of excess.

In the published novel, Poe tracks Pym's journey to the South Seas and often dramatizes the effects of drinking. The ship *Grampus* leaves Nantucket with Pym concealed in the hold, provisioned with food and drink. When his freshwater putrefies, he consumes "half a dozen bottles of cordials and liqueurs" (69). His alcohol-induced dehydration creates nightmares but later proves instructive: Pym avoids inebriation when, after a mutiny and a storm, he and three fellow survivors find some port wine. While Pym searches for other supplies, Augustus, Dirk Peters, and Richard Parker drain the bottle, leaving them shaking "as if with a violent ague" (128).[9] Augustus soon dies from gangrene, his decline hastened by extreme dehydration. His corpse quickly becomes "loathsome beyond expression" and falls apart when cast overboard to hungry sharks (142). The conscious pairing of Pym and Augustus earlier in the novel makes the latter's early death an unsettling surprise. But by discarding the often besotted Augustus, Poe also signals the emergence of a sober, more mature Pym, the scientist-ethnographer keen to explore the polar region. Never again would Poe depict a neat break between a narrator and an alcoholic alter ego.[10]

Poe's sporadic problems with alcohol in 1836 complicated his relationship with Thomas W. White, the owner of the *Southern Literary Messenger*, who dismissed Poe after the January 1837 issue rolled off the press. Writing years later, a classmate who knew Poe in Richmond during this time admitted he was occasionally "incapacitated" for work and "subject to intoxication" (Thomas and Jackson 237). Poe had apparently acquired a fondness for juleps. But a fellow lodger who took meals with Poe during his unproductive stay in New York the following year said that he had never seen the author "the least affected with liquor" (242).

After moving to Philadelphia in 1838, Poe again began writing tales, and in 1839 he found work with *Burton's Gentleman's Magazine*. The poet Thomas Dunn English, a young admirer, reported pulling Poe from the gutter one summer evening and accompanying him home, but in September, Poe assured former *Messenger* editor James Heath that he was abstaining from alcohol (263, 269). Both reports should be read with skepticism, but such details hint at his occasional insobriety at the very moment when the temperance movement was gaining popularity.

As Jeffrey Meyers points out, Poe's contemporaries perceived excessive drinking as a moral problem rather than a psychological disorder (87), and Stephen Rachman rightly credits Poe for intuiting that alcoholism often arose from an unresolved inner conflict (34–35). That insight lay at the heart of the brilliant tale Poe contributed to the October 1839 issue of *Burton's Gentleman's Magazine*. In "William Wilson," he portrayed a divided, conflicted self, projecting a clash between an arrogant, aristocratic youth and a plebian counterpart bearing an identical name. "William Wilson" shows Poe's incipient awareness of a yet-unnamed principle of self-destructiveness; it probes the uncanny self-alienation of seeming to be two persons at once, dramatizing the hatred a dissolute character feels for his sober, moralistic counterpart.

The tale begins at a boarding school in an English village (the same school Poe attended from 1818 to 1820), and it traces the growing resentment felt by the narrator at discovering that he has a rival, a boy who speaks only in a whisper. Drink enters the tale when, to escape his nemesis, Wilson leaves the boarding school, enrolls at Eton, and plunges into wild profligacy. Recalling Poe's drunken nights at the University of Virginia, Wilson caps a week of "soulless dissipation" with a night of "secret carousal" involving a handful of "dissolute" students.[11] While "madly flushed with cards and intoxication," he discovers the presence of his hated rival, dressed in identical clothes and shaking his finger as he whispers the narrator's name (Poe, *Collected Works* 2: 438). A similar intrusion occurs at Oxford, where the double interrupts an evening of gambling to expose Wilson as a cheater who has robbed a rich lord. Humiliated, the dissolute Wilson leaves Oxford, only to discover that in Vienna, Berlin, Moscow, Paris, Naples, and Egypt, his rival has pursued him to expose his misdeeds.

During the carnival at Rome, when the drunken Wilson tries to seduce the wife of a nobleman, a low whisper arrests his attention. Here, Poe stages a final encounter, when Wilson perceives his counterpart as a figure in a mirror. A sword thrust at this adversary leaves Wilson himself "dabbled with blood" (2: 448). He seems to hear his dying enemy say that, in killing his counterpart, Wilson has murdered himself. Levin attributes this "moral suicide" to the Imp of the Perverse, the urge for self-ruin that Poe elaborated in an 1845 tale so titled (143). Meyers similarly notes that Poe's story expresses his "dual impulses: to act destructively and to censure his own irrational behavior" (57). Poe's epigraph to "William Wilson," which alludes to "CONSCIENCE grim," suggests, however, a moral conflict between a corrupt man and his guilty conscience (Poe, *Collected Works* 2: 426).[12]

This intimation that the narrator has killed his moral intelligence casts new light on the tale's second paragraph, in which Wilson brands himself a victim of "circumstances beyond human control" (2: 427). He invites readers to discern a "fatality" in his downfall rather than ascribing it to immorality. But this preemptive rationalization, which casts Wilson as a victim of provocation and temptation, collapses at the revelation that he has destroyed his conscience. Like authors of popular sensational temperance tales, Wilson wants to blame his gambling and womanizing on a compulsion for strong drink. But Poe refuses this reductive logic. Liquor did not cause Wilson's misdeeds; he drank to disable the moral intelligence that might otherwise have thwarted his compulsions. Wilson's depravity arises not from alcohol per se but from a radically divided consciousness, a hatred of and opposition to his impulsive self that mirrors the assault on conscience ascribed to the profligate Wilson in the closing line.

Poe's meditation in "William Wilson" on the psychological mechanism that leads to self-ruin shows the inner turn that his narratives project from 1839 onward. Recurrently, alcohol becomes part of the formula for disaster, and prophetically so—Poe had an important relapse into intoxication after the onset of his wife's consumption in January 1842. His absences from the editorial office of *Graham's Magazine* (where he had been working since April 1841) finally compelled his resignation in May. In a letter to George Evelith, Poe later conceded that, after Virginia's hemorrhage, he drank "God only knows how often or how much," but he attributed that excess to the "insanity" of profound grief (Poe, *Collected Letters* 2: 641).

His erratic behavior extended through March 1843, when Poe traveled to Washington, DC, ostensibly to meet with President Tyler or his son about a government appointment. But a delay induced Poe to begin drinking, and his notorious debauch in a Washington hotel from March 10 to March 12 led him to berate his bedridden friend and sponsor, Frederick W. Thomas; offend the wife of another friend, Jesse E. Dow; and insult the aforementioned Thomas Dunn English, a Tyler supporter who happened to be staying at the hotel. Poe ridiculed English's mustache and in the process made a bitter enemy (Thomas and Jackson 403–6).

This period of grief, "insanity," and recurrent insobriety forms the background against which Poe composed a troubling tale of alcoholic self-ruin. He wrote it amid a flood of moralistic temperance publications and called it "The Black Cat." Like "William Wilson," "The Black Cat" appears compatible with the logic of the sensational temperance tale, in which chronic dissipation brings death and destruction. After gouging out the eye of his "favorite pet and playmate," Pluto, the narrator blames his downfall on drink: "Our friendship lasted . . . for several years, during which my general temperament and character—through the instrumentality of the Fiend Intemperance—had (I blush to confess it) experienced a radical alteration for the worse" (Poe, *Collected Works* 3: 850–51).

As this sentence suggests, the narrative vacillates between temperance tract and critique of temperance fiction. The parenthetical slip into self-dramatization—"(I blush to confess it)"—adopts a rhetoric of reform consistent with the genre's conventions, even as it undermines the narrator's announced intention "to place before the world, *plainly, succinctly, and without comment,* a series of mere household events" (3: 849, emphasis added). Later, boldly revising temperance logic, the narrator contradicts his claim that alcohol has caused his damnation: "I am above the weakness of seeking to establish a sequence of cause and effect, between the disaster and the atrocity. But I am detailing a chain of facts—and wish not to leave even a possible link imperfect" (3: 853). He bristles that his downfall could be reduced to a moral judgment based solely on drinking. The distinction between cause and effect and a "chain of facts" unsettles temperance logic; uncontrolled drinking always derives from something else.

Poe's narrator famously identifies the "spirit of PERVERSENESS" as the impetus for his fate. He contends, "I am not more sure that my soul lives, than I am that perverseness is one of the primitive impulses of the human heart—one of the indivisible primary faculties, or sentiments, which give direction to the character of Man." A "primary" faculty has no precedent, and so a primal urge for self-destruction propels the drinking: "This spirit of perverseness, I say, came to my final overthrow. It was this unfathomable longing of the soul *to vex itself*—to offer violence to its own nature—to do wrong for the wrong's sake only—that urged me to continue and finally to consummate the injury I had inflicted upon the unoffending brute" (3: 852, emphasis in original). His hanging of the cat completes a "gin-nurtured" attack that begins with the removal of an eye—an act that, following the logic of "The Tell-Tale Heart" (where a "vulture" eye incites an old man's murder), represents an assault upon himself, his "I." Because Poe figures intemperance as a product of perverseness, he rejects the notion of alcoholism as a curable "disease."[13]

Like Poe, the narrator of "The Black Cat" drinks to forget, "plung[ing] into excess, and soon drown[ing] in wine all memory" of unspeakable deeds and inescapable guilt (3: 851). His most horrific act, burying an ax in his wife's brain for protecting a second one-eyed black cat, epitomizes this perverseness. Ultimately, the narrator consigns himself to the hangman, completing his self-ruin by inadvertently walling up the feline embodiment of his guilt. Just as the police are leaving his house, the narrator makes a gratuitous boast about its construction and strikes the wall exactly where he has immured his wife's body. The howl of the cat—a creature bearing a mark resembling a gallows—betrays his crime and likewise his compulsion to destroy himself. The tale's symbolic "chain of events" acknowledges the effect of drink but portrays intemperance as the consequence of a deeper, self-destructive urge.

Poe wrote "The Black Cat" in late 1842, the same year that Walt Whitman published his temperance novel, *Franklin Evans, the Inebriate,* and Abraham Lincoln addressed the Washingtonian Society of Springfield, Illinois. Lincoln understood the new direction of social reform represented by the group, which had been founded by recovering alcoholics who emphasized outreach rather than moralizing or denunciation. Lincoln defended "habitual drunkards," comparing "their heads and their hearts" favorably to "those of any other class" and suggesting greater susceptibility to drink among the "brilliant and the warm-blooded" (88). In a sense, Poe's tale pushes the logic of Washingtonian reform to the breaking point and invites intimate understanding of a troubling inebriate who proves to be anything but good-hearted.

Between the story's composition and its eventual publication in August 1843, Poe's own need for temperance rehabilitation became a cause célèbre. Before his unfortunate trip to Washington, Poe had nearly secured financial backing for his long-projected monthly magazine, *The Stylus,* from Thomas Clarke, a wealthy Philadelphia publisher and temperance advocate. But news of Poe's debauch soured the deal. Quickly, Poe's erstwhile admirer English pounced on an opportunity to caricature his fellow poet in *The Doom of the Drinker,* which began serialization in Clarke's *Philadelphia Saturday Museum* in November 1843. English associated Poe's "excitement" under wine with the "bitter and apparently candid style" of his criticism, portraying an unnamed writer—recognizably Poe—as the "very incarnation of treachery and falsehood" (Thomas and Jackson 443). English also mocked Poe in "The Ghost of a Grey Tadpole," a parody of "The Black Cat," published in January 1844 (450). And in English's later novel *1844* (1846), Poe figures as the chronic inebriate Marmaduke Hammerhead.[14]

Poe's animus toward English unmistakably infused his 1846 tale of revenge, "The Cask of Amontillado."[15] After a physical altercation in New York in early

1846, the two traded vicious characterizations in print. In his series "The Literati of New York City" for *Godey's Lady's Book,* Poe accused English of "plagiarism" and "ignorance"; English attacked Poe in the *Morning Telegraph* as a "drunkard," so "base and depraved" that he was "an assassin in morals" and "a quack in literature" to boot (Thomas and Jackson 648). Like the fictional Montresor's rival, Fortunato, English had obviously "ventured upon insult" with great pertinacity (Poe, *Collected Works* 3: 1256).

Poe did not, however, allow the personal, professional feud to dictate the intricacies of his tale: Montresor's cold-blooded inhumation of his rival remains incomprehensible; of the "thousand injuries" attributed to Fortunato, the only acknowledged grievance is "insult." Montresor's craving for vengeance springs from a darker impulse. The intimate doubling insinuated by their tangled relationship provides clues: the two men inhabit the same social circles, possess similar pedigrees, bear names connoting wealth, and fancy themselves wine connoisseurs. As René Girard noted, rivalry feeds on mutual desires.[16]

Montresor understands exactly what Fortunato wants, and the promised amontillado satisfies both his thirst and the need to display expertise. Levin calls the story "almost . . . a temperance tract" (147), and in that sense it conveys the typical moral that an insatiable thirst for alcohol leads to death. The strange bond at the heart of the tale also manifests the logic of Washingtonian reform, the brotherhood of those who understand the lure of drink. Montresor exploits Fortunato's "weak point," his "connoisseurship in wine," but admits that he "did not differ from [Fortunato] materially" (Poe, *Collected Works* 3: 1257). They have both lived a life shaped by a knowledge and love of rare vintages, and despite their rivalry, they are also—like Poe and English—onetime friends.

After a doubly ironic toast to those buried in Montresor's vault and to Fortunato's long life, Montresor oddly reveals the arms of his family and its motto, "*Nemo me impune lacessit*" (No one provokes me with impunity) (3: 1260, 1264). The motto (also that of Poe's home state, Virginia) portends the crime and hints at implacable vengeance. It also prompts a question: Why does Montresor wish to bury his enemy in a place sacred to his family? His scheme curiously confers symbolic consanguinity. Reaching the supposed site of the cask, however, Montresor claps his victim in chains and (repeating the Freudian scheme of "The Black Cat") walls in the surrogate victim of his own self-destructiveness.

Determined to "punish with impunity," Montresor tellingly betrays remorse while entombing his friend. When Fortunato falls silent, Montresor becomes "impatient" for a reply to his taunts. When the bells on Fortunato's cap jingle one last time, Montresor admits, "my heart grew sick" (3: 1263). He feels his tie to Fortunato. From the tale's second sentence, we learn that his account may be a deathbed revelation to a confessor ("You, who so well know the nature of my soul"), and its next-to-last sentence confirms that the murder has weighed on the narrator for "half of a century" (3: 1256, 1263). Montresor perhaps realizes that he will soon join his victim in the family vault. His final sentence—"*In pace requiescat!*"—reflects belated pity for Fortunato or hope of lasting peace for himself, or perhaps it merges both meanings in a common plea (3: 1263). If Poe's contempt for English precipitated "The Cask of Amontillado" and its temperance plot, the story also allowed him to explore again the consequences of killing an intimate adversary, a figurative alter ego.

Although he commits a perfect crime, Montresor cannot free himself from memory or conscience. That is, he cannot injure his alter ego with impunity. Montresor's lingering guilt and inability to forget his counterpart marks Poe's deviation from the standard Washingtonian temperance plot. Typical "sensational" temperance logic operates through sentimentalism: the demise of the drinker produces emotional release; it resolves the linked problems of abuse, despair, and intemperance (at least fictionally) and supplies a moral for readers to ponder. Poe's narrators, conversely, cannot escape the double who evokes the spirit of perverseness. Its presence (whether as a whispering nemesis, a howling cat, or a walled-in rival) precludes a definitive triumph over alcohol or an implied didactic lesson. The author projects the hated counterpart as an inescapable, self-destructive presence.

Poe's last major tale of drink, "Hop-Frog," seems to depart from the doppelgänger plot, however, by depicting a clash between radically dissimilar characters. The revolting conclusion, incinerating the king and his seven counselors, reverses the palpable master–slave relationship. It also presents a dilemma for readers encouraged to sympathize with the persecuted dwarf jester.

First published in the abolitionist *Flag of Our Union* in 1849, the story responds to both temperance and antislavery reform, and its tonal ambiguity derives from that fusion. By the time Poe wrote "Hop-Frog," the two movements had to some extent coalesced to reinforce each other, portraying both drinkers and slaves as victims of bondage, exacting a terrible toll on the nation.[17] Although Poe identified with the South and opposed immediate abolition, his sympathies in this horrific narrative seem hard to locate, for while he offers good reason to cheer the putative slave's revolt against a heartless master, he also portrays an act of terrible cruelty.

Biographers have sometimes read the execution of the king and his ministers as Poe's figurative revenge on those who enabled his drinking, or on unsympathetic readers, or on tyrannical editors (Quinn 595; Silverman 406–7). But biographical readings crumble under the pressure of the tale's perverse logic. Why would Poe, who at times defended the South's "peculiar institution," align himself with a putative slave to arouse sympathy for a dwarf hypersensitive to alcohol? Why does Hop-Frog's brand of vengeance, down to the primate costumes and chains, so obviously play on then-pervasive racial fears and stereotypes? The shocking public execution thematically opens the idea, repellent to slaveholders, that Hop-Fog's yearning for self-liberation could be the same yearning that inflamed rebels such as Nat Turner. But such a conclusion must remain speculative, and the strangely enigmatic temperance plot only complicates this antislavery reading.

Hop-Frog rebels because the king and his court have abused both the dwarf and his beloved Trippetta, striking the latter and forcing the former to guzzle wine. The diminutive jester shares Poe's acute vulnerability to alcohol, and Poe understood the compulsion to drink as perverse. The narrator explains, "Hop-Frog was not fond of wine; for it excited the poor cripple almost to madness; and madness is no comfortable feeling" (Poe, *Collected Works* 3: 1347).[18] Although at first "his large eyes *gleamed,* rather than shone" with "the effect of wine on his excitable brain" (3: 1348), Hop-Frog conquers his inebriation after witnessing the king's assault on Trippetta. Explaining to the king the dramatic effect of the "Eight Chained Ourang-Outangs," he speaks "very tranquilly, and as if he had never tasted wine in his life." The narrator puns: "Having drained another bumper with no very perceptible ill effect, Hop-Frog entered at once, *and with spirit,* into the plans for the masquerade" (3: 1349–50, emphasis added). In this fantasy of mastery over alcohol, intoxicating spirits inspire cool revenge. Hop-Frog's ploy avenges Trippetta's humiliation and simultaneously destroys that which makes him a drunken fool.

But here the temperance plot, Hop-Frog's revolt against compulsory drinking, pushes the antislavery plot to the point of revulsion. The dwarf's vengeance—although provoked by palpable injustice—seems, in editor Thomas Ollive Mabbott's view, "too much for poetic justice" (3: 1343). The immolation of the king and his counselors creates a veritable act of terrorism; Hop-Frog reduces the eight supposed "ourang-outangs" to a "fetid, blackened, hideous, and indistinguishable mass" (3: 1354).

In "Hop-Frog," Poe seems to have jettisoned the motif of doubling used in earlier tales to stage the clash between two sides of the self. Yet the projection of a captive's overthrow of his master may indeed represent a symbolic resolution of internal conflict if we understand the relation between Poe's king and jester to represent the artistic tension between critical constraint and creative freedom. The bored king demands "characters" and "something novel" to relieve the "everlasting sameness" of court life (3: 1347). To liberate himself and Trippetta from the monarch's domination—an oppression intensified by forced consumption of wine—Hop-Frog devises a masquerade that will, he promises, leave spectators "terrified" (3: 1350). In chaining and then igniting his tormentors, Hop-Frog frees himself from slavery and from drink. Poe seems to envision a triumph over the perverse, alcoholic compulsion toward self-ruin.

But as the arc of his career suggests, Poe's thirst never abated. If his mysterious death in 1849 has contributed to the mythology of southern drinking, his status as a "southern" writer remains problematic. Born in Boston but raised in London and Richmond, he produced his best tales in Philadelphia and New York, remaining a man on the move, tied less to any region than to the Republic of Letters. He made a last temperance pledge in Richmond in 1849, shortly before departing for Baltimore, where his still-unexplained drinking binge perhaps triggered a fatal cerebral hemorrhage.

Evoking the pseudoscience of phrenology in "The Imp of the Perverse," Poe speculated that the "combativeness" rooted in one's survival instinct often battled an unnamed, irrational impulse toward self-ruin (Poe, *Collected Works* 3: 1220). In his tales of drink, Poe conjured this impulse, thus asserting an unconscious cause of insobriety, even as his narratives replicated the surface logic of alcoholic doom in temperance fiction.

Notes

1. Thomas and Jackson's *Poe Log* chronicles the life of Edgar Allan Poe through facts and excerpts from newspapers, legal records, letters, manuscripts, and other documents. It is an invaluable source for any scholar interested in the life and career of Poe.

2. Rachman, drawing from various accounts of the Jacksonian era, explains, "a 'national drinking binge' preoccupied the social life of men" (15). Further, he observes that Poe's drinking patterns

coincided with common drinking trends (in both communal and solo binge drinking) during his lifetime. These shifting patterns of consumption, Rachman argues, "in good measure, led to the temperance movements that came to prominence in the American 1830s and 40s" (16).

3. Poe famously outlines the "heresy of *The Didactic*" (emphasis and capitalization his) in "The Poetic Principle." See *Essays and Reviews,* particularly 75–77.

4. See Poe's May 25, 1826, letter to John Allan in *Collected Letters* 1: 5–6.

5. The pseudonym indirectly suggests a pun relevant to the tale: the protagonist kills himself at sunrise by quaffing several goblets of poisoned wine. "Convolvulus" refers to a flowering plant of the morning glory family.

6. For a convincing reading of how "A Descent into the Maelström" is built on a temperance trope, see Osborn 182–86.

7. Bruce I. Weiner has suggested, "Like many tales of effect, the first episode of *Pym* reads like a temperance tract, warning as much against unbridled imagination as against excessive drinking" (50).

8. For an argument that Augustus recalls Poe's brother, Henry, who died from consumption in 1831, an illness probably complicated by alcoholism, see Richard Kopley x–xxvi.

9. The novel's repeated emphasis on terrible thirst may reflect Poe's own anxiety about periodic cravings for drink.

10. Augustus is never mentioned after his death. His prompt dismissal (after Poe had alluded to Pym's conversations, years later, with Augustus [*Imaginary Voyages* 94]) could reflect Poe's attempt to defeat his thirst during the composition of the novel. Such a link between reality and fiction could also be made for his later fiction: after various binges evinced an inability to keep away from the bottle, later stories depict an inability to escape the double, whose life has become entwined with or whose remnants remain materially significant to the character's fate.

11. Several biographers and critics have noted this autobiographical connection, though Quinn claims to be the first to identify this (106–7). See also Hoffman 214–15, Meyers 26.

12. The tale thus displays sharp insight into the self-conflict Nathaniel P. Willis metaphorized as a struggle between angel and devil, when describing Poe in an obituary (94–99).

13. This reading seconds Rachman's identification of the tale as "a *perverse* Washingtonian temperance narrative, one that calls into question the possibility of reform, exploiting the new form of mass cultural discourse in order to display its contradictions" (26, emphasis in original).

14. This excerpt from *1844* exemplifies English's characterization of Poe: "That is Marmaduke Hammerhead—a very well-known writer for the sixpenny periodicals, who aspires to be a critic, but never presumes himself a gentleman. He is the author of a poem, called the 'Black Crow,' now making some stir, in the literary circles. . . . He never gets drunk more than five days out of the seven; tells the truth sometimes by mistake; has moral courage sufficient to flog his wife, when he thinks she deserves it, and occasionally without any thought upon the subject merely to keep his hand in; and has never, that I know of, been convicted of petit larceny" (Thomas and Jackson 664).

15. Kenneth Silverman suggests that Poe's malice could be aimed at Thomas Dunn English, Hiram Fuller, C. F. Briggs, Thomas C. Clark, Billy Burton, or his adopted father, John Allan, among other literary foes (316–17).

16. See Girard, especially chapter 1, "'Triangular' Desire."

17. For different arguments on the connection between temperance and abolitionism, see chapters by Robert S. Levine, John W. Crowley, and Nicholas O. Warner in *The Serpent in the Cup.*

18. Quinn suggests, "Perhaps Poe's own reaction to those who urged him, against his will, to drink the one glass that took away his self-control was the model for the behavior of the dwarf" (595).

Works Cited

Crowley, John W. "Slaves to the Bottle: Gough's *Autobiography* and Douglass's *Narrative*." *The Serpent in the Cup: Temperance in American Literature,* edited by David S. Reynolds and Debra J. Rosenthal, U of Massachusetts P, 1997, pp. 115–35.

Girard, René. *Deceit, Desire and the Novel: Self and Other in Literary Structure.* John Hopkins UP, 1965.

Hoffman, Daniel. *Poe Poe Poe Poe Poe Poe Poe.* Doubleday, 1972.

Kopley, Richard. Introduction. *The Narrative of Arthur Gordon Pym of Nantucket,* by Edgar Allan Poe. 1838. Penguin, 1999, pp. ix–xxix.

Levin, Harry. *The Power of Blackness: Hawthorne, Poe, Melville.* Knopf, 1958.

Levine, Robert S. "'Whiskey, Blacking, and All': Temperance and Race in William Wells Brown's *Clotel*." *The Serpent in the Cup: Temperance in American Literature,* edited by David S. Reynolds and Debra J. Rosenthal, U of Massachusetts P, 1997, pp. 93–114.

Lincoln, Abraham. *Lincoln: Speeches and Writings 1832–1858.* Edited by Don E. Fehrenbacher, Library of America, 1989.

Meyers, Jeffrey. *Edgar Allan Poe: His Life and Legacy.* Cooper Square, 1992.

Osborn, Matthew Warner. *Rum Maniacs: Alcoholic Insanity in the Early American Republic.* U of Chicago P, 2014.

Poe, Edgar Allan. *The Collected Letters of Edgar Allan Poe.* Edited by John Ward Ostrom, Burton R. Pollin, and Jeffrey A. Savoye, Gordian Press, 2008. 2 vols.

———. *The Collected Works of Edgar Allan Poe.* Edited by Thomas Ollive Mabbott, Harvard UP, 1978. 3 vols.

———. *Essays and Reviews.* Edited by G. R. Thompson, Library of America, 1984.

———. *The Imaginary Voyages.* Edited by Burton R. Pollin, Gordian, 1994.

Quinn, Arthur Hobson. *Edgar Allan Poe: A Critical Biography.* D. Appleton-Century, 1941.

Silverman, Kenneth. *Edgar A. Poe: Mourning and Never-Ending Remembrance.* HarperCollins, 1991.

Rachman, Stephen. "Poe's Drinking, Poe's Delirium: The Privacy of Imps." *Edgar Allan Poe Review,* vol. 12, no. 2 (Fall 2011), pp. 6–40.

Reynolds, David. "Black Cats and Delirium Tremens: Temperance and the American Renaissance." *The Serpent in the Cup: Temperance in American Literature,* edited by David S. Reynolds and Debra J. Rosenthal, U of Massachusetts P, 1997, pp. 22–59.

Rosenthal, Debra J., and David S. Reynolds. Introduction. *The Serpent in the Cup: Temperance in American Literature,* edited by David S. Reynolds and Debra J. Rosenthal, U of Massachusetts P, 1997, pp. 1–9.

Thomas, Dwight, and David K. Jackson. *The Poe Log: A Documentary Life of Edgar Allan Poe, 1809–1849.* G. K. Hall, 1987.

Warner, Michael. "Whitman Drunk." *Breaking Bounds: Whitman and American Cultural Studies,* edited by Betsy Erkkila and Jay Grossman, Oxford UP, 1996, pp. 30–43.

Warner, Nicholas O. "Temperance, Morality, and Medicine in the Fiction of Harriet Beecher Stowe." *The Serpent in the Cup,* edited by David S. Reynolds and Debra J. Rosenthal, U of Massachusetts P, 1997, pp. 136–52.

Weiner, Bruce. I. "Novels, Tales, and Problems of Form in *The Narrative of Arthur Gordon Pym.*" *Poe's Pym: Critical Explorations,* edited by Richard Kopley, Duke UP, 1992, pp. 44–56.

Willis, Nathaniel P. "'Death of Edgar A. Poe' (1850)." *Poe in His Own Time: A Biographical Chronicle of His Life, Drawn from Recollections, Interviews, and Memoirs by Family, Friends, and Associates,* edited by Benjamin F. Fisher, U of Iowa P, 2010, pp. 94–99.

The Methodical Drinker

Alcohol, Economics, and Regional Identity
in Early Virginian Literature

KATHARINE A. BURNETT

Midway through his 1824 novel *The Valley of Shenandoah; Or, Memoirs of the Graysons*, George Tucker depicts an outing of the Virginia aristocracy. A group of men gathers at Mr. McCulloch's plantation for a hunting party at dawn. Before they begin the day's festivities, and at McCulloch's strong urging, they each drink a portion of julep, "some of them repeatedly" (1: 161). Then again during their breakfast after the hunt. And again. When the scene ends and the men stagger off, it's a wonder they are able to stand at all. And it's not even noon.

At first glance, the scene is not surprising in a novel set in the post-Revolutionary South. After all, the popular image of the aristocratic Old South has become synonymous with mint juleps and glasses of bourbon leisurely sipped on a front porch while slaves labor in the fields.[1] As hedonistic as the hunting scene may appear, in this sense it actually follows a script for southern planation culture. Another text published the same year, Mary Randolph's cookbook *The Virginia Housewife; Or, Methodical Cook* (1824), lists pages of recipes to produce exactly this scenario. The cookbook, which was incredibly popular with American readers throughout the nineteenth century, emphasizes the importance of southern hospitality and leisure: "The husband [of such a house], who can ask a friend to partake of his dinner in full confidence of finding his wife unruffled by the petty vexations attendant on the neglect of household duties—who can usher his guest into the dining-room assured of seeing that methodical nicety which is the essence of true elegance . . ." (xii).[2]

The expectation is that company can arrive at any time and find the dinner table—including the spirits—at the ready and plentiful. The cookbook also includes a section dedicated to recipes for batch cordials, with notations such as "A Necessary Refreshment at All Parties" (170). These directives, coupled with the constant presence of alcohol in the recipes themselves, indicate that the inebriated hunting scene in Tucker's novel closely follows a formula for southern entertainment. These men are, indeed, the typical hard-drinking, hard-riding cavaliers that pervade nostalgic stereotypes of the Old South.

While alcohol and even excessive drinking are celebrated as markers of southern distinction in both texts, the planter elite's abuse of alcohol denotes the problems inherent in plantation culture. Throughout *Virginia Housewife,* Randolph expresses anxieties regarding control and financial moderation in a slave-based economy, beginning with the title *Methodical Cook* and the motto printed on the title page: "Method is the soul of management." The introduction then insists on "management" in every household, in which the wife and mistress must be vigilant in monitoring her slaves while controlling overconsumption and overspending. "Management" comes to mean not just regulation but also how elements of plantation culture are used and misused.

The ideal plantation household *should* have excess—an idea represented by the opulent table perpetually set for company. The problem becomes whether that excess can be maintained without running out of control. As Randolph puts it, "The prosperity and happiness of a family [that is, a plantation] depend greatly on the order and regularity established in it" (xii). Despite the fact that the aim of the cookbook is to create an atmosphere of southern comfort, with traditionally southern beverages as the constant accompaniments, Randolph's admonitions indicate that the ideal is always at risk of slipping away if the elements that define southern identity are "mismanaged."

The plantation elite's tendency toward mismanagement is brought to the forefront in fictional representations of the era's drinking culture. In the hunting scene from Tucker's *Valley of Shenandoah,* mismanagement of alcohol emulates the mismanagement of the plantation. In this case, it is not so much that the men drink excessively but that they cannot drink excessively and still perform their roles as heads of well-functioning plantations. There is no "management" taking place on McCulloch's estate, and the setting on the Virginia plantation indicates that all of the labor is supplied by slaves, with no oversight on McCullough's part. The plantation itself is in disrepair due to McCulloch's neglect of his finances; he plays the generous southern host at the expense of the estate. As the narrative observes, throughout the home are "evidences of the liberal thoughtless disposition, as well as the bad *management* of [the] host, and the easy good nature of his wife" (1: 168, my emphasis). The scene represents the plantation leisure so often associated with the antebellum South, yet the disorder of the McCulloch household is also a case study for what Randolph's cookbook aims to prevent.

These moments in which alcohol takes center stage in antebellum literature reveal the tenuous nature of southern society as a result of the plantation economy and its reliance on slave labor. Randolph's emphasis on "management" in her cookbook points to the ways in which the defining characteristics of southern plantation culture were apt to go awry—a trend that *Valley of Shenandoah* evokes in its representations of the region's drinking culture. In both the novel and the cookbook, the mismanagement of alcohol emerges in the moments that both define and destroy the region. It is not simply that alcohol and excessive drinking lead to dissolution; rather, how southerners can or cannot control the excessive drinking practices encouraged in the antebellum South indicates the problems inherent in a plantation society.

In these early Virginian texts, alcohol becomes a stand-in for the contradictions of the slaveholding antebellum South. On one hand, profuse quantities of alcohol and the ability to drink to excess are privileges enjoyed by the southern elite. On the other hand, mismanagement of both denotes the problems that simmer under the facade of the plantation ideal. As Frederick Douglass would observe in his 1855 *My Bondage, My Freedom*, the lavish tables and overconsumption of fine spirits in southern plantation households masked the obvious moral deficiencies of the society, which became manifest in the planters' physical ailments: "Lurking beneath all of their dishes, are invisible spirits of evil, ready to feed the self-deluded gormandizers with aches, pains, fierce temper, uncontrolled passions, dyspepsia, rheumatism, lumbago, and gout" (111). The choice of the word "spirits" is surely not accidental, and Douglass's observations parallel the consequences of mismanagement that characterize the hunting scene in Tucker's novel.

The handling of alcohol and excessive drinking in texts by upper-class, white southerners symbolizes the ambivalence of the South's social life and economy, particularly in the interregnum period represented by the cookbook and novel—right at the cusp of the 1830s cotton boom but after the region's initial prosperity in the post-Revolutionary era. Both Tucker and Randolph, Virginians of the planter class, were concerned with the preservation of an aristocratic plantation culture that later authors would depict nostalgically, but they were also acutely aware of the problems perpetuated by that culture.

In Tucker's novel, alcohol and its mismanagement become representative of a cultural shift, for better or for worse. He draws from the ideology represented in texts like *Virginia Housewife* to create a balance between a defense of slaveholding Virginia society and a prescient account of its downfall. Scenes that depict alcohol and excessive drinking are a way to critique the problems in southern plantation culture while still maintaining a unique regional identity. As such, "management" of the South's drinking practices becomes a proxy for debates over the state of the region itself, a way to acknowledge the problems without entirely changing the system or losing what many Virginians saw as a culture worthy of preservation.

Method and Madness: Mary Randolph and Southern Drinking Culture

When Tucker and Randolph published their respective works in 1824, the U.S. South, and Virginia in particular, were in a transitional moment. Immediately after the Revolutionary War, the region flourished economically and its population grew. However, that growth waned as the nineteenth century progressed. By the 1820s, Virginia was in a period of stasis: the region's planters could no longer rely on post-Revolutionary affluence, but the 1830s cotton boom was still a number of years away.

One constant during this period of limbo was the pervasiveness of alcohol. While the temperance movement gained ground in northern states at the beginning of the nineteenth century, it was not popular in the South, and alcohol was still a daily part of life up through the Civil War (Veit 27–28). Corn whiskey was the dominant drink—the reason the toddy and the julep became the cultural icons of the Old South. Even when all other supplies were scarce, whiskey was always plentiful (Farrish 6). Part of this trend was due to poor water quality, which meant that Virginia families in the early colonial and post-Revolutionary South often drank tea (for the women and children) and alcohol (for the men) (McColley 40–41). In all, as Joe Gray Taylor puts it in his history of southern food culture, "There can be little doubt that antebellum southerners drank too much" (46).

The only difference was that the upper classes would drink whiskey as the ever-popular julep rather than straight, like the lower classes. Despite the regional specificity of pervasive alcoholic consumption, this cultural marker of the antebellum South was, at its root, grounded in global economic and political patterns.[3] At the beginning of the nineteenth century, the sugar needed for the julep was not pervasive in the U.S. South because the type of sugarcane that flourished in the Caribbean and South America was much more difficult to cultivate in northern climates (Shields, *Southern Provisions* 255–56). However, the Haitian Revolution ending in 1804 and abolition of slave trade in the Atlantic forced European markets to seek out other spaces for sugar cultivation and other modes of labor to supply those markets (Galloway 122–23). The acquisition of land in the 1803 Louisiana Purchase, which had more suitable climates for sugar growth, combined with the introduction of the much heartier "ribbon cane" in 1814 fostered sugar agriculture in the United States (Sitterson 120). By the time Randolph's and Tucker's texts were published in the 1820s, access to sugar was much more common in the United States, and that access enabled southerners to create the juleps for which the region became known (Sitterson 9–12; Shields, *Southern Provisions* 256).

The designation of the julep as a southern cultural emblem highlights the marked class and racial distinctions that shaped plantation culture in the region. Socioeconomic and racial hierarchies always determined who drank what. Access to sugar, even though it was more available, was still limited by wealth and status in antebellum society, and providing a julep at a large gathering would have been an indication of privilege. As Tucker, Randolph, and even Douglass's autobiography suggest, tables were laid—especially for guests—to display the wealth and refinement of the family and to maintain racial divisions. Mary Titus observes, "If in the North, table rituals demarcated social classes, in the South they confirmed white aristocracy. . . . The elegance and even extravagance of these meals testify to the aristocratic status of their host and hostess and suggest that nature blesses their social order. . . . Ceremonial dining confirmed the white family's position in the hierarchical order of the plantation" (245). Douglass recalls these carefully orchestrated ceremonies in *My Bondage, My Freedom,* where "behind the tall-backed and elaborately wrought chairs, stand the servants," thus reinforcing the line between master and slave, black and white (109). The hierarchized drinking rituals and their association with privilege indicated a desire to maintain the facade of the planation ideal always under threat of deterioration.[4]

All of these factors contributed to pervasive drunkenness as a point of pride and regional identity, especially on the part of the men (Clinton 106; McColley 40–41). While many southerners recognized the problems with this lifestyle, drinking and inebriation were not necessarily censured. "Hard drinking" was a trait of a true southern gentleman, just as much as gambling, dueling, or hunting (Clinton 105–7). Bertram Wyatt-Brown observes, "Consumption of hard liquor signified virility. Convivial male drinking was intended to show affection and group solidarity in permissible fashion" (279). The form of southern hospitality and conviviality performed in such rituals sustained an idea of the South that defined the region's communal identity far beyond the antebellum period. Anthony Szczesiul notes that "this myth of southern hospitality has been an essential, foundational narrative within the larger national project of southern exceptionalism" (2). For elite southerners of the planter class, imbibing a certain style of drink and participating in the frequent and abundant drinking rituals were ways to maintain status and remain part of that distinct southern community.

This drunken context shaped Randolph's *Virginia Housewife,* and the cookbook incorporates alcohol and prolific drinking as a regular part of the southern household. However, the book's stress on the importance of management reveals the instability of these cultural markers. Randolph wrote the cookbook after she and her husband, who came from a wealthy Virginia family, suffered several financial setbacks. The couple was forced to sell their plantation in Richmond and open a boardinghouse, where Randolph became a famed cook and hostess of the planter style, yet in an urban setting. As Sarah Walden notes, Randolph's recipes demonstrate regional and French influences, indicating a transatlantic focus that emulates the global connections of the southern economy (Walden 48). As a result, Randolph's domestic management was both public and private, where she "was living in a world at the threshold of modern thinking," a blend of old-world Virginia and the emerging urban and global life of the nineteenth century (Harbury 29). These experiences meant that while Randolph recirculated in her cookbook the cultural markers that defined the South—the frequent and ritualized drinking, the ideal of plantation leisure— she also observed the potential excesses in such a culture.[5]

Randolph's place on the "threshold of modern thinking" with regard to dietary habits and alcohol consumption is never more evident than in her introduction to *Virginia Housewife,* in which she recreates the paradigm of the southern plantation but with reforms to account for the era's pervasive instability. The cookbook, a literal recipe for a generous and hospitable Virginia homestead, ultimately presents the ideal southern home as a well-managed and well-moderated business. Throughout her introduction, the emphasis on proper "management" counterbalances the constant demand that the southern plantation be "social and comfortable"—that is, plentiful in food and drink (xi). That balance is an attempt to find method in the chaotic Virginia social life drenched in alcohol and excess.

"Profusion is not elegance," Randolph admonishes later in the cookbook. "A dinner justly calculated for the company, and consisting for the greater part of small articles, correctly prepared, and neatly served up, will make a much more pleasing appearance to the sight, and give a far greater gratification to the appetite, than a table loaded with food, and from the multiplicity of dishes, unavoidably neglected in the preparation" (28).

There is no mention of alcohol in the passage, but the idea of "small articles, correctly prepared" versus "a table loaded with food" no doubt includes the corresponding beverages to accompany such a meal. "Profusion" calls up the regional habit of drinking to excess, and as Wyatt-Brown observes, the very rituals used to create cultural distinction and communal bonding "often led to the dangers of heavy and solitary drinking" if left unmanaged (279).

Although the cookbook became nationally popular, Randolph's emphasis on economical household management is very specifically directed to regional practices and how to moderate them. In the introduction, Randolph refers to her intended audience as "Virginia ladies," rather than housekeepers more generally: "The Virginia ladies, who are proverbially good managers, employ themselves, while their servants are eating, in washing the cups, glasses, etc." (xi). Randolph's pointed directive to Virginia ladies indicates a pattern in the slaveholding class at the time, in which southern households were prone to mismanagement. Many elite white women of the planter class had no direct knowledge of cooking or basic household chores and instead oversaw slaves who performed such tasks. Like the southern drinking and dining rituals, these habits maintained the racial and class hierarchies that defined plantation society and that would shape later characterizations of the southern kitchen in slave narratives and abolitionist texts such as *Uncle Tom's Cabin,* in which white mistresses are absentee managers (Titus 249–51).

As if to offset the trend, the recipes and instructions in *Virginia Housewife* rest on the assumption that a truly methodical housekeeper has made herself familiar with all of the inner workings of her kitchen and home yet still maintains her elevated position as a wealthy white mistress. Randolph was very open about the fact that the book was written to educate elite white women of the southern planter class. Unlike many southern authors of the time, in her writings she pointedly uses the term "slaves" rather than the more obfuscating "servants" when referring to enslaved men and women (Veit 33; Walden 49–50). Further, her emphasis on "method" makes a clear distinction between the "drudgery" of manual labor performed by slaves and the skilled management performed by white mistresses, if they are doing their jobs properly (Veit 33–34). By maintaining these hierarchies, yet warning against their abuse, Randolph indicates that the behaviors adopted by upper-class whites who rely on slave labor should be controlled, just as the excesses of southern culture in the form of inebriation must be moderated.

Domestic economy and methodical household management were compulsory for women like Randolph in the nineteenth century; men, in contrast, dealt with the "worldly" concerns of estate management. In most historical narratives, the business of running the planation structured the southern homestead. Katharine Harbury observes, "The men's economic base (plantation, crops, tobacco, wealth, furnishings, etc.) provided a springboard from which women were to conduct their supportive roles (elevation of status through cuisine) as hostesses" (137). Yet in *Valley of Shenandoah*, the reverse is true. Tucker makes domestic concerns part of the broader conversation about the region's economics and social governance. The emphasis on method and management within the household, especially with regard to southern drinking culture, serves as a model for the criticisms Tucker applies to the region's economic management more generally, including the practice of slavery.

A Recipe for Disaster: George Tucker and the Virginia Interregnum

As Randolph's advice in *Virginia Housewife* makes clear, the ubiquity of alcohol and the seemingly carefree attitude of white southerners toward it belied the problems they faced in managing the plantation system that prevailed at the time. Although popular conceptions of the antebellum South portray a thriving plantation, for Virginians in the post-Revolutionary era, it was a time of decline and gradual economic stagnation. In his study of Jeffersonian-era agriculture and writing, David Shields points out that the year 1820—just four years before both Tucker and Randolph published their works—is an overlooked turning point in the history of the antebellum period, particularly for Virginia: "Traditional agriculture in Virginia in 1820 was in crisis because of declining productivity, caused by farmers year after year planting the same cash crops, tobacco and corn, until the soil had been leached of nutriment." The crisis in soil depletion, coupled with the expansion of western territories and loss of population due to emigration to the West, "put pressure on eastern farming" (14–15).

But the most important factor in the decay of the Virginia economy rested on one trend: poor management. Planters relied on overseers or more senior slaves to run their estates and then turned their attention to "gentlemanly" (and noncompensatory) pursuits like government service, writing, and entertaining (McColley 22–23). Absentee management frequently led to abuses on the overseers' part, or to complete financial ignorance on the planters' part. In conjunction with the planters' reliance on a defective credit system and the depletion of soil, improper management practices meant that the state of the Virginian planter class by 1824 was tenuous at best (31).

As a member of that class and a contemporary of Randolph's, George Tucker was hyperaware of these self-inflicted problems while also benefiting from the hierarchies that defined the culture of the Old South. Like Randolph, Tucker married into a wealthy Virginia family with extensive plantation holdings, then experienced a series of financial setbacks (mostly self-induced) that ultimately led to his work as an author.[6] Ironically, his most well-read books were on economics. For most of his life, Tucker was a professor of political economy at the University of Virginia, during which time he published books studying national and regional economic development. Much of his writing focused on precisely the problems that defined 1820s Virginia: the region's overreliance on slave labor and one-crop agriculture, paired with rampant mismanagement. In his 1837 *The Laws of Wages, Profits, and Rent, Investigated,* he wrote, "A course of bad crops, a recurrence of epidemic diseases, and lastly, extreme indolence, ignorance, or improvidence in the people would all conduce to the same end" (62). The "end" in this case was the economic and cultural decline of the South.

In his ruminations on the state of the South's plantation economy, Tucker projects the injunctions for management in Randolph's cookbook onto discussions of southern economic development and the problems raised by the plantation system's reliance on slave labor. In particular, he targets the system of slavery itself as an indication of both economic and moral deficiency, declaring, "Slavery cannot exist in the most advanced stages of society, where the utmost degree of industry and economy are required in the great mass of the community to provide the means of subsistence" (*Laws* 48). Although *Laws* was published more than ten years after *Valley of Shenandoah*, at a time when the South was supposedly recovering from the 1820s slump, one of the first major financial crises in the United States took place in 1837, partially spurred on by the very practices Tucker identifies in the southern planter class, as well as by the same global economic and political shifts that led to the rise of sugar planting in the United States.

Tucker's critiques of Virginia's plantation economy are a consistent thread in *Valley of Shenandoah* and provide the backdrop for the alcohol-drenched hunting scene. The novel begins with a financial crisis: the Graysons, a wealthy family of the planter class, are recovering from the death of Colonel Grayson. The patriarch had accumulated a number of debts prior to his death, which forces the family to reduce its estate and restructure its finances. Despite the impetus to practice more economy in their lifestyle, the Graysons seem incapable of moderation and fail to adapt to their new circumstances. This is never more evident than in the frequent dining scenes at the homes of the elite, including the Grayson plantation, with an abundance of "good Madeira" wine and julep always at the ready.

The excessive drinking and dining are simply part of the role played by upper-class Virginians. Yet the Graysons' inability to control their finances in the midst of this excess makes the drinking in the novel a warning as well as an indication of regional or class distinction. Even Edward Grayson, the only son of the family, observes the problems and attributes them to the planters' inability to alter their expensive habits: "Consequently, in order to continue them, [the planter] is compelled to run in debt. . . . Brought up in ease and idleness, he has a taste for expensive pleasures and enjoyments—he loves good wine, liberal hospitality, fine horses, furniture, and dress" (Tucker, *Valley* 1: 110). Although Edward seems almost comically blind to his own foibles in this regard, his observations identify the contrast between the social expectations of the Old South—excessive drinking, immoderate lifestyles, overgenerous hospitality—and the reality—the economic mismanagement perpetuated by those expectations and by the structure of the plantation itself. That contrast is most evident in the drinking scenes that pepper the novel, in which the defining cultural traditions of the antebellum South collide with the increasingly dysfunctional operations of the slave-based plantation economy.

In light of the problems troubling the region at the time, it would be easy to interpret the revelers in the hunting scene as cautionary examples. The "liberal thoughtless disposition" and "bad management" on McCulloch's part typify the habits described by Edward Grayson, while the ramshackle McCulloch plantation, on which "every vestige of ornament and defence was nearly effaced," is evidence of the poor management Randolph's cookbook was designed to avoid (1: 168). These traits are paired with McCulloch's casual disregard for the slaves performing most of the labor on his farm: they only appear rarely in the scene, and usually through McCullough's casual mentions of "my negroes." As a result, the McCullough plantation represents some of the worst aspects of plantation culture out of control.

Yet McCulloch is also a sympathetic character in the novel and exemplifies the qualities of a somewhat respectable planter. The hunting party runs through the checklist of southern leisure: the sense of (white male) community created around the table, the semi-aristocratic sport of hunting, the abundant food, and above all, the repeated drinking rituals. The narrative also repeatedly refers to the julep, that bastion of elite plantation culture, rather than a basic, unadulterated whiskey drink. By imbibing the julep served by their host, the hunters' drinking at once represents everything that made Virginia planter aristocracy distinctive and everything that made it economically unstable and morally unsound, without denying any of those traits. As both a symbol of regional distinction and evidence of degeneracy, the characters' abuse of alcohol in the scene negotiates the tenuousness that runs throughout the novel with regard to the state of the Virginia planter class.

The hunting scene also adds another layer to the representations of early Virginia, touching on a subject that occupied Tucker in his nonfiction: the immorality of slavery. Mary Randolph's cookbook is predicated on the very existence of slave labor and assumes that a housewife's primary job is to monitor and manage the work of slaves. All of the aristocratic families in *Valley of Shenandoah*, including those in dire economic straits, like the Graysons, own slaves. And in both texts, the supervision—or, in most cases, lack of supervision—of a planter's slaves corresponds with the planter's consumption of alcohol and financial instability. In his ruminations on the state of the South in the novel, Edward Grayson rehashes a common and incredibly problematic argument taken up by both pro- and antislavery factions at the time: "No; it is in the effect which slavery has on the *whites*, that the chief mischief is produced. It consigns this half of the population to idleness, or tends to consign them, both by making their labour less necessary, and by making it degrading" (1: 69, my emphasis). Ridiculous as this line of thinking may be—the *white slave owners* are the victims?—it parallels *Virginia Housewife*'s admonitions for mistresses to be more involved in running the plantation household at the risk of losing the "true elegance" bred by "methodical nicety." Proper management, in both texts, means upholding the expectations of a slaveholding southern society but controlling its excesses.

A character's management of drinking becomes the avatar for those excesses. This is never more evident than in the language adopted when characters in *Valley of Shenandoah* discuss the importance of imposing proper management in both economics and regional politics. Several times throughout the novel, characters refer to the need for "sobriety" and "moderation" in the region's dealings (1: 205, 209). These are common enough terms, but given the decline of the region in the 1820s, paired with the drunken nature of southern social life, the need for "sobriety," both literally and figuratively, was of prime concern for southerners like Randolph and Tucker.

Thus, the hunting scene follows the script for southern entertainment outlined by Randolph's cookbook and the ideals of planter culture at the time, but the implied interjections of the slaves and the hints of the plantation's dilapidated state indicate that the script is flimsy at best. The realities of plantation management intrude into the romanticized depiction of aristocratic southern society, especially as the men grow drunker. The scene culminates in an episode of inebriated hog hunting: as the men dine, McCulloch is informed that a neighbor's hogs are loose in his fields (due to an ill-kept fence). What begins as a vision of Virginian leisure quickly turns into a slapstick comedy.

This pairing of dissipation and dysfunction with supposed cultural tradition creates an unstable dynamic that is revealed in how the novel's narrator treats this scene—with a blend of bemusement and disapproval, heroism and imminent ruin. Throughout, the narrator emphasizes the "distinctly Virginian" elements of the gathering, shown in the careful description of the drink, the native julep, and the heroic portrayal of the hunt, which stylizes the slightly tipsy hunters as noble "marksmen" (1: 160–66). Yet these passages contrast with the critical description of the decadence and mismanagement of the plantation itself, including a critique leveled at McCulloch in particular: "Their [the Mc-Cullochs'] occasional display of luxury, together with the abundance with which their table was supplied, with a fare rather substantially good than remarkably nice, removed the impression of poverty, which the exterior of the house was calculated to convey; but left that of bad management in all its original force" (1: 169).

McCulloch's situation is a microcosm of the events taking place throughout the novel, wherein formerly prosperous Virginian families slowly fall into financial decline due to mismanagement and the failure of plantation agriculture in the region. The characters' abuse of alcohol highlights the fact that antebellum Virginia's slave-based plantation economy is always on the brink of falling into complete chaos.

Reflecting the South and Virginia as a whole, the way in which individuals participate in the South's drinking culture in *Valley of Shenandoah* and *Virginia Housewife* signifies the contradictions underlying the decline of the planter class in the 1820s. The planters' financial ills and their almost willful ignorance of management are presented as symptoms of the inherent problems with a plantation economy reliant on slave labor. Yet, as members of this very class, Mary Randolph and George Tucker had a stake in maintaining the society that benefited from these institutions. Like many white southerners of the era, these authors' positions in antebellum Virginia placed them at the very nexus of southern social life, where they relied on the conventions of southern society while witnessing the inherent problems. With their representations of alcohol and excessive drinking, both authors balanced the pull between identifying with the cultural symbols of the Old South and criticizing the problems those symbols created. Just as the classic julep remains the cultural gateway to the era for contemporary audiences, alcohol consumption in the post-Revolutionary South bundled together the pride and anxieties that defined the region.

Notes

1. In the context of early Virginia and the early antebellum South, a "julep" refers to any sweetened hard alcoholic drink, not necessarily the mint julep that would become part of popular representations of the South in the late nineteenth and early twentieth centuries.

2. All references to *The Virginia Housewife* indicate the 1836 edition of the text, which is identical to the 1824 version.

3. As Matthew Guterl argues, planters in the U.S. South were very aware of and influenced by the culture, politics, and economics of nations in the Caribbean and South America, to the extent that to understand the development of the antebellum South as a region, one must locate it first within a global framework.

4. The forced performance of southern elites never really disappears in fictional representations of the South. In his interpretation of Eudora Welty's *Delta Wedding* (1946), Brannon Costello observes, "The spectacle of privilege and unity belies the fact that their spectacular performance is . . . necessary to maintain the illusion of freedom" (42).

5. While running the boardinghouse, Mary Randolph also invented the first prototype for a refrigerator (Harbury 29).

6. In addition to *The Valley of Shenandoah,* Tucker also published two other novels in an attempt to recover the family finances. (It didn't work.)

Works Cited

Clinton, Catherine. *The Plantation Mistress: Woman's World in the Old South.* Pantheon, 1982.

Costello, Brannon. *Plantation Airs: Racial Paternalism and the Transformations of Class in Southern Fiction, 1945–1971.* Louisiana State UP, 2007.

Douglass, Frederick. *My Bondage, My Freedom.* Miller, Orten, and Mulligan, 1855.

Farrish, Chris. "Food in the Antebellum South and the Confederacy." *Food in the Civil War Era: The South,* edited by Helen Zoe Veit, Michigan State UP, 2015, pp. 1–18.

Galloway, J. H. *The Sugar Cane Industry: An Historical Geography from Its Origins to 1914.* Cambridge UP, 1989.

Guterl, Matthew Pratt. *American Mediterranean: Southern Slaveholders in the Age of Emancipation.* Harvard UP, 2008.

Harbury, Katharine E. *Colonial Virginia's Cooking Dynasty.* U of South Carolina P, 2004.

McColley, Robert. *Slavery and Jeffersonian Virginia.* 2nd ed. U of Illinois P, 1973.

Randolph, Mary. *The Virginia Housewife; Or, Methodical Cook.* 1824. John Plaskitt, 1836.

Shields, David S. "Book Farming: Thomas Jefferson and the Necessity of Reading in the Agrarian South." *Writing in the Kitchen: Essays on Southern Literature and Foodways,* edited by David A. Davis and Tara Powell, UP of Mississippi, 2014, pp. 13–28.

———. *Southern Provisions: The Creation and Revival of a Cuisine.* U of Chicago P, 2015.

Sitterson, J. Carlyle. *Sugar Country: The Cane Sugar Industry in the South, 1753–1950.* U of Kentucky P, 1953.

Szczesiul, Anthony. *The Southern Hospitality Myth: Ethics, Politics, Race, and American Memory.* U of Georgia P, 2017.

Taylor, Joe Gray. *Eating, Drinking, and Visiting in the South: An Informal History.* Louisiana State UP, 1982.

Titus, Mary. "The Dining Room Door Swings Both Ways: Food, Race, and Domestic

Space in the Nineteenth-Century South." *Haunted Bodies: Gender and Southern Texts*, edited by Anne Goodwyn Jones and Susan V. Donaldson, UP of Virginia, 1997, pp. 243–56.

Tucker, George. *The Laws of Wages, Profits, and Rent, Investigated.* E. L. Carey and A. Hart, 1837.

———. *The Valley of Shenandoah; Or, Memoirs of the Graysons.* 1824. Edited by Donald R. Noble Jr., U of North Carolina P, 1970. 2 vols.

Veit, Helen Zoe, editor. *Food in the Civil War Era: The South.* Michigan State UP, 2015.

Walden, Sarah W. *Tasteful Domesticity: Women's Rhetoric and the American Cookbook, 1790–1940.* U of Pittsburgh P, 2018.

Wyatt-Brown, Bertram. *Southern Honor: Ethics and Behavior in the Old South.* 25th anniversary edition. Oxford UP, 2007.

The Inebriation and Adaptation
of Larry Brown's *Big Bad Love*

ZACKARY VERNON

Since D. W. Griffith's infamous 1915 racist melodrama *The Birth of a Nation*, which many scholars consider the first feature-length film, the U.S. South has been a common setting and thematic focus for both Hollywood and independent filmmakers. In tracing the history of southern cinema, Deborah E. Barker and Kathryn McKee note that most films about the South have been adaptations of literary works, particularly novels and plays, written by southern authors: "It would be only a slight exaggeration to say that the majority of prominent films set in the South have been literary adaptations and even less of an exaggeration to say that the works of most prominent southern writers have been adapted for the screen" (11–12).

This is true of Mississippi writer Larry Brown, who rose to literary stardom in the late 1980s and the 1990s with the publication of books like *Facing the Music* (1988), *Dirty Work* (1990), and *Father and Son* (1996). Brown's *Big Bad Love* (1990) and *Joe* (1991) both have been adapted into films, with *Joe* being far more successful, both critically and commercially, and Brown himself has been the subject of a much-hailed documentary, Gary Hawkins's *The Rough South of Larry Brown* (2002), which also adapts three of Brown's short stories and weaves them into the narrative of Brown's struggle for literary success. Taken together, these works suggest that Brown has served—as, Barker and McKee argue, many southern writers before him have—as a guide through an often exoticized region, "taking us into the fictional world of the South and at the same time ensuring its authenticity" (12). Filmmakers' desire to adapt Brown's works likely derives from their perception of him as an authority, one who can write authentically about a purportedly "rough South" peopled with hard-living and hard-drinking southerners, which exists at the margins of both national and regional mainstream cultures.

Director and writer Arliss Howard's 2001 film *Big Bad Love* is an adaptation, albeit a loose one, of Brown's 1990 short story collection of the same name. Based principally on Brown's final story of the collection "92 Days," *Big Bad Love* focuses on Leon "Bobby" Barlow, a housepainter and Vietnam veteran, who struggles to write and publish fiction while also battling with alcoholism and its far-ranging ramifications in his personal life. *Big Bad Love,* both the book and film, is an appropriate topic to discuss in *Southern Comforts* because they are inhabited by characters who are incessantly drinking. The protagonist, Leon, in particular, remains drunk throughout most of the narrative, and it is his inebriation that guides much of Howard's adaptation.

While many critics—for example, A. O. Scott of the *New York Times* and David Rooney of *Variety*—argue that Howard's adaptation is overly self-indulgent, I contend that such critiques often misconstrue attempted innovation for indulgence. By focalizing the film through Leon, Howard's unconventional stylistic choices work effectively to give viewers a peek into the mind of a struggling alcoholic and, at the same time, engender in viewers a similar sense of inebriation. Leon's drunkenness is mirrored on-screen through the use of disorienting jump cuts and unexpected plot turns that are only cogent if they are understood as being filtered through Leon's intoxicated perspective. Indeed, the film adaptation's most interesting moments, which often teeter on the verge of being impressionistic and surrealistic, are those that feature Barlow's intoxication. This intimate portrayal of alcoholism presents a feeling and a state of mind, rather than attempting to faithfully adapt Brown's short stories.

I use the term "inebriated adaptation" to suggest not only that Howard's cinematic aesthetic highlights a sense of intoxication but also that Howard's crafting of the adaptation has a drunken quality to it, in that fragments of several short stories are intertwined, sometimes seemingly at random, thus reflecting the oblique and disjointed memory of a book recalled while under the influence. Although the inebriated adaptation adds aesthetic value, however, the film misses a broader mark in its refusal to portray Leon's drinking as something endemic to or resulting from his working-class experience. Therefore, Howard's film may be an unsuccessful adaptation, but not for the reasons most critics maintain. His portrayal of Leon, far from reflecting the self-indulgence critics have identified, is an innovative approach to representing cinematically an inebriated perception of the world. Yet Howard alters Brown's version of Leon, changing his economic status from working class to middle or even upper class and, in doing so, fails to inspire empathy or sympathy between viewers and his alcoholic protagonist.

The Intersection of Alcohol and Class in Larry Brown's Fiction

Because Larry Brown is from Oxford, Mississippi, comparisons between him and earlier Oxford resident William Faulkner are inevitable. However, the types of Delta citizens that Brown wrote about differ significantly from Faulkner's, and these differences are largely based on each writer's own background. Jean W. Cash notes that Brown's family was of "the yeoman class," while "Faulkner was of Oxford's upper-middle class" ("Larry Brown" xx). The southern literary progenitor that is a more apt comparison to Brown is Harry Crews, a writer whom Brown considered his literary hero. Cash posits, "Following in the tradition of Crews, arguably the first southern writer to sympathetically depict the region's working class, Brown produced a body of work that still further humanizes its members" (xix). While this statement about Crews as the original author to depict sympathetically the working-class South may seem somewhat hyperbolic, other scholars do agree. For example, Amy E. Weldon argues that Crews's *A Childhood: The Biography of a Place* (1978) is "the first major Southern autobiography in which a member of the 'poor white' class derided by [William Alexander] Percy speaks up for himself and his people" (91; see also Bledsoe, Gray, and Guinn).

Brown's accounts of his native Mississippi depict working-class people struggling to gain economic security while also battling cultural pathologies ranging from broken families and violent relationships to depression and alcoholism. During childhood, Brown experienced firsthand the effects of alcohol and alcoholism on his family life. According to Cash, "His father's drinking and the consequent lack of money continued to disrupt the family: as Brown told one interviewer [Judith Weinraub], 'Let's just say I [had] . . . a childhood that had some hard times.'" Brown also remarks, "Maybe my early life is why I wrote so many things about drinking and trouble and violence" ("Larry Brown" xxi).

Brown himself was no stranger to drinking and no stranger to bars. In Gary Hawkins's documentary *The Rough South of Larry Brown*, Brown's wife, Mary Annie, states that, when he was not at home, "he was usually out at a bar." Following this in the documentary, Brown says, "There's so much material in there," to which Mary Annie dubiously responds, "Yeah, that's what he says." Brown retorts, "But that's what I've been around and what I'm still around. It's one of the things I know the best." Mary Annie concludes, "I'm sure that's where most of his stories come from—sitting in a bar. The slimier the better, you know." Mary Annie's allegation here conveys a great deal about why Brown's characters' life conditions all too often lead them to drink excessively. Both the catalysts for and dangers of drinking are among the chief overarching concerns that Brown's fiction explores. Joe Samuel Starnes asserts, "Characters who drink more than is good for them, as Brown often did, populate his work, and beer and liquor frequently fuel characters' bad decisions." Starnes even proposes that "a river of alcohol runs through . . . all of Brown's work" (53–54), and this is certainly true of *Big Bad Love*. The stories in this collection almost all concern down-and-out men (and occasionally women) who incessantly pursue alcohol in order to anesthetize themselves against their desperate, unrequited desires and their poverty-stricken lives.

By the late 1980s, when he was writing *Big Bad Love*, Brown's success as a writer had reached an all-time peak, and he was retiring from his position with the fire department in order to write full time. While the extra time to write proved beneficial for Brown, Cash notes that his editor, Shannon Ravenel, "feared that without a regular work schedule, Brown would increase his drinking. She was right" (*Larry Brown* 99). It seems, then, that the characters' incessant drinking in Brown's work did not just come from his observations in bars; Brown himself was known to drink often, and at times heavily (Starnes 52). In one interview with fellow writers Barry Hannah and Brad Watson, Brown admits that drinking was the greatest obstacle to his writing.

To be clear, I am not suggesting, as some critics have (Cash, "Saving Them" 36), that there is a direct parallel between Brown and his characters. Instead, I simply posit that Brown's life experiences and his penchant for drinking likely led to a thematic preoccupation with alcohol and alcoholism that runs throughout his oeuvre and that impacted his sympathetic depictions of high rates of alcoholism among the lower classes of his native Mississippi.

Arliss Howard's Inebriated Adaptation of *Big Bad Love*

Despite the mixed reviews the collection received, Brown's *Big Bad Love* piqued the interest of Arliss Howard shortly after it appeared in 1990, as he believed that the stories were "strange and new and completely familiar" (Cash, *Larry Brown* 198). However, it would take Howard more than a decade to begin filming the adaptation. Howard is best known for his performance as Robert "Cowboy" Evans in Stanley Kubrick's 1987 *Full Metal Jacket,* and *Big Bad Love* was his directorial debut. The adaptation was cowritten by Howard and his brother, James Howard, and coproduced by Howard and his wife, Debra Winger. Howard filmed the adaptation in Oxford and nearby Holly Springs, Mississippi, and Brown was personally involved with the filmmaking process, showing up on set for most of the shooting and even appearing in a brief cameo (199).

The film adaptation of *Big Bad Love* premiered at several film festivals in 2001, including Cannes, and it had a wider commercial release in February 2002 (Cash, *Larry Brown* 205, 209). During its February opening weekend, *Big Bad Love* earned only $5,293, and by April it had grossed a paltry $100,420 (209–10). While the film did garner some positive press on the festival circuit, it received far more negative reviews after its commercial release. As of May 2017, according to the review aggregate website Rotten Tomatoes, only twenty-four of the fifty-eight surveyed reviews of *Big Bad Love* were "Fresh," while thirty-four were "Rotten." Likewise, another aggregate website, Metacritic, gave the film a "metascore" of only forty-nine out of one hundred. This figure was based on twenty-four surveyed reviews—nine positive, eleven mixed, and four negative.

When he was asked how he thought the film turned out, Brown's own response was positive, if also reserved: "Sure. It was fine. I was there for most of the production. They gave me a small part. I had a small role. We got a great soundtrack out of it. We had a bunch of North Mississippi blues players: R. L. Burnside, Junior Kimbrough, and Tom Waits had a couple of songs. I was happy with how it turned out. It didn't get a wide distribution for it" (Fitten and Hetrick 189). Brown's focus on the soundtrack may suggest that his own perception of the adaptation, like that of most critics, was tepid at best.

Many critics take aim at the filmmaking style Howard uses throughout *Big Bad Love.* A. O. Scott, for instance, says that the film is "overly stylized" and that its "literary self-consciousness suffocates lived reality." Scott goes on to assert that "beneath its stylistic and structural quirks, *Big Bad Love* . . . is a self-indulgent celebration of self-indulgence." David Rooney also notes the "self-indulgence" of Howard's directorial sensibility, arguing that the film is "compromised" by this. Steven G. Kellman, reviewing the film in *Southern Quarterly,* states, "It is a film about attitude more than incident, and whatever story lurks in Bobby's life is camouflaged by Howard's fondness for ostentatious camera work and editing. The narrative is both understated and overwrought" (179). Ed Gonzalez shares Kellman's concern: "Howard conjures the past via surrealist flourishes so overwrought you'd swear he just stepped out of a Buñuel retrospective." The reference to filmmaker Luis Buñuel here, although clearly meant as a slight, is fitting in that Howard, like Buñuel, brings to his film a surrealist quality, augmenting the dreamlike feeling of the film rather than sticking closely to the plot of Brown's short story collection.

Most critics neglect to consider how heavy and prolonged drinking affects the way in which the film's characters perceive the world and experience memory, as well as how central these issues are to Howard's adaptation of *Big Bad Love.* What results is an adaptation that not only is about alcoholism but also is itself inebriated, by which I mean that it often feels like it was constructed by someone under the influence of alcohol and that its construction serves to mimic the protagonists' intoxication. Despite the inebriated quality of the adaptation, though, the characters and scenes in the disparate stories of the collection come together to form a more unified, overarching narrative than Brown's book contains.

In order to overcome the rather difficult problem of adapting a short story collection without it ending up being a mere episodic series of vaguely related narratives, Howard relies on viewers to fill in holes and to suspend disbelief even when the narrative seems disorienting. Leon's drunken dreams and meditations, for example, often contain fragments of various narratives from Brown's book; viewers do not necessarily need to be familiar with Brown's stories to understand these fragmented and often incoherent narratives as reflecting Leon's intoxicated perception of reality. Howard also creates a composite of characters from the stories, so that, in the end, they too possess a distinctly inebriated quality, as if observed and recalled by a mind far from sober. Leon, in particular, contains characteristics from all the protagonists in the collection, and Howard draws heavily from the plot and dialogue of several stories other than "92 Days," such as the comically bad writer in "The Apprentice," the flasher narrative in

"Waiting for the Ladies," the drunken lovemaking in "Falling out of Love," and Mr. Aaron's war stories in "Old Soldiers."

Howard's film opens with a scene in which a mailman is removing from and returning to Barlow's mailbox large manila envelopes that contain fiction that he has submitted for publication. This simple scene cuts back and forth to close-up shots—a thigh here, a foot there—of Leon (Arliss Howard) making love in a bathtub with his (ex-)wife Marilyn (Debra Winger), who is wearing a wedding dress and veil. As the mailman leaves and Leon's friend Monroe (Paul Le Mat) pulls up and begins knocking on the door, Marilyn, seemingly inside Leon's house, vanishes, and we see Leon alone in the bathtub, dirty and hungover. The scene of him making love with his wife has been a dream, probably a drunken dream of his wedding day. Barlow says, "Some dreams ruin being awake, if you know the difference. Best not to know." Although this scene does not appear in Brown's book, it is a fitting place to begin a film in which reality and fantasy are constantly blurred, particularly due to Leon's frequent intoxication.

The following scene in the film is similar to the opening scene in "92 Days," in which Monroe offers Leon beers and condolences, since he has recently divorced Marilyn. Subsequently, in the film, after Monroe and Leon paint a house in order to procure enough money to stock Leon up on booze for his long and feverish bouts of writing, there is a scene in which Leon reads rejection letters from various presses. This is also similar to the book, except that Howard adds to the basic scene by dramatizing the connection between Leon's drinking and his shifting grasp of reality. As Leon pounds one beer after another and begins to become drunk, the cinematic techniques employed by Howard increasingly mimic Leon's inebriated state of mind. For example, the editors' words, presumably heard in their own voices in Leon's mind, blur together, creating a cacophony that leaves Leon increasingly agitated. The music from Leon's radio also begins to fuse with the editors' voices, and ultimately they seem to be singing their rejections to him. Finally, Leon, now clearly both intoxicated and enraged, hears the voices on the radio narrating his own life, conveying to him not only his literary rejections but also the fact that his ex-wife's lawyer has sent him a bill.

This focus on Leon's perception of reality is also apparent in an experimental scene in which Leon's mother (Angie Dickinson) comes to check on him. This scene in the book is rendered in a rather straightforward linear and objective manner, and the film follows the dialogue quite closely. However, like so much of the film, the scene is rendered through Leon's perspective—a perspective that is considerably addled by the Maker's Mark that he guzzles as his mother arrives—so that what the viewer sees is precisely what Leon feels. As his mother heaps blame on him for being a bad father and husband, the soundtrack, which has consisted of a light orchestral song, slowly comes to a crescendo, complete with a roaring timpani. At its peak, Leon, ashamed of causing so much pain in the lives of his family members, looks increasingly guilty, and although they are sitting inside, the skies seem to open and a rainstorm breaks out over his head, showering him with water and flooding the house. It is only after his mother leaves that Leon, although still drinking bourbon, dries out and the rainstorm ends.

Another significant scene that conveys Leon's drunken perception of reality occurs after the death of his young daughter. During the funeral, the camera pans around the gathering, showing various people, including the family members, in mourning. When the camera finally lands on Leon, though, the entire scene becomes focalized through him, and the somber tone shifts. Notably, the preacher, who had previously been delivering a standard Christian funeral service, radically alters his tone and message, as the service is filtered through Leon's intoxicated and grief-stricken perspective. Thus, the preacher says, or at least Leon perceives him to say, "Blah, blah. She shall suffer no more. Blah, blah. Platitude about the mysterious ways in which God works. Platitude about faith. Platitude about grief. Cliché about God calling his children home. Cliché about angels. Blah, blah. She shall suffer no more. Blah, blah. In the twinkling of an eye. Blah. For the trumpet shall sound. Blah, blah. And the dead shall be raised incorruptible. Blah, blah, blah. And we shall be changed."

While this scene could have become ironic or even comic, in Howard's hands it is powerfully moving. Leon, for all his faults, is genuinely in mourning, and Howard invites viewers to mourn along with him. Even though his consciousness seems to have been altered by substance abuse, Leon's perception of his daughter's funeral is poignant in that he hears only the clichés of a Christian burial and from them gleans no solace. In the final line of the sermon, the preacher looks Leon in the eyes and says, "And we shall be changed." In this moment, even in his inebriated state, Leon, the look on his face suggests, knows that this is true, that the death of his daughter is a wound that will not heal.

Much like this scene, the moments throughout the film that appear most self-indulgent invariably occur when Leon is drunk, thus mirroring his mental state. In Leon's moments of sobriety, however, the film is far from self-indulgent; instead, the pace slows, and the film often becomes lyrical in an understated way. For example, in one sequence of the film, Leon is imprisoned for public drunkenness following the death of his daughter. While in prison, Leon is, of course, not drinking, and, as a result, the tone of the film shifts dramatically, becoming sober along with Leon. The scenes during this sequence are quiet and meditative, following Leon as he ruminates on the state of his broken family. In other words, Howard uses the tonal shifts that are linked to Leon's clarity of mind throughout the film to invite viewers into the consciousness of the main character and to enable them to see the world as he sees it. This form of cinematographic empathy may not make viewers like Leon any more, but at the very least it does force them to experience the world as he does—that is, as a desperately unhappy alcoholic. Nonetheless, the difficulty in establishing lasting sympathy for Leon remains, largely due to the way in which Howard alters the class status that Brown assigns to Leon in the short story collection.

Drinking in "Rough South" Literature and Film

Even while Howard's adaptation is more stylistically innovative than critics have given it credit for, *Big Bad Love* ultimately fails in its attempts to create a sympathetic connection between viewers and the film's frequently intoxicated characters. Roger Ebert's assessment is particularly damning: "It all comes down to whether you can tolerate Leon Barlow. I can't. *Big Bad Love* can, and is filled with characters who love and accept him, even though he is a full-time, gold-plated pain in the can. . . . The movie has patience with his narcissistic self-pity. My diagnosis: Send Barlow to rehab, haul him to some AA meetings, and find out in a year if he has anything worth saying."

Other reviewers also focus on Leon's unlikability or his lack of character development. Steven G. Kellman argues that Leon "is a very hard man to like" (179). Similarly, Christy Lemire of the *Seattle Post-Intelligencer* states that the film "catalogs Leon's self-destructive behavior without hinting at its origin. We're simply expected to accept that that's the way he is, which makes it difficult to sympathize or connect with him on any level" (in Cash, *Larry Brown* 209). Several other reviewers, including Kellman, critique the film for its tendency to romanticize the myth of the self-destructive, alcoholic artist. According to Cash, the characters' lack of likability is linked to their class: "Part of the problem arose from the film's transplantation of Leon Barlow from working-class origins to a middle-class background. Since both Leon and his friend, Monroe, are portrayed as less economically down-and-out, they seem less sympathetic" (*Larry Brown* 209). Cash's contention here is valid but warrants further investigation; in particular, it is important to contextualize her critique of the film within a broader lineage of "rough South" literature and film.

Larry Brown's fiction has in recent years come to be associated with "grit lit" and rough South literature, two often overlapping (sub)genres of southern literature. In the introduction to *Grit Lit: A Rough South Reader* (2012), Brian Carpenter writes, "We have defined 'Grit Lit' as typically blue collar or working class, mostly small town, sometimes rural, occasionally but not always violent, usually but not necessarily Southern." Carpenter distinguishes grit lit from the rough South by defining the latter as "mostly poor, white, rural, and unquestionably violent—Grit Lit's wilder kin" (xvii; see also Gingher).

Although grit lit and rough South literature may occasionally deserve critique for their tendency to romanticize and commodify working-class cultures, the emergence of writers like Brown within these genres is significant in giving voice to a marginalized class that has historically not been well represented in the southern literary canon. Erik Bledsoe states that lower-class culture "until recently has lacked its own recognized storytellers. This new generation of southern writers is giving voice to a different group of southerners, and in doing so it is forcing its readers to reexamine long-held stereotypes and beliefs while challenging the literary roles traditionally assigned poor whites" (68). Richard Gray, in *Southern Aberrations: Writers of the American South and the Problems of Regionalism* (2000), notes that, between the two world wars, there were writers like Erskine Caldwell and Richard Wright who wrote about issues of rural southern poverty.

Beginning in the last quarter of the twentieth century and continuing to the present, grit lit could be interpreted as an extension of this earlier work, although grit lit does signal a significantly larger expansion of the canon in this vein. Therefore, grit lit and rough South literature, at their best, expand the literary canon by adding new voices, while also highlighting the cultural heterogeneity of the U.S. South. Matthew Guinn asserts that Brown's meteoric rise to literary success should not be seen as a "fluke but merely the harbinger of many such new voices, the prologue to a new chapter in southern literature in which lower-class and blue-collar whites, aided by Sun Belt prosperity, have belatedly joined the southern literary consciousness" (36).

Brown's fiction does significant cultural work in that it deconstructs lingering misconceptions about lower-class white southerners and gives them the
"dignity historically denied them in literature and film" (Watkins 18). In culti-
vating characters with whom readers can empathize, regardless of the readers'
own life circumstances, Brown humanizes a class of people that has often been
vilified or mocked, and he accomplishes this without peddling idealizations of
this class. This is clear in the way Brown writes about alcohol use among lower-
class southerners. He presents them in neither an idealized nor a demeaning
way, and he manages to convey to readers how and why such a population may
be particularly vulnerable to substance abuse. Most of the characters in Brown's
Big Bad Love drink to escape, however briefly, the difficult circumstances of
their lives. For example, in the story "Wild Thing," a man stuck working as a
forklift driver says, "It was a hard life, and I didn't know if I was going to be able
to keep on living it" (41). In another story, "Gold Nuggets," a character describes
his menial job, saying, "The job I had wasn't worth a damn anyway, just putting
washers in little holes. It wasn't anything that made me feel real fulfilled" (77).
Additionally, in "Old Soldiers," a character who is specifically called a "drunk" is
also described as "a good man," and yet he too suffers from alcoholism that may
be directly linked to his occupation: "He's worked hard all his life laying brick,
but he's had his troubles with the bottle" (97).

Countless such characters throughout *Big Bad Love* seem to suffer from a
compulsion to drink as a means of lessening the hopelessness of their lives,
though Brown reminds us that this escape is fleeting for his working-class characters: "But the whiskey will make you want to cry after it makes you want to
laugh" (93). However, the cinematic counterparts of Brown's characters, especially Leon Barlow, seem to lack such dark catalysts motivating the dissat-
isfaction with their lives and their subsequent desire to drink. The film, then,
disarticulates Brown's characters' alcohol use and addiction from broader social
factors such as poverty.

Bledsoe puts alcoholism and various other forms of excess at the center of
lower-class southern literature: "In the public imagination, and arguably in reality, it is a world of excess—excessive alcohol, excessive sex, excessive violence"
(68). This centering of rough South literature—and by extension cinema—on
excess need not suggest that the genre condones stereotypes or fetishizes cultural pathologies like alcoholism that disproportionately affect the working
class. Rather, the focus on drinking and other excesses in the genre reflects social realities of region and class and, in doing so, could lead readers and viewers

to understand the hardships faced by those disadvantaged by a severe lack of economic opportunities in the region and the nation.

Howard's adaptation of *Big Bad Love,* however, utterly fails in this regard. Howard's Leon Barlow, despite periodically working menial jobs for his beer money, seems middle class, and any hardships he faces seem to result from his unwillingness to allow a job to compete with his writing and drinking rather than from any structural barriers between him and economic opportunities. Moreover, his upbringing seems solidly upper class; his parents' house, his childhood home, is a mansion—and could even be an antebellum plantation. Leon's friend Monroe is also so wealthy that at one point in the film Leon says that he is "sitting on Fort Knox."

As a result of his associations with and the opportunities provided by friends and family in the film, Leon is more difficult to sympathize with than his alcoholic literary antecedents, given that he never grasps the privilege he possesses as a white, straight man from an apparently affluent family and with extremely affluent friends. Therefore, *Big Bad Love* is an unsuccessful adaptation because it does not provide viewers with the best that rough South literature and film have to offer—a realistic and evenhanded portrayal of the lower classes and the cultural pathologies, such as alcoholism, that they sometimes face. Howard's film, inhabited by narcissistic alcoholics of the middle and upper classes, ultimately portrays characters who exist at the cultural center and thus possess a privilege that insulates them from the hardships with which Brown's marginalized characters must constantly contend.

Works Cited

Barker, Deborah E., and Kathryn McKee. "Introduction: The Southern Imaginary." *American Cinema and the Southern Imaginary,* edited by Deborah E. Barker and Kathryn McKee, U of Georgia P, 2011, pp. 1–23.

Bledsoe, Erik. "The Rise of Southern Redneck and White Trash Writers." *Southern Cultures,* vol. 6, no. 1 (Spring 2000), pp. 68–90.

Brown, Larry. *Big Bad Love.* Vintage Contemporaries, 1990.

Carpenter, Brian. "Introduction: Blood and Bone." *Grit Lit: A Rough South Reader,* edited by Brian Carpenter and Tom Franklin, U of South Carolina P, 2012, pp. xiii–xxxii.

Cash, Jean W. "Larry Brown: An Introduction." *Larry Brown and the Blue-Collar South,* edited by Jean W. Cash and Keith Perry, UP of Mississippi, 2008, pp. xix–xxxvi.

———. *Larry Brown: A Writer's Life.* UP of Mississippi, 2011.

————. "'Saving Them from Their Lives': Storytelling and Self-Fulfillment in *Big Bad Love*." *Larry Brown and the Blue-Collar South*, edited by Jean W. Cash and Keith Perry, UP of Mississippi, 2008, pp. 36–48.

Ebert, Roger. "*Big Bad Love*." Rogerebert.com, 15 March 2002, www.rogerebert.com /reviews/big-bad-love-2002.

Fitten, Marc, and Lawrence Hetrick. "An Interview with Larry Brown." 2003. *Conversations with Larry Brown*, edited by Jay Watson, UP of Mississippi, 2007, pp. 180–89.

Gingher, Robert. "Grit Lit." *The Companion to Southern Literature*, edited by Joseph M. Flora, Lucinda H. MacKethan, and Todd Taylor, Louisiana State UP, 2002, pp. 319–20.

Gonzalez, Ed. "Review: *Big Bad Love*." *Slant*, 4 February 2002, www.slantmagazine.com /film/review/big-bad-love.

Gray, Richard. *Southern Aberrations: Writers of the American South and the Problems of Regionalism*. Louisiana State UP, 2000.

Guinn, Matthew. *After Southern Modernism: Fiction of the Contemporary South*. UP of Mississippi, 2000.

Hawkins, Gary, director. *The Rough South of Larry Brown*. Blue Moon Filmed Productions, 2002.

Howard, Arliss, director. *Big Bad Love*. IFC Films, 2002.

Kellman, Steven G. "Portrait of the Artist as a Boozy Screwup." *Southern Quarterly*, vol. 40, no. 3 (Spring 2002), pp. 178–79.

Rooney, David. "*Big Bad Love*." *Variety*, 12 May 2001, variety.com/2001/film/reviews /big-bad-love-1200468406.

Scott, A. O. "A Writer Holds It All In, at Least from His Family." *New York Times*, 22 February 2002, www.nytimes.com/2002/02/22/movies/film-review-a-writer-holds -it-all-in-at-least-from-his-family.html.

Starnes, Joe Samuel. "Larry Brown: A Firefighter Finds His Voice." *Rough South, Rural South: Region and Class in Recent Southern Literature*, edited by Jean W. Cash and Keith Perry. UP of Mississippi, 2016, pp. 50–58.

Weldon, Amy E. "'When Fantasy Meant Survival': Writing, Class, and the Oral Tradition in the Autobiographies of Rick Bragg and Harry Crews." *Mississippi Quarterly*, vol. 53, no. 1 (1999), pp. 89–110.

Flannery O'Connor, "Interleckchuls," and Cocktail Culture

MONICA C. MILLER

While she was a resident of the Yaddo artist colony, author Flannery O'Connor reported in a letter to a friend on the behavior of her fellow writers: "In any collection of so-called artists you will find a good percentage alcoholic in one degree or another." To the chaste, teetotalist O'Connor, Yaddo was a den of iniquity: "In such a place you have to expect them all to sleep around. This is not sin but Experience, and if you do not sleep with the opposite sex, it is assumed that you sleep with your own" (*Habit* 363). For O'Connor, whose drink of choice was "Coca-Colas laced with black coffee" (Gooch 242),[1] the drunken debauchery of this New England artist's colony was emblematic of the kind of atheistic, "interleckshul" (see Powell) life of the mind against which she held herself apart, in her claims of being a "Hillbilly Thomist." Rather than sit in the same cocktail parties, dulling her senses with drink, O'Connor wanted a true life of the mind—sharpened, open, and active, not sardonic and static.

This essay is not a biographical reading of O'Connor's works through the lens of her attitudes toward alcoholic excesses. Rather, I argue that O'Connor's personal values regarding teetotalism and intellectualism are related not only to each other but also to her understanding of meaning-making itself. Reading O'Connor's experiences with intellectual cocktail culture as biographical details informing her stories would be a critically unproductive approach. Rather, I propose that O'Connor's criticism of the intellectual approach that she saw as characteristic of intellectual cocktail culture offers a tantalizing new way of understanding her work. Specifically, O'Connor depicts the intellectual tendency to employ a metaphoric understanding of the world as a contrast to a literal—or what O'Connor would discuss as anagogic—approach to making sense of the world, an approach that was fundamental to her Christ-centered worldview.

With regard to questions of interpretation, O'Connor herself was clear. In her essay "The Nature and Aim of Fiction," O'Connor calls upon the tradition of scriptural analysis to delineate an exegetical approach. O'Connor reports, "The medieval commentators on Scripture found three kinds of meaning in the literal level of the sacred text: one they called allegorical, in which one fact pointed to another; one they called tropological, or moral, which had to do with what should be done; and one they called anagogical, which had to do with the Divine life and our participation in it" (*Mystery and Manners* 72). To O'Connor, the most important aspect of these, for the fiction writer, was the anagogic vision, what she further explained as "the kind of vision that is able to see different levels of reality in one image or one situation." Contrary to her claims of anti-intellectualism, O'Connor's approach to both literary production and interpretation were, in fact, quite intellectually complex and informed by scholarship.

O'Connor's claims to anti-intellectualism become specious when considered in light of her own rigorous education and pursuit of learning and of her lived experience. It's often overlooked that, before her diagnosis of lupus forced her to move home to Milledgeville, Georgia, O'Connor expected to be a part of this urban life of the mind, making plans while a graduate student at Iowa to live in New York City as a working artist. And while O'Connor was dismissive of cocktail-fueled, intellectual environments such as Yaddo and university English departments, we should not forget that Yaddo was where she wrote a significant amount of her breakthrough novel *Wise Blood,* and she spent a great deal of time, even after her diagnosis, in the company of nonteetotalist artists and intellectuals.

While much has been written about the ways in which her later life in Milledgeville, living at Andalusia farm with her mother, informed her work,[2] much less attention has been paid to the influence of her pre-Andalusia life. Given how formative this time was for O'Connor—a period during which she befriended people such as Allen Tate, Caroline Gordon, and Robert and Sally Fitzgerald (who would play major roles in both her personal and her professional life)—O'Connor's experiences with cocktail-fueled intellectual culture should be considered a significant influence on her writing, as much as her relationship with her mother or her experience with disability. Generally, critical attention has focused on the significance of her life "spent between the house and the chicken yard"—the rural, the southern, and the autobiographical details of her life on the farm in Milledgeville (see *Habit* 290–91). By broadening our vision of O'Connor's life, other influences emerge—such as the role that cocktail culture played in her own life and work.

I argue here that O'Connor's critique of cocktail culture intelligentsia's prioritization of the metaphoric over the literal provides an important heuristic for our own analysis of her work. Specifically, this insight allows us a new approach to her story "The River" by emphasizing the nihilistic cocktail culture that forms a backdrop to the story's tragedy. Little scholarly attention has been paid to the presence of alcohol in O'Connor's work, likely because little alcohol appears— the moonshine and unmarked liquor in *The Violent Bear It Away* being one notable exception.[3] Unlike the "burning arm [that] slid down Tarwater's throat as if the devil were already reaching inside him to finger his soul" in *The Violent Bear It Away* (*Collected Works* 358), however, there is an alternate, intellectual version of drinking culture that exists in O'Connor's letters and in "The River."

"The River," published in O'Connor's 1955 short story collection *A Good Man Is Hard to Find,* tells the story of four- or five-year-old Harry Ashfield. Driven out of his home by his parents' constant cocktail parties, Harry is taken by his babysitter, Mrs. Connin, to a religious healing ceremony, where Harry is baptized in the river of the story's title. Once home, he braves his way through his drunk, neglectful parents and their friends to bed. The next day, while his parents sleep off their hangovers, Harry makes his way back to the river, where, in seeking to permanently baptize himself, he drowns.

Much of the scholarship on this story focuses on the meaning of Harry's baptism and drowning. Often, "The River" is compared to *The Violent Bear It Away,* which also ends with a fatal baptism death of a child, or "The Lame Shall Enter First," in which an undernourished, neglected child also ends his life. In scholarship addressing these works, the focus is often on the meaning of the child's death as a puncturing means of salvation or the parents' confrontation with the violence of grace. Unlike these other texts, however, in which the experiences of the parents are as significant as that of the children, the parents in "The River" are unnamed—presumably, they are Mr. and Mrs. Ashfield, though they are referred to as "the father" and "his mother" (or even "the woman") throughout the story—and they are generally dismissed by scholars as bad parents who set the stage for Harry's need for escape. Joy A. Farmer, for example, notes, "Instead of loving parents, Harry has a mother and father too hungover from the previous evening's revels to take proper notice of him" (59). While scholarship on these other texts considers the role of Rayber in young Bishop's death in *The Violent Bear It Away*, for instance, or the culpability of Norton in his son's suicide in "The Lame Shall Enter First," the passivity and anonymity of Harry's parents in "The River" means that little scholarly attention has been paid to them, other than as the cause of Harry's neglect.

However, I maintain that the details we are given about their cocktail-fueled, intelligentsia-filled revels are significant. Shifting our focus from Harry to his parents alters our understanding of the intellectual in O'Connor's fiction. While plenty has been written about O'Connor's own ambivalence toward the intellectual in both her own life and her fiction, such studies generally focus on O'Connor's "three distinct intellectual character types," which Tara Powell identifies in *The Intellectual in Twentieth-Century Southern Literature*: "The student intellectuals, unable to perceive the religious mystery central to O'Connor's own intellectual life, [who] elevate reason to be the definitive aspect of humanity. The 'Educationists,' or teachers, [who] perceive mystery but believe one's 'great dignity' is the ability to eradicate it. Finally, the 'artists' are educated thinkers who attempt to experience or even shape mystical reality through intellect" (20). Indeed, characters in both *The Violent Bear It Away* and "The Lame Shall Enter First" exemplify the kind of "Educationist" intellectual described by Powell.

However, I believe that Harry's parents in "The River" are in a category of their own, unique in O'Connor's writing and consonant with O'Connor's experiences in sardonic, cocktail-fueled, intellectual cultures such as those at Yaddo, at the University of Iowa, during her brief time living in New York City, and on the many speaking tours she made after her initial literary success. The story's urban setting, signified by apartment living and city buses, places it less in a specifically southern tradition of intellectual life than in an urban one. The drunkenness and hangovers omnipresent in the apartment designate it as a place of confusion, but I argue that it is a very specific kind of confusion: the confusion of the metaphoric for the anagogic. In other words, in "The River," O'Connor uses the dangers of decadent cocktail culture to dramatize the dangers that intellectualization poses to spiritual salvation—specifically through its fascination with metaphor at the expense of other methods of understanding the nature of reality.

O'Connor explained her own trouble with the American intellectual attachment to a metaphoric understanding of the world in her well-known anecdote about meeting author Mary McCarthy at a cocktail party. Characterizing McCarthy as a "Big Intellectual" who left the Church at the age of fifteen, O'Connor describes her experience of the party to her friend Betty Hester (identified as "A" in her published correspondence) as one of absolute discomfort. She reported that she felt so out of her element that, at one in the morning, having been there for five hours, the usually loquacious O'Connor still had not said a word. Her subsequent depiction of her clash with McCarthy not only resonates with the description of the Ashfields' party but also provides the foundation for the anagogic approach to meaning-making and understanding for which I am arguing:

> Well, toward morning the conversation turned on the Eucharist, which I, being the Catholic, was obviously supposed to defend. [Mary McCarthy] said when she was a child and received the Host, she thought of it as the Holy Ghost, He being the "most portable" person of the Trinity; now she thought of it as a symbol and implied that it was a pretty good one. I then said, in a very shaky voice, "Well, if it's a symbol, to hell with it." That was all the defense I was capable of but I realize now that this is all I will ever be able to say about it, outside of a story, except that it is the center of existence for me; all the rest of life is expendable. (*Habit* 124–25)

O'Connor understood the presence of the ineffable as very real and very much not symbolic or metaphoric. The cold, abstracting distance that distinguishes McCarthy's "Big Intellectual" stance in this anecdote is anathema to O'Connor's understanding of the world. Indeed, it supports the reading of "The River" as something more than a story of metaphoric loneliness and redemption, framing it as a story of simultaneous tragedy and salvation. Harry dies in his pursuit of communion (both emotional and spiritual), and O'Connor's rejection of metaphoric readings in general (as the Mary McCarthy anecdote illustrates) encourages an uncomfortable reading of the end of "The River" as one in which the triumph of salvation rests uncomfortably with the reality of the death of a neglected child.[4]

Throughout her correspondence and essays, O'Connor sets herself apart from the sophisticated, intellectual mind-sets that characterize Harry's home life. However, in her discussion of O'Connor's ambivalence toward the intellectual lifestyle, Powell points out, "Any discussions of O'Connor's attitudes toward education must acknowledge that she was intellectual in every meaningful sense. O'Connor often maintained that she never really learned anything until she went to the Iowa Writers' Workshop" (27). O'Connor admitted to trying out the cocktail culture during her time at Yaddo, in 1948 and 1949, but she felt as alienated at those parties as she did when she met Mary McCarthy. Indeed, as Sally Fitzgerald reports in her editorial comments in *Habit of Being*, "Flannery seemed fated to asceticism. The one time she decided that she should contribute to the frolics at Yaddo, she tripped and broke her bottle on her way to the party" (310).

Although her experiences at Yaddo were not quite as confrontational as her dinner with McCarthy, she later reported to her friend Cecil Dawkins, "There were a good many parties at which everybody contributed something for the liquor. I went to one or two of these but always left before they began to break things. . . . This was in pre-beatnik days but I assume it is about the same. At the breakfast table they talked about seconal and barbiturates and now maybe it's marijuana. You survive in this atmosphere by minding your own business . . . and by not being afraid to be different from the rest of them" (*Habit* 364). Here, O'Connor describes how her original interest in arty cocktail parties quickly waned when she discovered that cocktail-fueled revelry quickly turns to debauchery and "breaking things."[5]

I find her references in this letter to "beatniks" enlightening with respect to Harry's parents in "The River," as the Ashfields' abstract art and sardonic attitudes surely might categorize them as such beatniks. The reality of intellectual cocktail parties is not engaging discussion, artistic collaboration, or the forging of new friendships based on shared values and aesthetic appreciation—in fact, it is more about destruction and "breaking things" than it is about productivity of any kind, whether of art or discourse.

The destructive reality of intellectual cocktail culture is an important force in "The River." The Ashfields' party lifestyle comes at the cost of the safety and well-being of their child, Harry, whose life is one of neglect and malnourishment. The story's opening sets the scene of parental impatience and disinterest: "The child stood glum and limp in the middle of the dark living room while his father pulled him into a plaid coat. His right arm was hung in the sleeve but the father buttoned the coat anyway and pushed him forward toward a pale spotted hand that stuck through the half-open door." When the babysitter, Mrs. Connin, the owner of the disembodied hand who has arrived to pick up Harry, complains that the child's coat isn't fixed right, "'Well then for Christ's sake fix him,' the father muttered. 'It's six in the morning.' He was in his bathrobe and barefooted" (*Collected Works* 154).

In this opening scene, the foundation of Harry's young existence is established. He is "glum and limp," being picked up at six in the morning by a babysitter from a dark apartment, barely tended to by an impatient, barefoot, undressed father who halfheartedly tries to dress his son. Harry's father makes reference to Harry's mother being sick, and he tells the sitter that they expect them to stay out until eight or nine that night. Mrs. Connin's naïveté is revealed over the course of the day, as she takes seriously that Harry's mother has some sort of serious affliction which requires her young son to be away an entire day. However, when she later remembers to ask the preacher, Mr. Paradise, to pray for Harry's mother, Harry explains that his mother is neither in the hospital nor in pain, but simply "hasn't got up yet. . . . She has a hangover" (165).

When not under the care of a babysitter, the young Harry is completely on his own. The day after his baptism, for example, he awakens late to a "dark and close" apartment, where his parents are still asleep. His search for food is particularly poignant, as he ends up eating two cracker-and-anchovy-paste canapés still on the coffee table from the night before, with some leftover ginger ale (168). Still hungry, the description of the kitchen drives home the characterization of cocktail culture as one of neglect and malnourishment:

> The apartment was silent except for the faint humming of the refrigerator. He went into the kitchen and found some raisin bread heels and spread a half jar of peanut butter between them and climbed up on the tall kitchen stool and sat chewing the sandwich slowly, wiping his nose every now and then on his shoulder. When his finished he found some chocolate milk and drank that. He would rather have had the ginger ale he saw but they left the bottle openers where he couldn't reach them. He studied what was left in the refrigerator for a while—some shriveled vegetables that she had forgot were there and a lot of brown oranges that she bought and didn't squeeze; there were three or four kinds of cheese and something fishy in a paper bag; the rest was a pork bone. (168–69)

Such morning-after barrenness is nothing new for the preschool-age boy; indeed, his parents' drunken parties are common enough that he is familiar with the concept of the hangover.

Harry's grasp of the seriousness of his baptism in the river causes him to realize how much his apartment life is not: "He had a sudden feeling that that this was not a joke. Where he lived everything was a joke" (165). Part of his pre-baptism, untethered identity can be attributed to the apartment's barrenness, both materially and spiritually. O'Connor describes a similar lack of serious-ness among her colleagues at Yaddo, when she tells Betty Hester, "After a few weeks at Yaddo, you long to talk to talk to an insurance agent, dog-catcher, bricklayer—anybody who isn't talking about Form or sleeping pills" (*Habit* 487).

Both the author and her character crave connection with those who are se-rious and nondestructive. This story constructs a version of cocktail culture that fails to deliver on the promise of intellectual stimulation and productive dis-course that it seems to offer. "Cocktail parties," by their nature, imply a higher level of engagement than other types of drinking environments, including more careful attention to dress (as "cocktail" itself designates a rather formal style) as well as drinks that are crafted from often complicated recipes, requiring both myriad ingredients and artful presentation, with accessories such as paper um-brellas and fruit garnishes and even performative displays involving fire.

As both O'Connor's and Harry's experiences reflect, however, such appear-ances often belie an unengaged and even destructive reality. Rather than foster-ing artistic engagement, such parties instead lead to disappointment and disen-gagement. Like O'Connor at Yaddo, Harry suffers from a lack of connection to anyone engaged with the real world. Rather, he has picked up on the nihilism of his parents' cocktail culture, which is in large part responsible for the desolation of the apartment. The day after his baptism, he wanders the apartment while his parents sleep, bored. "In his own room he had picture books and blocks but they were for the most part torn up; he found the way to get new ones was to tear up the ones he had. There was very little to do at any time but eat; how-ever, he was not a fat boy" (*Collected Works* 169). The only kinds of consumption possible in the apartment are mindless, nonnourishing ones: tearing up books rather than reading them and eating stale canapés rather than healthy food. Even the air is unhealthy, as Mrs. Connin complains: "I couldn't smell those dead cigarette butts long if I was ever to come sit with you" (154). The day af-ter the party, as Harry wanders around the quiet apartment, he is described as "looking into the ashtrays at the butts as if this might be a habit" (168–69). He then empties ashtrays on the floor and rubs the ashes into the carpet.[6]

The significance of their last name, Ashfield, seems almost overdetermined, as it emphasizes the desolation and barrenness of the family's party-filled apartment life. And while it is certainly possible to read this name as metaphoric, I read the name as coexisting on both metaphoric and anagogic levels. Yes, there are metaphoric meanings to be drawn from "Ashfield," with regard to barrenness and emptiness, but there is also a literal field of ash in the apartment, left behind by clumsy smokers. Harry's playing with the ashes in the ashtrays can be read even further, as the charnel grounds suggested by this name are simultaneously metaphoric (in their symbolic suggestion of death), literal (in the danger posed to Harry in playing with dirty cigarette butts), and anagogic (as a reference to and representation of the realm of death in which Harry dallies on the outskirts).

This desolation manifests in Harry's mother's affliction as well. We first hear her calling from the bedroom while Mr. Ashfield impatiently tries to dress Harry:

> A toneless voice called from the bedroom, "Bring me an icepack."
> "Too bad his mamma's sick," Mrs. Connin said. "What's her trouble?"
> "We don't know," he muttered.
> "We'll ask the preacher to pray for her. He's healed a lot of folks." (155)

The comical ambiguities of this scene—readers realize the nature of Mrs. Ashfield's "illness," whereas Mrs. Connin believes her to be so afflicted that she is in need of divine healing—also reveal the deeper confusion at the heart of the Ashfields' lives. Specifically, when Mr. Ashfield replies "We don't know" to Mrs. Connin's question about the nature of his wife's illness, which we might read as a sardonic reply to the babysitter's naïveté, we might also take seriously his admission of not understanding the root cause of their nihilistic malaise spawned by cocktail party intelligentsia life.

Indeed, Mr. Ashfield's answer that he doesn't know the cause of his wife's affliction resonates with the story's later scene between Harry and his mother. After Harry returns from his day with Mrs. Connin (during which time he not only undergoes the baptism with Mr. Paradise but also steals Mrs. Connin's heirloom Bible), he encounters his parents and their friends in a lethargic and mocking state of drunkenness, representing the kinds of "arrogant intellectuals" in O'Connor's work that Powell describes as "critiqued fiercely in recurring character types portraying what the author saw as the pitfalls of an intellectual life untempered by spiritual humility" (20). In this scene, we finally see Mrs. Ashfield, and our first vision of her, focalized through Mrs. Connin's perspective, is an especially negative one: "'That would be her,' Mrs. Connin decided, in the black britches—long black satin britches and barefoot sandals and red toenails. She was lying on half the sofa, with her knees crossed in the air and her head propped on the arm. She didn't get up" (*Collected Works* 166).

In fact, Mrs. Ashfield is only roused from her lethargic stupor when she learns of her son's baptism and the preacher's prayers for her affliction. Although she is not moved enough to behave maternally—after Harry escapes from his parents and their mocking friends, he gets undressed and puts himself to bed, alone[7]—she does eventually follow him to his room, and she seems to feel threatened by the possibility of another force having sway over her son: "'What did that dolt of a preacher say about me?' she whispered. 'What lies have you been telling today, honey?'" She shakes him awake and pulls him into a sitting position. "'Tell me,' she whispered and her bitter breath covered his face" (168).

The urban, sophisticated disregard and neglect of the apartment stands in stark contrast to the "long gentle hand" of the river (171). And while it is tempting to want to attribute this contrast to an urban/rural, atheist/Christian split, I believe the story points to a more complex understanding of the cocktail culture that pervades Harry's apartment life. Specifically, the story asserts that the nihilism and futility at the heart of this culture is a problem of *interpretation*.

Within "The River" are two material objects that are the subject of interpretation by both Mrs. Connin and Mrs. Ashfield and her friends: the Ashfields' abstract art painting and Mrs. Connin's heirloom Bible. When Mrs. Connin picks up Harry at the Ashfields' apartment, she walks "over to a watercolor hanging near the phonograph" and "peer[s] closely at the black lines crossing into broken planes of violent color" (154). The presence of this presumably abstract painting leaves Mrs. Connin unimpressed, and she tells Mr. Ashfield, "I wouldn't have paid for that . . . I would have drew it myself" (154). The modern art painting is contrasted with Mrs. Connin's house, which has walls "filled with pictures and calendars," including a picture of her husband, and "a colored picture over the bed of a man wearing a white sheet. He had long hair and a gold circle around his head and he was sawing on a board while some children stood watching him" (158).

This contrast highlights what I have characterized as a contrast in interpretation, as Mrs. Connin responds to the literal rather than the abstract. This is notably demonstrated by the education that Harry attributes to his exposure to Mrs. Connin's world: "He had found out already this morning that he had been made by a carpenter named Jesus Christ. Before he had thought it had been a doctor named Sladewall, a fat man with a yellow mustache who gave him shots and thought his name was Herbert, but this must have been a joke. They joked a lot where he lived. If he had thought about it before, he would have thought Jesus Christ was a word like 'oh' or 'damm' or 'God,' or maybe somebody who had cheated them out of something sometime" (160). Again, a passage ostensibly about comic misunderstanding contains deeper revelations, as Harry's misunderstanding about who made him—either a doctor or Christ—echoes the theme of misinterpretation.[8]

As her encounter with Mary McCarthy demonstrates, O'Connor rejected metaphoric understandings of the sublime outright; rather, she embraced this anagogic vision. Her distinction between the metaphoric and the anagogic is in keeping with her fiction's critique of intellectual cocktail culture. Just as Mrs. Connin's rejection of the Ashfields' abstract painting highlights the rejection of strictly metaphoric interpretation, the reaction of Mrs. Ashfield and her friends to the antique Bible that Harry stole from Mrs. Connin's house similarly demonstrates the problem of misinterpretation. Mrs. Ashfield's face assumes "an exaggerated comical expression. . . . 'My God,' somebody said. One of the men peered at it sharply from behind a thick pair of glasses. 'That's valuable,' he said. 'That's a collector's item. . . . I tell you it's valuable. . . . 1832'" (167).

O'Connor infuses this exchange with irony, from the profane expression of "My God" to the man's repeated insistence on the book's value. Of course, to the understanding reader, the Bible will be understood to have value as a sacred text as well as a valuable family heirloom of Mrs. Connin's. Mrs. Ashfield's friends, however, only see the Bible's value in its material nature, as an antique book dating back to 1832. Here, the Ashfields and their friends exemplify the kind of intellectuals in O'Connor's work who "perceive the world through the brainy lens of scholarship [and] find themselves, time and again, regarded with amusement, caution, suspicion, ridicule, and even disdain as they each come to grief . . . on the horns of O'Connor's pen" (Powell 26). They are what Powell characterizes as, "exemplify[ing] the ugliest mental excesses of the modern world."

In "The River," the mental excesses obfuscate the kind of anagogic interpretation that O'Connor espoused. Unlike what Powell characterizes as the "interleckchul education" of the arty, cocktail party types satirized here, an education that "defines each person by his or her own reason, positing the human mind as the singular context through which that person may experience the surrounding world," O'Connor did, in fact, approve of an education that "places individuals in a variety of contexts, thoughts, and experiences—most specifically, spiritual experiences" (Powell 28). Despite their apparent worldliness and world-weariness, the Ashfields never actually leave their apartment; they are stuck in a singular, hazy, alcohol-scrimmed place. Indeed, in yet another comically ironic insight, Harry notes that "he was lucky this time that they had found Mrs. Connin who would take you away for the day instead of an ordinary sitter who only sat where you lived or went to the park. You found out more when you left where you lived" (160). Read anagogically, the story's end leaves us with a sense of tragic ambivalence: yes, Harry's two different baptisms hold out the promise of salvation and eternal life, but they also represent the senseless death of a neglected child. "The River" is O'Connor's indictment of intellectual cocktail culture as an impediment to learning, creativity, and even life.

Notes

1. Indeed, in a letter to Robert Lowell, O'Connor explained, "In our house the liquor is kept in the bathroom closet between the Draino and the plunger, and you don't get any unless you are about dead. The last time I had any was when I dropped the side of the chicken brooder on my foot and broke my toe" (*Habit of Being* 311).

2. See, for instance, her letter to "A" (*Letters*), in which O'Connor explains how the mother–daughter relationship in "Good Country People" was influenced by her own relationship with her mother, or the myriad scholarly analyses (such as Bernard or Westling) of how their relationship manifests in her work. See also O'Connor's anecdotes about the black tenant workers at Andalusia and the anecdotes that make their way into her fiction, such as the story related in her letter to Sally and Robert Fitzgerald (*Letters*).

3. Some scholars have begun examining the appearance of moonshine in O'Connor works such as *The Violent Bear It Away*, but they have yet to look at appearances of more upscale alcohol. *See* Donahoo.

4. I realize that using O'Connor's own explanations of her work poses the danger of falling prey to the intentional fallacy; it certainly is not my intention to confuse O'Connor's personal statements and life experiences with her fiction. However, I do think that considering not only the ways in which her life resonates with her fiction but also the strategies for literary exegesis that she proposes is a productive approach to her work. I agree with O'Connor that strictly metaphoric readings of her work often fail, in that such readings typically undercut the violence of her work. Because violence is such a pervasive element in her fiction, to explain it away as metaphoric ultimately diminishes the power of her work.

5. However, as her later letter to her friend Betty Boyd reveals, O'Connor never completely dismissed cocktail culture. An autograph party was held for her in Milledgeville after the publication of *Wise Blood*, and O'Connor describes the ordeal of being feted by nearly three hundred guests: "Cocktails were not served but I lived through it anyway" (*Habit* 36). So, while O'Connor may have generally eschewed alcoholic spirits in favor of more ineffable ones, she did express an understanding of their charms.

6. Despite his ultimate drowning in the story, Harry's casual neglect in the story is almost benign when compared to the fate of other children in O'Connor's work, which encourages me to see his parents as a different type of character than other parents in her fiction, who function as much clearer actors in the violence of grace. See Joy A. Farmer, "Suffer, the Little Children: Child Abuse and the Violent Atonement in the Fiction of Flannery O'Connor," for an exhaustive list of these characters, from "Enoch Emery of *Wise Blood*, forced by his daddy to come to the city and then abandoned" to "Sarah Ham of 'The Comforts of Home,' rejected by her biological mother and sexually molested by an older stepbrother" to "the unborn child in 'A Stroke of Good Fortune,' hated even before conception and, therefore, likely to become the next victim in this disheartening litany" (62).

7. It is important to remember that Harry is described as being "four or five"—an awfully young age to be putting himself to bed.

8. And, in fact, Harry's confusion between the literal and the abstract demonstrates the efficacy of O'Connor's own anagogic approach to analysis, as it complicates this apparent binary approach to analysis.

Works Cited

Bernard, Gretchen Dobrott. "Flannery O'Connor's Fractured Families: Mothers and Daughters in Conflict." *Revista de Estudios Norteamericanos* 10 (2004): 71–82.

Donahoo, Robert. "Making Moonshine: O'Connor's Use of Regional Culture in *The Violent Bear It Away*." Presented at Flannery O'Connor and Other Southern Women Writers Conference, Millidgeville, Georgia, 18 September 2015.

Farmer, Joy A. "Suffer, the Little Children: Child Abuse and the Violent Atonement in the Fiction of Flannery O'Connor." *Texas Review*, vol. 24, no. 1–2 (Spring/Summer 2003), pp. 58–76.

Gooch, Brad. *Flannery: A Life of Flannery O'Connor*. Little, Brown, 2009.

O'Connor, Flannery. *Flannery O'Connor: Collected Works*. Library of America, 1988.

———. *The Habit of Being: Letters of Flannery O'Connor*. Edited by Sally Fitzgerald, Farrar, Strauss, and Giroux, 1979.

———. Letter to "A." 5 August 1955. *Letters*. Library of America, 1988, p. 946.

———. Letter to Sally and Robert Fitzgerald. 20 September 1951. *Letters*. Library of America, 1988, p. 890.

———. *Mystery and Manners: Occasional Prose*. Edited by Sally and Robert Fitzgerald, Farrar, Strauss, and Giroux, 1970.

Powell, Tara. *The Intellectual in Twentieth-Century Southern Literature.* Louisiana State UP, 2012.

Westling, Louise. "Flannery O'Connor's Mothers and Daughters." *Twentieth-Century Literature,* vol. 24, no. 4 (Winter 1978), pp. 510–22.

Trashed

Women Under the Influence of Alcohol
in Wright's Native Son

ELLEN LANSKY

Early in his autobiography, *Black Boy*, Richard Wright recalls his experience as a very young drinker. People who were evidently already drinking to escape the misery of their everyday lives in Mississippi would buy him drinks in the local saloon, and he would entertain them with his drunken tricks, usually verbal sleights. It did not take long before alcohol had claimed the child. He recalls, "To beg drinks in the saloon became an obsession. . . . I was a drunkard in my sixth year, before I had begun school" (22). In the Memphis saloons, Wright recalls that men (and sometimes women) encouraged him to get drunk in a fashion that recalls the uses of alcohol on plantations. On many plantations, as Douglass describes in *Narrative of the Life of Frederick Douglass*, "slaveholders not only like to see the slave drink of his own accord but will adopt various plans to make him drunk" with what Douglass calls "a dose of vicious liberty" so that slaves "felt, and very properly too, that [they] had almost as well be slaves to man as to rum" (256). In this recollection from *Black Boy*, Wright demonstrates his understanding of alcohol's ability to raise one's spirits, especially from experience of an onerous daily existence, and also to demean, exploit, and disempower somebody else—usually someone vulnerable in a culture that privileges white men: a slave, a woman, a child.

This image of Wright as child alcoholic serves as a guide or a heuristic for examining the role and function of alcohol in his work, especially *Native Son* (1940). Indeed, examining the presence of alcohol and its consequences enables contemporary readers to contextualize *Native Son* and to read alcohol into the novel's project as a protest novel, with alcohol revealed not so much as a social lubricant or a party supply but as a technology of oppression. In *Native Son*,

Wright illustrates the particularly insidious effects of alcohol when the forces of gender and power are at work and men ply women with alcohol for entertainment and sex. Young Richard Wright was able to leave the saloon and go to school, and the influence of alcohol did not follow him into adulthood. The drinking women characters in *Native Son* are not as fortunate.

Wright's understanding of the role and function of alcohol is clearly inscribed, if mostly unremarked, in the first two books of *Native Son*, "Fear" and "Flight." His careful deployment of details in the novel's scenes of drinking show the role and significance of alcohol and drinking as an exercise of power, with its origins in the African slave trade and on plantations in the U.S. South. Wright also shows that the effects of alcohol upon the bodies of women include manipulation, theft, sexual assault, violence, and death. African American women are particularly vulnerable to these effects. To draw a corollary, in *Incidents in the Life of a Slave Girl*, Harriet Jacobs, writing as Linda Brent, notes that "slavery is terrible for men; but it is far more terrible for women" (77). Wright's novel demonstrates that alcohol can have terrible consequences for men, but the consequences are far more terrible for women.

The Deaths of Bessies

Wright's novel exhibits his interest in "current events" and situations that not only give his novel the available force of verisimilitude but also strengthen the novel's engagement with the powerful influence of alcohol. One well-known fact about the composition of *Native Son* is that Wright drafted his novel in New York, and his friend Margaret Walker sent him newspaper clippings from Chicago about a notorious murderer, Robert Nixon. Nixon, described in a June 5, 1938, *Chicago Sunday Tribune* front-page news item, was an eighteen-year-old bricklayer who had confessed to "five savage murders" that were "accomplished with a ferocity suggestive of Poe's 'Murders in the Rue Morgue'—the work of a giant ape" (Leavelle). Wright took this clipping as a starting point, rather like a creative writing exercise, and created a scene in which Bigger Thomas, Wright's protagonist, is called an "ape" in the sensational press. A mob calls out, as a real-life mob did for Nixon, to lynch him.

Another connection between contemporaneous events and characters in Wright's novel can be drawn between the sensational death of the real-life "Empress of the Blues," Bessie Smith, and Bessie Mears, Bigger's girlfriend in *Native*

Son. Until now, the connections between Bessie Mears and Bessie Smith have been implied but not fully elaborated. Both Smith and Mears are prodigious drinkers, and the tragedy of their lives is transmitted through the blues: Smith in song, Mears in her manner of speech. For example, in his essay "Bessie's Blues," Edward A. Watson connects Bessie Mears's speeches with characteristics of the blues. He notes that Bessie's speech "in keeping with traditional blues, reveals a pathetic autobiography which is flashed across the screen, as it were, in a moment of personal catastrophe" (57).

Bessie Smith's moment of personal catastrophe came in an alcohol-related car accident on a dark Mississippi road, which resulted in her death. Bessie Mears's blues-speeches can be linked, as a sort of echo, to Smith's fatal catastrophe and its implications for African Americans and all women under the influence of alcohol. This link complicates and enriches the characterization and significance of Bessie Mears in Wright's novel as well as his project as a writer. The specter of Bessie Smith's sensational, alcohol-related death also brings to view the presence and influence of alcohol in the novel, a significant factor in the deaths of Mary Dalton and Bessie Mears.

Alcohol and the Plantation Tale

Robert Stepto provides a critical framework for reading *Native Son* as a "plantation tale." Stepto describes the cast of characters and their roles and notes that they "are recognizably those of a nineteenth-century American plantation society" (62). First, Mr. Dalton "may not be a slave-holding captain of early agribusiness, but [as a real estate magnate] his immense profits do come from the land and from the hard toil of blacks." Mrs. Dalton, white and stately, serves her role as the mistress of the Big House. Her blindness is both actual and symbolic of the ways in which plantation mistresses and wives of slave owners turned a "blind eye" to the depredations of slavery.[1]

Stepto goes on to explain that Mary Dalton, the daughter, plays the role of "the young, white . . . virginal belle on the pedestal," and Bigger Thomas, a twenty-year-old African American man, is the house servant/slave. In smaller, supporting roles, Stepto classifies Max, the communist attorney who does his best to defend Bigger, as the character who "resembles the sympathetic white found in the slave narratives who is somewhat removed from the system" (163). One could argue that Jan, Mary's communist boyfriend, occupies a similar position, though as the narrative unfolds, he shows himself to be a participant in a system based on white male privilege and power.

Wright's novel also bears significant links to another kind of plantation tale: nineteenth-century African American slave narratives. Slave narratives such as *Narrative of the Life of Frederick Douglass* document the ways in which slave owners used alcohol to manipulate and control slaves on the plantation. Wright's novel shows a similar dynamic in the twentieth-century South Side of Chicago. In his iteration, men who desire power use alcohol to control and manipulate women. However, as the characterizations of Bessie Mears and Mary Dalton suggest, women drinkers might be useful to these men in providing cash or sex, but women who get drunk also lose their worth. As the contents of the bottle of liquor enters the bodies of women and they become drunk, their bodies become the value equivalent of an empty bottle: trash.

The plantation society's social dynamics suggest both a clear-cut "master/slave" order and then a range of transgressions, usually initiated by white people in power, against the disempowered black servants who cannot protest. Wright shows how both social and physical transgressions are complicated by the role that alcohol plays in them. For example, Mr. Dalton, the master, tells Bigger that his first duty in his job as the Daltons' chauffeur/servant is to drive Mary to a lecture at the university. Mary gets in the backseat of the car, the conventional place for one who is being driven. However, within the distance of two stoplights, she violates the boundaries that govern the expectations among her, Mr. Dalton, and Bigger. She tells him to drive her somewhere else and then to lie if he is asked about it. She may not be the boss, but she is the boss's daughter, and she is white, and, as such, Bigger implicitly understands that he cannot say no to her. When she tells Bigger that she is "going to meet a friend of [hers] who's also a friend of [his]," it is now also in her purview to manage his friendships.

When Mary introduces her friend Jan to Bigger, Jan also transgresses the social order in his interactions with Bigger. While it is possible to interpret Jan's actions in terms of his desire for equality among the races and between individuals, it is also clear that Jan issues orders. He demands a handshake, tells Bigger not to call him "sir," and directs Bigger, the black chauffeur, to move over so that he, the white boyfriend of the boss's white daughter, can drive the white boss man's big blue Buick. Jan may think of himself as a comrade, but his actions illustrate a person taking the role of the white man in charge. Though the implications of his actions are probably not visible to himself, for Mary, he asserts his privilege and power as a white man over the white woman and the black servant, despite his enthusiastic desire to disavow these things.

In the scene at Ernie's Kitchen Shack, Wright complicates the fluid social dynamics with the appearance of a bottle of rum. The use of alcohol here is part of an exercise of white male power over black and female bodies, with consequences that are, as Harriet Jacobs might put it, terrible for Bigger but far more terrible for Mary Dalton. The bottle of rum on the table stands as an invitation for camaraderie and conviviality among Bigger, Mary, and Jan. The bottle of rum is also an artifact from the slave trade, a souvenir from plantation culture in the South, brought to Chicago's South Side and doled out by the white man who has assumed a power position.[2]

Furthermore, the bottle of rum that Jan orders, opens, serves, stoppers, and brings back to the car—as if it were the fourth member of their party—is not just a symbol but an embodiment, a glass homunculus, an ewer of white male power, especially power over women's bodies and bodies of color. In Jan's hand, the bottle of rum works on the characters to lower inhibitions and blur the boundaries between the white plantation family, its deputies and ancillaries, and its slaves. Jan pours the rounds in Ernie's Kitchen Shack and, as the rum eases all of them, especially Bigger, into a conversation, he refills Bigger's glass until Bigger "is drunk enough to look straight at them" (75), something he's been conditioned not to do.

In his presumed position of power, Jan decides when they are finished at Ernie's, and he stoppers the bottle and pays the bill. Conjuring the old plantation order, Mary directs Bigger to take her trunk to the train station in advance of her trip to Detroit the following morning. When they return to the car, Jan and Mary affirm their role as privileged passengers (not equal riders) and get in the backseat. From this power position, Jan gives orders to Bigger to drive them around the park, and then he takes control of the bottle.

Jan's attention to Mary's alcohol intake illustrates the double standards and dangers that befall women who drink alcohol, regardless of class or race. As Jean-Charles Sournia notes in *A History of Alcoholism*, "female drunkenness has always been seen as more serious and degrading than the equivalent male excess" (22), and his observation is borne out in Wright's scene. Jan first facilitates Mary's drinking and then passes judgment on her drinking style, admonishing her that she's "going heavy tonight." When Jan leaves the car to catch a street-car home, he offers Bigger another drink, even though Bigger has already had "two huge swallows" in addition to the beers and rum he has drunk at Ernie's Kitchen Shack. In contrast, when Mary asks for another, Jan cautions her. He asks whether she has had enough, a rhetorical question that provides its own answer. When she takes the bottle from him, he exclaims "Whoa!" when she drinks. He finishes off the bottle and lurches. He is drunk, and so is Bigger, but he reserves his judgments and admonishments for Mary Dalton (Wright, *Native Son* 77–79).

Beyond reenacting social roles from the plantation in this scene, Wright updates the same tropes used by Douglass and others to illustrate how intoxication allows white men to dominate women in the same way that white men used alcohol to dominate black bodies. Jan uses alcohol to ensure Mary's compliance with his desires, in a manner that parallels the ways in which slave owners used alcohol to ensure compliance on the plantation. For example, Frederick Douglass depicts the ways that slave owners and overseers encouraged slaves to drink to excess during holiday periods so that going back to work would seem to be almost a relief and they would continue to deliver their unremunerated labor with compliance rather than defiance. In a similar manner, Jan seems to like Mary, but she's also useful to him, and he uses alcohol to access her body and her money in way that is similar to Douglass's depiction of the slaveholders who aim to "cheat [the slave] with a dose of vicious dissipation" (300).

Granted, Wright does not characterize Jan as a deliberately cruel white man; however, Jan's ends are the same as that of the cruel slaveholders encouraging their slaves to drink themselves sick. Jan encourages Mary to drink enough of the rum so that she complies when he asks her for bail money, and she is also compliant, or at least she does not protest vigorously, when he wants to have sex in the back of the Buick. Also, he knows that if she is caught and punished for being drunk, her parents will limit her access to him and his access to her body and her money, so he admonishes her not to pass out when they are ready to part company (*Native Son* 79). Before he catches a streetcar, he leaves the empty bottle of rum—now a glass body of evidence that points to everybody's drunkenness and to Jan's facilitation of it—in the gutter, now a piece of trash.

What happens next is well rehearsed and well known among Wright's readers, and the ensuing scenes in "Fear" map the consequences of social and physical transgressions between a white woman and a black man, all complicated and intensified by the influence of alcohol, and all the more severe for the drunk white woman. After Jan leaves the scene, Bigger steps in and replicates Jan's actions, using alcohol to get what he wants from Mary. By the time Mary and Bigger return to the Daltons' big white house, both of them are drunk, and Mary is too drunk to walk. Bigger wonders if he "ought to call Mr. Dalton or Peggy," but he decides not to, thinking that "in spite of his hate for her, he was excited standing here watching her like this." He manages to maneuver her to the kitchen, at which point she can no longer walk or speak; he discovers that he can move her "only by lifting her bodily" (82–83). In a gesture that could appear in a soft porn romance, the drunk black chauffeur catches the drunk white daughter of the house in his arms and carries her across the threshold of her bedroom, managing to grope and fondle her in the process.[3] Earlier in the evening, Bigger couldn't say no to Mary, and she had her way. Now she is drunk and can't say no to him.

When Mrs. Dalton reaches the already-crossed threshold of Mary's bedroom, she enacts the role of plantation mistress and its concomitant class and gender biases associated with alcohol and female bodies. First, Mrs. Dalton encounters the beer and rum miasma that Bigger and Mary have been exhaling. The smell is clearly an affront to Mrs. Dalton; she "straightened suddenly and took a quick step back," as if she had come upon something truly foul. To her daughter, she says, "You're dead drunk! You *stink* with whiskey" (86).

Here, Mrs. Dalton's exclamations evince her dismay at the way her daughter has violated class and gender expectations. Whiskey is clearly not an appropriate drink for the daughter of the owner of the South Side Real Estate Company, a twentieth-century urban plantation, nor, clearly, does Mrs. Dalton consider it anything but a social disgrace that this daughter is "dead drunk." She leaves the room. The irony in this scene is rank: Mary is certainly drunk (and dead, after Bigger, in a panic, suffocates her), though the stench comes not from whiskey but from rum—the toast of the slave trade.

Under the influence of alcohol and a toxic combination of fear, loathing, excitement, and panic, Bigger's solution to the problem of the rum-soaked corpse on the bed is to put Mary's body in a trunk, drag the trunk downstairs, stuff her body in the furnace, and then go home to bed. Left to burn in the bottom of the furnace, Mary's body becomes part of the trash that, per the terms of his employment, Bigger is supposed to put in the furnace each morning to incinerate. Her body, full of rum but empty of life, is no longer useful to Bigger, who has used her body for his own pleasure (as Jan does earlier). Mary Dalton's drunk, dead body becomes an iteration of the empty bottle of rum: first a useless piece of trash that Jan leaves in the gutter and now a pile of ashes in a furnace.

Another Bessie, Another Bottle/Body

Bigger's actions with regard to Mary's body foreshadow his actions with regard to his equally dead drunk girlfriend, Bessie Mears. It also repeats the dynamic of a more powerful man (first Jan, now Bigger) using alcohol as a tool to get what he wants from a woman (first Mary, now Bessie) and then discarding her as trash. Both Mary Dalton and Bessie Mears are on the receiving end of Bigger's physical violence, though it is worth noting that Bessie Mears is still alive to experience it. Mary Dalton is already dead when Bigger attacks her body. In a situation that recalls the dynamic of slave culture, the violence perpetrated on Mary's body is terrible, but it is far more terrible for Bessie, who lives to feel it.

For Bigger, Bessie is a disposable commodity that he can use to serve his needs or desires and then discard. When she first appears in the novel, Bigger thinks of Bessie as one option in a list of distractions to take his mind off the fear and panic he feels over the plan to rob a delicatessen. A bit later, when he and his friend Jack are busy masturbating in the movie theater (combining two distractions), Bigger says he "wished [he] had Bessie here now" (Wright, *Native Son* 30). He thinks of Bessie again, briefly, in his new room at the Daltons' house, telling himself that he "would bring Bessie here some night"—in the same way that he would "bring a pint of liquor up here and drink it in peace" (59). Even Bigger's little brother, Buddy, participates in the debasement of Bessie. When Bigger goes back to his family's crowded apartment after his eventful first day on the job, Buddy tells Bigger, "'You got a good job now. You can get a better gal than Bessie'" (104). Bigger clearly does not consider Bessie to be anything more than something he can use and then discard, in the same way that Jan leaves the empty bottle of rum in the gutter.

Bigger's actions and thoughts also replicate a dynamic that Wright has earlier engineered between Jan and Mary. Like Jan, who gets bail money and sex from Mary after he gives her alcohol, Bigger knows that a bottle of liquor is a powerful tool he can use to get what he wants from Bessie. Bigger understands that the terms of his relationship with Bessie pivot on her ability to give him what he wants (usually sex) due to his ability to procure alcohol for her. Bigger also understands how to manipulate Bessie's dependence on alcohol. The procedure is not complicated: "Most nights she was too tired to go out; she only wanted to get drunk. She wanted liquor and he wanted her. So he would give her the liquor and she would give him herself. . . . He knew why she liked him; he gave her money for drinks" (139).

The exchanges between Bigger and Bessie are an only slightly less sophisticated version of the dynamic between Jan and Mary: he gets her a bottle of alcohol and she gives him what he wants. The scenes with Bigger and Bessie also further underpin Wright's demonstration that women, and especially African American women, under the influence of alcohol are particularly vulnerable to sexual assault, violence, and death. Again, the effects of alcohol are terrible for men but far more terrible for women, especially African American women.

The scene at the Paris Grill enlarges the influence of alcohol in *Native Son* and its especially deleterious effects for African American women. Bigger, flush with money stolen from Mary Dalton's purse, takes Bessie to the Paris Grill, a venue whose name suggests a more sophisticated environment than the homely Ernie's Kitchen Shack. In manner that recalls Jan ordering, serving, and paying for the bottle of rum at Ernie's Kitchen Shack, Bigger uses Mary's money to procure and pay for the cocktails that he uses to manipulate Bessie and take what he wants from her.

The scene also suggests another remnant of plantation society: a slave uprising, replete with "oath drinks." Frederick H. Smith explains that "oath drinks were an important feature of slave uprisings. . . . The combination of rum and other powerful ingredients in these oath drinks included blood, which made the drinks red (131). At the Paris Grill, the red oath drinks do not gain their hue from the red color of rum; instead, Bigger orders "two sloe gin fizzes," a cocktail that is effervescent, sweet, and blood red (Wright, *Native Son* 140). The switch from rum to gin also brings the remnants of plantation society into the twentieth century and creates a more substantial link to Bessie Smith, whose catalog includes "Gin House Blues" and "Me and My Gin."

As they imbibe their blood-colored oath drinks, Bigger foments his twentieth-century South Side slave uprising: a plan, which now includes Bessie Mears, to swindle ransom money from the Daltons and leave town. Though Bessie thinks that Bigger's plan is "crazy" and suspects that something has happened to Mary, she knows that he has money and she wants liquor (144). At the beginning of the scene, she lifts her first red oath drink and says, "Here's to you." After a second round, they part company. She has drunk two of the red oath cocktails, and she is in on the uprising. He needs to return to the Daltons' to check the furnace; she says she is "going to get a pint" (148). Bigger gives Bessie some of Mary Dalton's money, which now implicates Bessie in the theft. Bessie uses Mary's money to buy whiskey—the stinking cheap form of alcohol that so affronts rich, white, socially upstanding (and blind) Mrs. Dalton.

Though Bigger consistently demeans Bessie and thinks she is as blind as the Daltons and everyone else around him, she is clearly much more clear-eyed than he is—about the ransom scheme, about Mary Dalton, and about her own relationship to alcohol. Drunk as she is, she not only correctly describes the ransom plan as "crazy" but also, when he tells her what he did with Mary Dalton, immediately perceives that law enforcement, the Daltons, and the monolith of white power will claim that Bigger raped Mary Dalton. She also knows that going along with him in his uprising will result in her own death. She shows that she understands how her demise is related to alcohol when says to him, "All you ever did since we been knowing each other was to get me drunk so's you could have me. . . . You got me into this murder and I see it all now. I been a fool, just a blind dumb black drunk fool" (230). Nevertheless, the red oath drinks are in her bloodstream, and she must play the fool.

The sensational slave uprising plot plays into a blues-like scene of personal catastrophe for Bessie Mears. After Bigger writes a ransom note which he signs "Red," which is meant to finger Jan for Mary Dalton's disappearance and also recalls the red sloe gin fizz oath drinks at the Paris Grill, the uprising is quashed. Ensuing events repeat the situation in Mary Dalton's bedroom, in which influence of alcohol turns a woman into trash. After the reporters and detectives in the Daltons' basement find Mary's bones among the ashes in the furnace, Bigger sneaks away from the "big house" and makes his way to the slave quarters/tenements to find his blood oath accomplice, Bessie. Bigger asks Bessie for the bottle that she has bought with the money from Mary Dalton's purse, and then, in a way that recalls Jan urging Mary to drink (but not too much), Bigger drinks, and urges Bessie to drink as well, before they flee Bessie's tenement to hide out in a freezing empty building.

Again, in a repetition of the earlier scene in "Fear," in which a female body is filled with alcohol and then turned to trash, Bigger "got the half-filled flask and drained it," after which he starts kissing and touching Bessie, in a manner reminiscent of the way first Jan and then Bigger groped and fondled Mary Dalton (231). Bessie, however, is not drunk, and she tells him "Please, Bigger. . . .

Bigger. . . . *Don't!*" (234–35). This time, there is no white plantation mistress to interrupt Bigger, and he rapes Bessie. After he finishes, he decides that "he could not take her with him and he could not leave her behind." He quickly determines a course of action: he will kill her. Then, in an amazing feat of pronoun repetition, deploying "it" in order to show, and show again, that Bigger perceives Bessie not as a woman ("she") but as a nonhuman entity ("it"), Wright renders the scene: "Yes, that was what he could do with it [Bessie], throw it out of the window, down the narrow air-shaft where nobody would find it until, perhaps, it had begun to smell" (235). Bigger bludgeons Bessie with a brick and, in a repetition of his actions turning Mary Dalton's body into garbage to be burned, Bigger tosses Bessie's body down an air shaft, where she freezes to death. Bessie's body is nothing more than a cold, sodden lump of litter.

Conclusion: "Me and My Gin"

When one considers the presence and influence of alcohol in the novel's two carefully wrought death scenes, one sees that alcohol functions with more complexity and gravity than simply an intoxicating spirit that people drink to celebrate, lift their moods, and feel free. Instead, Wright reminds readers that alcohol was part of the slave economy and that its role and function in American and African American communities contributed to the disempowerment of both African Americans and white people, especially women.

The death scenes have also suggested to some readers an unpleasant streak of misogyny and an inability on the part of the author to imagine female characters that go beyond stereotypes. In fact, in her essay "Talking to Bessie: Richard Wright's Female Servants," Julieann Veronica Ulm reviews the history of feminist criticism of *Native Son* and notes that "one does not have to look far to find a host of critics decrying Wright's portrayal of Bessie" (152). However, Wright's portrayal of the drunk, truly miserable Bessie Mears, drawn from the boozy life and songs of Bessie Smith, indicates that he understood the stakes for African American women in a culture that privileges men, especially white, rich, heterosexual, Christian men. As the novel shows, (African American) women remained in peril at the hands of the South Side plantation owner. The stakes for women were especially high, and the consequences grim, when alcohol was a factor.

Finally, though Wright claimed in "How 'Bigger' Was Born" that he was "launching out upon another novel, this time about the status of women in modern American society" (461), and though he never published that novel, *Native Son* still offers an important critique of the status of women in midcentury American society. Wright brings to light the harsh consequences of alcohol and drinking for American women, especially African American women, in the same way that Harriet Jacobs illuminated slavery's culture of rape and sexual violence. Mary Dalton's drunken death is terrible, but Bessie Mears's death is far more terrible—riven as it is with disregard for her status as a woman and also heaped with disregard for her status as a person of color. Wright conveys that critique through Bessie Mears, an African American female character literally soaked with alcohol, a character imbued with the spectral presence of Bessie Smith.

Notes

1. The wives of slave owners and plantation owners in *Narrative of the Life of Frederick Douglass* and the wife of the truly awful Dr. Flint in Harriet Jacobs's *Incidents in the Life of a Slave Girl* are excellent examples of this character.

2. Stewart Royce King explains that "the Atlantic slave trade . . . involved the whole of the European global trade network, bringing . . . rum and other plantation products, such as cotton, from the Americas; and some manufactured goods from Europe to Africa to exchange for slaves." Indeed, in his book *The Alcoholic Republic,* W. J. Rorabaugh notes that "rum was the currency of the age" (64) at the height of the Atlantic slave trade that underpinned plantation culture in the U.S. South.

3. In a scene deleted from the original 1940 edition of *Native Son* but returned to the text in the restored version (1998), Mary's actions might suggest to some readers that she actually wants to have sex with Bigger: "He tightened his arms as his lips pressed tightly against hers and he felt her body moving strongly. The thought and conviction that Jan had had her a lot flashed through his mind. He kissed her again and felt the sharp bones of her hips move in a hard and veritable grind" (84). The grind may be "veritable," but it doesn't amount to consent; she's drunk. Unfortunately, because she is drunk, it is easy to castigate her and suggest that she "asked for it."

Works Cited

Douglass, Frederick. *Narrative of the Life of Frederick Douglass: An American Slave, Written by Himself. The Classic Slave Narratives,* edited by Henry Louis Gates Jr., New American Library, 1987, pp. 243–331.

Jacobs, Harriet. *Incidents in the Life of a Slave Girl. The Classic Slave Narratives,* edited by Henry Louis Gates Jr., New American Library, 1987, pp. 333–513.

King, Stewart Royce. "Atlantic Slave Trade." *Encyclopedia of Race and Racism,* 2nd ed., vol. 1, edited by Patrick L. Mason, Macmillan Reference, 2013, pp. 181–94.

Leavelle, Charles. "Bricklayer Is Likened to Jungle Beast." *Chicago Sunday Tribune,* June 5, 1938.

Rorabaugh, W. J. *The Alcoholic Republic: An American Tradition.* Oxford UP, 1979.

Smith, Frederick H. *The Archaeology of Alcohol and Drinking.* UP of Florida, 2008.

Sournia, Jean-Charles. *A History of Alcoholism.* B. Blackwell, 1990.

Stepto, Robert. "'I Thought I Knew These People': Wright and the Afro-American Literary Tradition." *Richard Wright,* edited by Harold Bloom, Chelsea House, 1989, pp. 57–74.

Ulm, Julieann Veronica. "Talking to Bessie: Richard Wright's Domestic Servants." *American Literature,* vol. 85, no. 1 (March 2013), pp. 151–76.

Watson, Edward A. "Bessie's Blues." *Bigger Thomas,* edited by Harold Bloom, Chelsea House, 1990, pp. 54–59.

Wright, Richard. *Black Boy.* Harper Perennial, 2006.

———. "How 'Bigger' Was Born." *Native Son.* Restored text, Perennial Classics, 1998, pp. 431–62.

———. *Native Son.* Restored text, Perennial Classics, 1998.

Miss Amelia's Liquor

"The Ballad of the Sad Café" and Surregionalism

DAVID A. DAVIS

"The Ballad of the Sad Café" (1951) is weird. The story about a bizarre love triangle involving Miss Amelia, her felonious ex-husband, and the hunchback Cousin Lymon is strange and grotesque because of the unusual characters and the irrational events of the plot, and the story's inherent weirdness begs for interpretation. In the story, Carson McCullers uses surrealist technique, juxtaposing elements of realism with dreamlike images, but the story's absurdity also distracts readers from the deeper message about a dysfunctional outlier community adhering to a defunct economic system in midcentury America.

The story juxtaposes a background plot about a system of commodity production based on labor exploitation with a foreground plot about a set of ridiculous characters, and the story's background is often overlooked. Alcohol bridges the middle distance between the story's realistic background and its surreal foreground, connecting Miss Amelia, through the café where she sells liquor, to the tenant farmers who work her fields, to her deformed alleged cousin, and to the community. In this story, alcohol functions as an ordering feature that both constructs and distorts space between reality and absurdity. "Ballad of the Sad Café" exemplifies the literary subgenre I call surregionalism, a form of midcentury southern modernism that depicts the South as a distorted, deviant literary cartography within the United States.

The story's spatial construction pivots on Miss Amelia's liquor. On the night Cousin Lymon arrives, Miss Amelia uncharacteristically shares her liquor with him and the others gathered around her store for free, and the liquor has a peculiarly transformative effect on the characters and the setting.

> Perhaps without it there would never have been a café. For the liquor of Miss Amelia has a special quality of its own. It is clean and sharp on the

tongue, but once down a man it glows inside him for a long time afterward. And that is not all. It is known that if a message is written with lemon juice on a clean sheet of paper there will be no sign of it. But if the paper is held for a moment to the fire then the letters turn brown and the meaning becomes clear. Imagine that the whisky is the fire and that the message is that which is known only in the soul of a man—then the worth of Miss Amelia's liquor can be understood. Things that have gone unnoticed, thoughts that have been harbored far back in the dark mind, are suddenly recognized and comprehended. (10)

Miss Amelia's liquor changes the person who consumes it, but it also changes how a person perceives and uses the space where it is consumed, and it is the relationship between alcohol and the construction of space that I intend to explore here. The story of the café illustrates that spatial construction is dynamic and contingent, and the café functions in the story as a microcosm of the South in midcentury America. Analyzing the interaction of alcohol and space in the story reveals connections among real space, imaginative space, narrative space, and the spatial construction of the South.

The notion that alcohol changes personal behavior is the foundation of addiction studies. Drinking causes a host of physiological changes in the body that affect function and psychological changes in the brain that affect cognition, which can lead to impaired judgment or irrational actions. In some people, drinking habits develop into a disorder with deleterious effects on the body and the mind. These empirical facts are well known, yet the image of the alcoholic is a frequently recurring trope in literature in which alcohol serves a metaphoric purpose, often to challenge the foundation of empiricism, the experience of time and space, and the social morals and mores that define polite society. Usually, the alcoholic is a degenerate character, as Susan Zieger describes in *Inventing the Addict,* who defines the social values of a particular time and place through transgression and, occasionally, redemption (16).

McCullers herself was a severe alcoholic. Virginia Spencer Carr documents that "Carson nursed sherry through most of the day while she worked, for she needed a certain amount of alcohol in her system to function creatively" (143). In a typical day, she would consume a prodigious amount of alcohol, moving from sherry in the morning to beer in the afternoon to cocktails in the evening. Her binges and parties were legendary for their inebriation and, occasionally, for their violence.

Considering McCullers's personal history of alcoholism and her sense of marginalization within midcentury America's prevailing conservatism, one fact seems unusual: she never writes a major character who suffers from alcoholism. Her characters drink, to be sure, and some of her short stories feature excessively drunk characters in certain scenes, but the protagonists are never alcoholics, especially when compared to the overt inebriates who carouse through the work of William Faulkner, F. Scott Fitzgerald, Ernest Hemingway, and other modernist writers. Ellen Lansky speculates that "McCullers may well have decided not to write about drinking female characters in order to protect the privacy and sanctity of her own relationship with alcohol" (4). In this sense, I argue that McCullers's use of alcohol as a story device is more complicated than that of most modernist writers, which invites us to look beyond the obvious elements of characterization and metaphor and to focus more deeply on the background and examine the function of alcohol in the setting of a story.

The environment in which people live, both as a physical reality and as an imaginary construct, is dynamic and contingent, and alcohol illustrates that spatial construction is not absolute and can be distorted. Alcohol changes the function of space, the use of space, the meaning of space, and the perception of space. In *Postmodern Geographies,* Edward Soja offers a theoretical framework for spatial construction. Two of his central premises are "Spatiality is a substantiated and recognizable social product, part of a 'second nature' which incorporates as it socializes and transforms physical and psychological spaces" and "As a social product, spatiality is simultaneously the medium and outcome, presupposition and embodiment, of social action and relationship" (129). His argument contends that people and the places and spaces they inhabit and encounter function in a mutually constitutive relationship, with neither entity occupying a static or stable position. Space thus changes both in the sense of the actual, tangible land and structures through which our bodies move and in the sense of the imaginary relationships that people develop with place that influence human behaviors and social practices.

Soja reconciles real space and imaginary space into real-as-imagined spaces. He explains that we understand space in three ways: "firstspace" is the physical environment that can be mapped, seen, and touched; "secondspace" is the representational space in the imagination that determines how a space is used; and "thirdspace" is "a fully lived space, a simultaneously real-and-imagined, actual-and-virtual locus of structured individuality and collective experience and agency" (*Postmetropolis* 11).[1] To illustrate the distinctions, imagine a two-story wooden structure as firstspace, consider the concept of "home" as a dwelling for human families as secondspace, and recognize a family living in a specific home as thirdspace.

Soja's ideas about spatial construction are useful to literary criticism because they explicitly acknowledge the role that imagination plays in the experience of space, and his ideas, along with theories from Henri Lefebvre, Michel Foucault, bell hooks, Michel de Certeau, and a host of other human geographers, including David Harvey and Doreen Massey, are at the core of the spatial turn in literary and cultural studies. The spatial turn refocuses attention on how humans relate to space and place.[2] Writers create an imaginative cartography that the characters and the reader inhabit during the narrative, which draws upon elements of real space and perceived space to produce a literary thirdspace, a metaphoric, experiential terrain.[3]

"The Ballad of the Sad Café," for example, begins with a description of an isolated southern community: "The town itself is dreary; not much is there except the cotton mill, the two-room houses where the workers live, a few peach trees, a church with two colored windows, and a miserable main street only a hundred yards long" (3). McCullers's description of the town corresponds to numerous southern crossroads communities and draws on common features, such as a main street and a church, that readers would immediately recognize, but her description seems slightly askew because she uses adjectives such as "dreary" and "miserable" to characterize the landscape. Doreen Fowler, recognizing the strange atmosphere that McCullers describes, labels the setting a "terrain of the unconscious" (260). In this imaginative terrain, a boarded-up building leaning "so far to the right that it seems bound to collapse any minute" dominates the miserable main street, and this unstable building was once the eponymous café, which "was unlike any place for miles around" (McCullers 3–4). McCullers's literary cartography juxtaposes elements of the real, rural southern landscape with surrealistic imaginative elements to produce a metaphoric setting that situates the reader within a real-as-imagined community of grotesque characters and strange events.

Most of the story's action takes place within the now boarded-up building that had once been a store, which functions as the central focus of the literary cartography, and the action demonstrates how and why socially constructed spaces change. At the earliest point in time in the story, the building was "a store that carried mostly feed, guano, and staples such as meal and snuff" (4). The store signifies Miss Amelia's role within the community's economy. She sells goods to local farmers, usually for a lien on their crops, which gives her considerable control over their farms. She holds the mortgage to many farms and rents land to some farmers, making her store the commercial and financial center for the community, where she also sells "the best liquor in the county" (4). Observing Prohibition in the breach, she sells liquor out the back door of the store, and she "never allowed liquor to be opened or drunk by anyone but herself" inside her store (21).

The building's previous use as a store serves as the story's temporal background and establishes a baseline of normal social structures for the story. When her strange cousin Lymon arrives, she changes her liquor policy and, to everyone's surprise, she offers him a drink for free and then serves drinks along with a tray of crackers inside the store. "This was the beginning of the café," and over time it expands to include a few tables where Miss Amelia serves fried catfish suppers and "liquor by the drink" (22–23). Here we see the spatial construction change, so "within two years the place was a store no longer, but had converted into a proper café, open every evening from six until twelve o'clock" (23). Serving liquor changes the real-as-imagined function of the space from commercial and financial, as a store, to cultural and communal, as a café.

Miss Amelia lives in the building, but "during the four years in which the store became a café the rooms upstairs were unchanged" (34). She maintains the separation between public and private space within the structure and keeps her private rooms as they had been all her life, and immaculately clean.[4] Cousin Lymon occupies her father's bedroom, which is elaborately furnished with a large chifforobe and a four-poster bed made of carved rosewood. Miss Amelia's room, in contrast, is sparsely furnished with a narrow pine bed, a bureau, and "two nails in the closet wall on which to hang her swamp boots" (35). As the café downstairs prospers, she remains a private person, and this space reflects her character.

In a work of literature, spatial description is often an element of characterization as much as a feature of setting. This description tells us that Miss Amelia cares little for material comfort and human contact. The one obvious exception is her relationship with Cousin Lymon, with whom Amelia shares her bankbook, the money from the cash register, and "the chart that showed where certain barrels of whisky were buried on a piece of property nearby" (37). The fact that Miss Amelia's private space remains unchanged even as Cousin Lymon occupies it is significant because it indicates that his presence does not change the experience of space. Cousin Lymon's presence does not change the store into a café. Serving and drinking liquor is the cause for the change in space.

The café, in turn, changes the community. McCullers writes, "It was not only the warmth, the decorations, and the brightness that made the café what it was. There is a deeper reason why the café was so precious to this town. And this deeper reason has to do with a certain pride that had not hitherto been known in these parts. To understand this new pride the cheapness of human life must be kept in mind. There were always plenty of people clustered around a mill—but it was seldom that every family had enough meal, garments, and fat back to go the rounds" (54).

Poverty robs many people of their personal pride and their sense of self-worth, but at the café, they can feel valued. "The new pride that the café brought to this town had an effect on almost everyone, even the children. For in order to come to the café you did not have to buy the dinner, or a portion of liquor." Miss Amelia provided cold drinks for a nickel, so everyone except the Baptist preacher came to the café at least once a week. "There, for a few hours at least, the deep bitter knowing that you are not worth much could be laid low" (54–55). Liquor served changes the function of the space, creating a communal center that changes the community, making it more cohesive. The effect on the community does not depend directly upon the presence of liquor but upon the functionality of the space, which, as the notable absence of the Baptist preacher makes clear, does depend upon the presence of liquor.

The café's role in the community changes after the inevitable fight between Miss Amelia and her ex-husband, Marvin Macy, who has been incarcerated in Atlanta. Soon after he returns to harass her, they have an elaborate and extended brawl through the café and across the town, and at the end of the fight, Cousin Lymon turns on her. Together, he and Macy beat her and spitefully destroy the café. Before they leave, "they went out in the swamp and completely wrecked the still, ruining the big new condenser and the cooler, and setting fire to the shack itself" (68).

After they leave, the café changes in a strange way. It does not close immediately. For a while, at least, it remains open, but "everything in the café had suddenly risen in price to be worth one dollar. And what sort of café is that?" (68). The price change makes the café inaccessible. Effectively, it violates the perception of how a café should function, so that it no longer coheres to the secondspace imagination of a communal space where people can share food and drinks and feel a sense of self-worth. Eventually, the café closes, the building falls into disrepair, and occasionally a "terrible dim" face is seen peering from the upstairs window (3).

McCullers's dynamic literary cartography illustrates how constructed spaces change in response to a complex set of uses, perceptions, and experiences. In this particular case, alcohol functions as the catalyst for change, but the story's message is much greater than one specific café in one isolated community. The community in the story is an exaggerated and distorted microcosm of the region, and McCuller's literary cartography can be read as a commentary on the midcentury U.S. South.

As Pete Daniel documents in *Lost Revolutions,* the South during the 1950s stood outside the mainstream of American life, but massive social forces were coming to bear on the region, creating tension that rippled through American culture. Many of these forces are evident in "The Ballad of the Sad Café." The story of Miss Amelia, Cousin Lymon, and the café takes place in the foreground, but the background is a representative, rural southern community. The economy centers on cotton production, most of the people in the town are exploited laborers working either on small farms or in the textile mill, and races are segregated. By 1951, when the story was published, millions of sharecroppers were leaving the land, pushed out by tractors and mechanical cotton pickers, and the National Association for the Advancement of Colored People was beginning its campaign of challenging segregation in the courts, which focused the nation's attention on the region's institutionalized racism. In the story, the community's economy is based on sharecropping, with Miss Amelia as a landowner. The café itself is segregated, and Jeff, "an old Negro," does the domestic work and the cooking for the café (30).

The strange characters and bizarre events taking place in the foreground distract from the story's actual setting, and most of the criticism of the story has focused on the story's weirdness rather than on its spatial construction. I contend, however, that the story's literary cartography, its weirdness, and its depiction of alcohol function together to achieve a surreal effect that is characteristic of surregionalism. The story's aesthetic features mimic the distorted perception of drunkenness, creating an inebriating effect while reading the story, in which all of the actions and characters seem to be strange and irrational. This inebriated perception, moreover, comments on the South as a socially constructed space that deviates from the norms of American culture. In the story, the South is surreal.

Like all spaces, the South is socially constructed, and, as Soja's theory suggests, its space functions on several levels. The South has a real, physical space in the form of a land and terrain that exists in the actual world. The boundaries of this space are contested and unclear, and the physical features of this space are various and indistinct, so the real space of the South is less important to the concept of "the South" than the land itself. The representational South, the way the South functions in the imagination, has been the focus, whether explicitly or implicitly, of most southern literary criticism.[5]

While southern literary criticism has mostly missed the spatial turn that reverberated through many other discourses in the humanities and social sciences in the past decade, southern critics have always been examining the imaginative construction of the region.[6] The real-as-imagined South, the region as thirdspace, is complicated in many southern texts, such as "The Ballad of the Sad Café," because the imaginary deviates substantially from reality. The South, in other words, exists more in imagination than in reality, so it is inherently unstable and prone to distorted perception. How, then, do we understand this particular experience of literary cartography?

A common approach to understanding McCullers's work, as well as the work of her midcentury contemporaries—including Flannery O'Connor, Tennessee Williams, Truman Capote, and Eudora Welty—has been to draw upon references to the Gothic and the grotesque and to label them Southern Gothic.[7] I worry, though, that this invocation of nineteenth-century aesthetics decontextualizes southern writing from its actual time and place. Using the term "Southern Gothic" to describe twentieth-century texts implies that southern writing is a closed system that does not respond to social, political, or artistic currents happening outside the region, which is entirely untrue. Midcentury southern writers were clearly influenced by the surrealist art that was in vogue elsewhere in America at the time.

Patricia Yaeger addresses this issue in *Dirt and Desire*. She describes McCullers's surrealist influences in *The Member of the Wedding* and suggests that McCullers's tendency to describe bizarre pictures and distorted images is consistent with James Clifford's definition of surrealism as "an aesthetic that values fragments, curious collections, unexpected juxtapositions—that works to provoke the manifestation of extraordinary realities drawn from the domains of the erotic, the exotic, and the unconscious" (quoted in Yaeger 159).[8] McCullers constructs a surreal landscape of the South, projecting extraordinary realities, such as the strange characters of Miss Amelia and Cousin Lymon, onto an imaginary map of the South. "The Ballad of the Sad Café" is an example of a subgenre of midcentury southern literature that I would label surregionalism, which are works that incorporate surrealist elements into a depiction of the South as an inherently strange region, a real-as-imagined landscape that distorts perceptions of reality.

To better understand how surregionalism works, think of the most iconic work of surrealist art: Salvador Dali's 1931 painting *The Persistence of Memory*. Most viewers focus immediately on the objects in the painting's foreground— the melting clocks draped on a tree limb, a ledge, and bizarre monstrous creature. We are inclined to respond to the painting's weirdness by concentrating our attention on the items that are recognizable yet deformed. The painting's background, meanwhile, is a landscape of a fishing village in Dali's native Catalonia. His paintings often juxtapose banal backgrounds with bizarre foregrounds to achieve an effect that is disorienting because it is based in both reality and fantasy simultaneously. McCullers and the other authors of surregionalism, I argue, are using similar techniques for a similar purpose. They construct imaginative landscapes that are recognizable and realistic and then project bizarre characters and events onto the literary cartography.

In McCullers's surreal literary cartography, the spaces are strange and distorted, amplifying the bizarreness of the characters and the actions taking place in the story. For example, the building that houses the café reflects the story's surrealist effects. In the frame narrative that opens the story, the building leans too far to the right, and "there is about it curious, cracked look that is very puzzling until you realize that at one time, and long ago, the right side of the front porch had been painted, and part of the wall—but the painting was left unfinished and one portion of the house is darker and dingier than the other" (3). We eventually learn that, on the day of the fight, Cousin Lymon decided that "he might as well paint the front porch." While Miss Amelia, Marvin Macy, and the people of the town are preparing for the fight, Cousin Lymon "painted half of the porch a gay bright green . . . . Typically enough he did not even finish the floor, but changed over to the walls, painting as high as he could reach and then standing on a crate to get a foot higher. When the paint ran out, the right side of the porch was bright green and there was a jagged portion of the wall that had been painted. Cousin Lymon left it at that" (63).

This image of the bright green paint smeared around the porch serves a few purposes in the text. First, it enhances the tension of the moment before the climactic action; second, it comments on Cousin Lymon's unstable state of mind, and his "childish satisfaction" with the work leads to speculation about his age, which people figure to be between "ten years or a hundred" (63); and third, the image itself is surrealistic, adding an element of extraordinary imagery to the scenery. The paint does not function in any rational way, and it does not invoke a common trope. It is strange, and it is placed in context with other strange images, characters, and actions to constitute a surreal narrative.

A habitué of the New York art scene, McCullers was familiar with surrealism in America. In 1940, during one of many separations from her husband, Reeves McCullers, she lived in an apartment in Brooklyn at 7 Middagh Street with poet W. H. Auden and burlesque dancer Gypsy Rose Lee. The apartment was a literary and intellectual hub, and among the visitors and guests were Salvador Dali and Pavel Tchelitchew, two of the most important figures in surrealism. Tchelitchew decorated the walls of the apartment with "a great surrealistic mural, a splash of color and grotesque form" (Carr 126). The following year, McCullers wrote "The Ballad of the Sad Café," and the image of Cousin Lymon painting the porch in a fit of inspiration perhaps alludes to this incident.

At the time that she wrote the story, surrealism was a strong influence in American culture, recognizable not only in artistic circles but also in advertising and other fields of vernacular discourse. In *Consuming Surrealism in American Culture*, Sandra Zalman explains that "surrealism was a site where high and low existed in a collaborative, rather than oppositional, dialogue, where avant-garde production mixed readily, if at times uneasily, with the vernacular, and as such, was actively absorbed into American mass culture" (11).[9] Surrealism, in other words, was a mainstream component of American culture at the time that McCullers wrote "The Ballad of the Sad Café," so the story's surrealistic aesthetics make sense in the context of the time.

Surrealistic aesthetics also make sense in the context of the place. In the midcentury American imagination, the South was a strange place, a landscape populated with chain gangs and snake handlers, a place lagging behind the rest of the nation in economic development and social progress, a region adhering to racial segregation and religious orthodoxy, a part of the country where many counties remained dry decades after the end of Prohibition, and a site of alterity onto which images of deviance and exoticism were projected. In the United States, the South was a region that was simultaneously the same yet different, normal yet strange.

Mab Segrest uses the term "Georgia Surreal" to describe the way the South "occupies this slippage between the particular avant-garde twentieth-century movement and its use in everyday language to mark the recognition of some instance of heightened or depressed reality in excess of what political ideologies admit and their institutions allow" (124). The South has often functioned as an imaginary space of Otherness where reality and unreality coexist. McCullers's literary cartography in "The Ballad of the Sad Café" takes place within this slippage, so her representation of spatial construction reflects the juxtapositions inherent in surreal forms.

"Ballad of the Sad Café," therefore, is weird for a reason. It represents an actual South, an imaginary South, and a sur/real-as-imagined South. As such, Miss Amelia's liquor serves several purposes in the story. It connects the characters in the foreground to the social and economic structure in the background. It changes and distorts the construction of space. It contributes to the elements of surreal aesthetics that challenge the reader's perception of the text. It makes the exaggerated characters and strange events in the story appear more believable in context. The story simulates the experience of drunkenness by distorting the reader's perception of reality with grotesque characters and distorted spaces.

Shifting the reader's focus to the strange events in the story distracts from the banal South in the background, but the region bleeds through at the edges of text, specifically in the frame narrative situated on the temporal boundaries of the story, years after Marvin Macy and Cousin Lymon have left town. Just as the initial description of the building leaning too far to the right opens the story with distortion of reality, the story ends with a sobering version of the same image: "The house of Miss Amelia leans so much to the right that it is now only a question of time when it will collapse completely, and people are careful not to walk around the yard. There is no good liquor to be bought in the town; the nearest still is eight miles away, and the liquor is such that those who drink it grow warts on their livers the size of goobers, and dream themselves into a dangerous inward world" (70). With this final surreal image, the "dangerous inward world" recedes, resolving into an image of the South as a dangerous actual place, a scene of twelve mortal men shackled together like slaves, working on a chain gang to repair a road that will inevitably connect this surreal terrain to the real world.

Notes

1. Edward Soja, *Thirdspace*, expands on the theory and gives multiple examples. His ideas about the social construction of space are influenced by Henri Lefebrve's work *The Production of Space*.

2. Robert Tally, *Spatiality*, gives a useful history and overview of the spatial turn in cultural studies.

3. In *The Postsouthern Sense of Place in Contemporary Fiction*, Martyn Bone interrogates southern writers' commitment to the concept of place. By the 1950s, he argues, the concept of place blinded many writers to changes taking place in the region.

4. Gaston Bachelard, *The Poetics of Space*, plumbs the emotional and phenomenological associations with interior spaces.

5. Scott Romine, *The Real South*, explores the imaginary representation of the South in the age of cultural reproduction, and Jennifer Greeson, *Our South*, argues that American writers constructed the South as a national Other.

6. Two of the most significant studies of the South as a real-as-experienced space are *The Nation's Region* by Leigh Anne Duck and *Southscapes* by Thadious M. Davis. Duck uses the theory of the chronotope to analyze the ways in which the South was perceived to deviate from the United States, and Davis conceptualizes the black experience of space in the South.

7. There are numerous readings of McCullers's work as grotesque according to various criteria. Some examples are Carmen Skaggs, "'A House of Freaks': Performance and the Grotesque in McCullers's 'The Ballad of the Sad Café'"; Clare Whatling, "Reading Miss Amelia: Critical Strategies in the Construction of Sex, Gender, Sexuality, the Gothic, and Grotesque"; and Sarah Gleeson-White, *Strange Bodies: Gender and Identity in the Novels of Carson McCullers*.

8. Although often associated with visual art, surrealism originated with writing. Andre Breton defines surrealism as "psychic automatism in its pure state, by which one proposes to express—verbally, by means of the written word, or in any other manner—the actual functioning of thought. Dictated by thought, in the absence of any control exercised by reason, exempt from any aesthetic or moral concern" (24).

9. Surrealism had a significant impact on American culture in the mid-twentieth century, affecting both highbrow and lowbrow culture. Dickran Tashjian, *Boatload of Madmen*, explains that fascist disdain for decadent art forced many European surrealists into exile in America, and Angela Miller, "With Eyes Wide Open," explains how surrealism was incorporated into American culture.

Works Cited

Bachelard, Gaston. *The Poetics of Space.* Translated by Maria Jolas, Beacon, 1994.

Bone, Martyn. *The Postsouthern Sense of Place in Contemporary Fiction.* Louisiana State UP, 2005.

Breton, André. *Manifestoes of Surrealism*. Translated by Richard Seaver and Helen R. Lane, U of Michigan P, 1969.

Carr, Virginia Spencer. *The Lonely Hunter: A Biography of Carson McCullers*. Doubleday, 1975.

Daniel, Pete. *Lost Revolutions: The South in the 1950s*. U of North Carolina P, 2000.

Davis, Thadious M. *Southscapes: Geographies of Race, Region, and Literature*. U of North Carolina P, 2011.

Duck, Leigh Anne. *The Nation's Region: Southern Modernism, Segregation, and U.S. Nationalism*. U of Georgia P, 2009.

Fowler, Doreen. "Carson McCullers's Primal Scenes: 'The Ballad of the Sad Café.'" *Critique: Studies in Contemporary Fiction*, vol. 43, no. 3 (Spring 2002), pp. 260–71.

Gleeson-White, Sarah. *Strange Bodies: Gender and Identity in the Novels of Carson McCullers*. U of Alabama P, 2003.

Greeson, Jennifer Rae. *Our South: Geographic Fantasy and the Rise of National Literature*. Harvard UP, 2010.

Lanksy, Ellen. "'A Bottle of Whiskey between Them': Williams, McCullers, and the Influence of Alcohol." *Carson McCullers Society Newsletter*, no. 7 (2005), pp. 4–6.

Lefebrve, Henri. *The Production of Space*. Translated by Donald Nicholson-Smith, Wiley-Blackwell, 1992.

McCullers, Carson. "The Ballad of the Sad Café." *The Ballad of the Sad Café and Other Stories* (1951), Mariner Books, 2005, pp. 1–72.

Miller, Angela. "'With Eyes Wide Open': The American Reception of Surrealism." *Caught by Politics: Hitler Exiles and American Visual Culture in the 1930s and 1940s*, edited by Sabine Eckmann and Lutz Koepnick, Palgrave Macmillan, 2007, pp. 61–94.

Romine, Scott. *The Real South: Southern Narrative in the Age of Cultural Reproduction*. Louisiana State UP, 2008.

Segrest, Mab. "The Milledgeville Asylum and the Georgia Surreal." *Southern Quarterly*, vol. 48, no. 3 (Spring 2011), pp. 114–50.

Skaggs, Carmen. "'A House of Freaks': Performance and the Grotesque in McCullers's 'The Ballad of the Sad Café.'" *ANQ*, vol. 26, no. 2 (2013), pp. 134–38.

Soja, Edward. *Postmetropolis: Critical Studies of Cities and Regions*. Wiley-Blackwell, 2000.

———. *Postmodern Geographies: The Reassertion of Space in Critical Social Theory*. Verso, 1989.

———. *Thirdspace: Journeys to Los Angeles and Other Real-and-Imagined Places*. Blackwell, 1996.

Tally, Robert. *Spatiality*. Taylor and Francis, 2012.

Tashjian, Dickran. *A Boatload of Madmen: Surrealism and the American Avant-Garde, 1920–1950*. Thames and Hudson, 2001.

Whatling, Clare. "Reading Miss Amelia: Critical Strategies in the Construction of Sex, Gender, Sexuality, the Gothic, and Grotesque." *Modernist Sexualities*, edited by Hugh Stevens and Caroline Howlett, Manchester UP, 2000, pp. 239–50.

Yaeger, Patricia. *Dirt and Desire: Reconstructing Southern Women's Writing, 1930–1990.* U of Chicago P, 2000.

Zalman, Sandra. *Consuming Surrealism in American Culture: Dissident Modernism.* Ashgate, 2015.

Zieger, Susan. *Inventing the Addict: Drugs, Race, and Sexuality in Nineteenth-Century British and American Literature.* U of Massachusetts P, 2008.

PART III

ALCOHOL'S PRODUCTION,
COMMODIFICATION, AND CIRCULATION
IN THE SOUTH

Racial Ambiguity, Bootlegging, and the Subversion of Plantation Hierarchies in Faulkner's South

JENNA GRACE SCIUTO

I n William Faulkner's South, bootlegging is a profitable criminal enterprise that enables alternative power structures to form. Through the illegal character of the enterprise (and consequent disruption of the natural order) and its universally desired product (indicating the egalitarian nature of alcoholism), bootlegging has the capacity to disrupt racial hierarchies and class relationships in Faulkner's fiction. The majority of the bootleggers present in Faulkner's work are racially ambiguous, such as Popeye of *Sanctuary* (1931), who is white yet repeatedly described as "that black man" (42); the "parchment color" (34) Joe Christmas of *Light in August* (1932); and Lucas Beauchamp of *Go Down, Moses* (1942)—a financially well-off biracial man who carries himself as if he were white.

What is Faulkner saying about the social construction of race through these characters? Or about the construction of criminality? Through his racially ambiguous bootleggers, Faulkner speaks to the entanglement of race, class, and criminality in Yoknapatawpha County and their relationship to the southern society and plantation culture that they both grow out of and disrupt. Whereas scholars such as Greg Forter and Seth Moglen have rightly pointed toward Faulkner's melancholic tendencies, I argue that tracing bootlegging throughout his oeuvre reveals a progressive social arc that may complicate our understanding of Faulkner more generally.[1]

Race relations in Mississippi did not change significantly during the early decades of the twentieth century. While the years between World War I and the 1940s saw a gradual lessening of its grip, the plantation economy remained intact in the South (Mandle 82), with the white planter class retaining its power. Lynch culture and the myth of the black rapist used to justify it persisted: 2,462 blacks were lynched between 1882 and 1930 (Tolnay and Beck 272). Thus, the post-Reconstruction, Prohibition, and World War II periods share an association between race and criminality in the American public consciousness, which had remained constant since the 1890s, unlike the fluctuations around the legality of alcohol.[2]

In fact, the criminalization of African Americans was linked to the enthusiasm for Prohibition in the South, as a result of the "fear that black men, stimulated by alcohol, would attack white women" (Barr 253, note 12). These widespread myths of African American criminality were in part what led southern states to ratify the Eighteenth Amendment (McGirr 75), which in turn enabled law enforcement to police "communities already identified as prone to 'criminality'" (xix). Nonetheless, an unexpected consequence of the bootlegging in reaction to Prohibition was "the blurring of the lines of segregation" (81) in the Jim Crow South, with federal agents remarking on the frequency with which both blacks and whites were found on the premises during raids.[3] Lisa McGirr argues that beneath "this veneer of racial harmony, however, was an entrenched imbalance of power that consigned whites and poor African-Americans to quite divergent roles in the subaltern economy," which frequently took the form of black employees working for white still owners (81).

Regardless, the illegality of the trade—operating outside of mainstream society—allowed for more fluid race and class relations. Lucas Beauchamp's still operation, for example, breaks a pattern of domination by whites, specifically against the backdrop of the 1940s—a period more open to these shifts than the 1920s or 1930s. Lucas's enterprise is a challenge to these common hierarchies, as well as to the reductive, decontextualized stereotypes of inherent black criminality.[4]

Pushing this further still, for Faulkner's ambiguous bootleggers, bootlegging itself aids in the social construction of race. Historically, blackness has often been constructed through illicit behavior, and thus the decision to bootleg has racial implications for Popeye, Joe, and Lucas.[5] According to the introduction to *Beyond Slavery*, Rebecca Scott argues that race is not "a determinant of human interaction" but "a construct whose political meaning could shift sharply over time and space, rendering inclusion or exclusion in the polity historically contingent" (Cooper et al. 10).

If, like other social categories, race is a construct contingent on time and space, then the role of criminality in the social construction of race in early twentieth-century Mississippi leads to the positioning of racially indeterminate figures such as Joe Christmas as black. Through choosing to work as a bootlegger, Joe endeavors to make himself socially recognizable as black. I argue that racial identities are both constructed by and illuminated through the production of liquor in Faulkner's work. An eye to the role of alcohol in this trio of novels (*Sanctuary, Light in August,* and *Go Down, Moses*), which span the Prohibition era and beyond, reveals shifting configurations of race and class made possible by the social subversion enabled by bootlegging, as well as the egalitarian potential that accompanied the move away from the traditional planation economy.

Two early short stories help to establish bootlegging as an undercurrent throughout Faulkner's works; however, in "Once Aboard the Lugger" (I) and (II) (1928), race and class relations are clearly defined through a bootlegger's failed attempt to subvert racial hierarchies during the Prohibition era.[6] Faulkner's *Sanctuary,* published a few years later, focuses on the representation of a bootlegging operation during the same period. In this novel, the illegal production of alcohol facilitates the advance of one group who did not financially benefit from the plantation system: poor whites. Frenchman's Bend, a former plantation/site of colonial control, is recast in the 1920s as a space where lower-class whites, such as moonshiners Lee Goodwin and Popeye, now hold power over those from higher-class positions, like Horace Benbow, Gowan Stevens, and Temple Drake. The desire for alcohol draws Gowan and Temple out to Frenchman's Bend, placing them under the control of lower-class whites disempowered by traditional social hierarchies.

Deliberately engaging with the Prohibition era, Faulkner includes important distinctions between *Sanctuary*'s two central bootleggers. When we are introduced to Popeye, he is in a black suit "with a tight, high-waisted coat" (4), while Goodwin with his "lean, weathered face" wears "muddy overalls" (12). The fact that Popeye is able to afford a car and stylish clothes while Goodwin hardly seems able to provide food for his child speaks to the class differences that accompany their roles in the economy of alcohol.[7] Goodwin operates a still in rural Yoknapatawpha County, primarily selling his alcohol to country folks. On the other hand, Popeye, with his connections to organized crime, approaches bootlegging as big business, benefiting from "the tremendous new opportunities created by the criminalization of alcohol traffic" (McGirr 54). Through including these subtle differences, Faulkner engages with the complexities of the period: Popeye's rise in class status, subverting the hierarchies in place, is an exception resulting from his particular locus in the bootlegging enterprise.

As an added complication, the moonshiners are repeatedly depicted in racially ambiguous terms by the narrator—Popeye is "prosperous, quiet, thin, black, and uncommunicative" (Faulkner, *Sanctuary* 309), while Lee Goodwin has a "black head and gaunt brown face" (281)—and by other characters—Horace Benbow thinks that Popeye "smells black" (7) and Temple Drake refers to Popeye throughout as "that black man" (42). Conor Picken is interested in the relationship between race, class, and criminality in *Sanctuary*, arguing that Gowan Stevens's alcoholic drinking positions him as "white trash" through his failed performance of whiteness, at the same time that it blackens him: "Figuratively blackened and emasculated by his habitual drunkenness, Gowan appears less like a gentleman and more like the character frequently described with images of blackness . . . the impotent 'black' bootlegger, Popeye" (446, 450). According to Picken, it is not only bootlegging and criminal activity that blackens characters but also alcoholic drinking, such as Gowan's, which represents "the (perceived) threat to the bastion of Southern social stability" (450).

I want to push further on the association between blackness and criminality here. Popeye, the "black" bootlegger, whose given name, as we learn in *Requiem for a Nun*, is Vitelli, is not racially black. Therefore, while his blackness must be metaphoric—that is, he has a "black presence" (Faulkner, *Sanctuary* 121)—it is nevertheless described in physical terms throughout the text. Why does Faulkner repeatedly position a racially white character as black? Is he simply speaking to the potential of criminality to blacken characters or to the entwinement of race and class in the novel?

For Popeye and Goodwin, bootlegging itself aids in the social construction of racially white characters as black.[8] Writing about the law's capacity to construct race in the United States, Ian Haney López argues that "whiteness is contingent, changeable, partial, inconstant, and ultimately social" (xxi). Popeye demonstrates this through the critical role his identity as a bootlegger plays in positioning him as black in the eyes of his southern community during the Prohibition era. Popeye's overt participation in the bootlegging economy races him differently than Joe Christmas, for instance, since Faulkner makes no secret of his profession. Further, through the depiction of the "black" bootlegger figure as an Italian named Vitelli, Faulkner also directly challenges the stereotypical associations between race and criminality.[9]

While this ambiguity could alternatively be used to confirm stereotypes by demonstrating that Popeye's criminality causes his exclusion from whiteness, I argue that the instability itself, in Popeye's example, plays a part in the challenge to stereotypical racial associations. In this way, Faulkner reveals the potential of both racial fluidity and the illegal manufacture of alcohol to destabilize the South's traditional social structures. Thus, tracing the role of alcohol in the novel uniquely illuminates social issues, such as the construction of racial identities in relation to criminality, as opposed to merely being illuminated by them.

In addition to the subversive effects of the illicit production of alcohol—and the benefits of operating outside of the traditional economy—racial ambiguity likewise works to destabilize southern social hierarchies. Biracial individuals disrupt the binary understanding of race that resulted from the one-drop rule of the 1830s (Ladd 28), which defined anyone with any degree of African lineage as black, as well as the attempts of scientific racism or racial anthropology to prove that the black and white races are different species (Mohammed 23).[10] The existence of mixed-race figures directly refuted these claims, challenging the very foundation upon which the slave system was built: the notion that African Americans were less than human—more specifically, that they were three-fifths of a person—and thus not entitled to the same rights. Therefore, biracial identity itself is a disruptive force for the plantation culture in the South. One's identity as biracial, like one's identity as a bootlegger, may not be visually observable in the body; both contain the threat of potentially passing undetected by respectable white southern society.

The number of African Americans passing for white reached a peak between 1880 and 1925 (J. Davis 56), and passing demonstrates the constructed, fluid nature of racial groups. Bootlegging disrupted race in a unique way during this period and, like the passing of forbidden liquor from one point to another, this racial ambiguity allowed black men to permeate social boundaries. For instance, Lucas's race is observable in his body but his moonlighting as a moonshiner passes undetected for twenty years. In Joe Christmas's case, neither his possible biracial origins nor his work as a bootlegger are immediately apparent to the community. Popeye's whiteness likewise does not seem to be observable in his physical body, perhaps as a result of the role of class anxieties in this equation.

While they are categorized in different ways based on class distinctions, Popeye and Goodwin both are white men who are socially constructed as black due to their identities as bootleggers, their lower-class origins, and their unsavory lifestyles. Both racial passing and the criminality of bootlegging pose a threat to the norms and hierarchies of Faulkner's early twentieth-century southern community through their social disruption, which is heightened by the potential of passing undetected.

In addition, due to the early twentieth-century southern setting, it is not surprising that the racially ambiguous bootleggers across all three novels are the victims of lynching, or a lynching attempt, in an effort to contain their disruptive potential. In *Sanctuary*, Lee Goodwin is lynched and sexually violated for the rape of Temple Drake.[11] Similarly, in *Light in August*, Joe Christmas is castrated and lynched.[12] The last words of vigilante Percy Grimm—"Now you'll let white women alone, even in hell" (464)—more than anything else in his life, connect Christmas to the myth of the black rapist.

Faulkner complicates stereotypical associations, however, by inverting the figure of the black rapist: both Lee Goodwin, the accused rapist, and Popeye, the actual rapist (though impotent, he rapes Temple Drake with a corncob), are racially white, though they are socially constructed as black in the novel. Joe Christmas is portrayed as a black rapist by his white southern community, but his racial background is unknown, and he had a consensual, ongoing sexual relationship with the white woman, Joanna Burden, he is accused of raping.[13] Lastly, Lucas Beauchamp is wrongly accused of murder and nearly lynched by a white mob in *Intruder in the Dust* (1948); the fact that Lucas is ultimately not killed may speak to the novel's later historical setting, one that shows a South in transition. For Faulkner's racially ambiguous bootleggers, this shared experience underscores their subversive power and threat to southern social hierarchies: the criminal enterprise of bootlegging, coupled with racial ambiguity, runs counter to Jefferson's social and racial hegemony. Alcohol-related criminality and indistinct racial construction can have deadly consequences. Indeed, this resistance is not welcomed by mainstream society.

Unlike the others, however, Joe Christmas's bootlegging does not initially appear to be intentionally subversive. In contrast to *Sanctuary*, the historical context for *Light in August* is both less certain and less central. Published in 1932, the novel presumably takes place in the early 1930s—the final years of national Prohibition. While the trade in alcohol is present in the novel, it is not a key aspect of the plot; however, it helps to develop the reader's understanding of Christmas as a character.

Bootlegging is depicted as something that Joe passively falls into as a result of his deceptive nature: "In the meantime he had begun to sell a little whiskey, very judiciously, restricting himself to a few discreet customers none of whom knew the others. . . . He could almost believe that it was not to make money that he sold the whiskey but because he was doomed to conceal always something from the women who surrounded him" (261–62). The language of this passage takes agency away from Joe, locating it with a vague type of fate, perhaps in anticipation of the "Player," who is later revealed to be directing the actions of Joe and of Percy Grimm (462). Joe does not appear to manufacture alcohol to actively disrupt society's positioning of him but instead because of a nebulous belief that he is "doomed" to deceive the women with whom he is close. He does not actively take up bootlegging due to his blackness but passively falls into it as a result of the prewritten script for blackness, illustrating in a direct way the social construction of identity, and of blackness more specifically. Joe positions himself as black through this choice of profession, in addition to his choice to inhabit a former slave cabin on the property of Joanna Burden, a white woman. His ideas of blackness are linked to social fictions and stereotypes like black criminality and are not grounded in his body or individual self.

Thus, Joe's decision to bootleg helps to socially construct him as black, and his selection of a racial identity—despite having no evidence either way—is a consciously subversive decision. The racial fluidity that allows him to choose is a direct challenge to the binary system of race, mobilized through alternatives to the plantation system such as the bootlegging economy. Joe acknowledges this element of choice himself, thinking, "If I'm not [black], damned if I haven't wasted a lot of time" (254), and later, in response to believing that Joanna wants to get married, he thinks, "No. If I give in now, I will deny all thirty years that I have lived to make me what I chose to be" (265).

Although Joe positions his bootlegging as a consequence of that which he is doomed to do—to deceive the women close to him—he also acknowledges the agency he has to construct his identity, which, given the context of the novel, is entwined with the bootlegging itself. In other words, through its central role in constructing his identity, Joe's bootlegging *can* be categorized as subversive. Moreover, the question of agency remains an interesting one throughout the novel: when Percy Grimm kills and castrates Christmas, he is described as moving "with that lean, swift, blind obedience to whatever Player moved him on the Board" (462). In opposition to Lucas's deliberate actions, both Grimm and Christmas, to different extents, fall into the patterns constructed for their lives by the Player or by an elusive fate, complicating the control they have over their actions.

Lucas Beauchamp, however, in "The Fire and the Hearth" (1942), from *Go Down, Moses*, overtly demonstrates the disruptive potential of the illegal production of alcohol. Lucas acts with intention, and, like his father, Tomey's Turl, will not be controlled by fate or society.[14] In Thadious Davis's words, Lucas "attempts as a game player to manipulate an oppressive legal system to his own ends" (135).[15] A foil to Percy Grimm, Lucas will not be moved by the Player but becomes a player himself. Here, running his still "carefully and discreetly" for twenty years (Faulkner, *Go Down, Moses* 35) enables Lucas to subvert the white planter's authority over his labor, his earning capacity, and thus his identity.

Lucas began his operation in the 1920s and continued during the post-Prohibition era, when alcohol was still outlawed in Mississippi. The longevity of the enterprise and the seeming quality of his goods—given the expensive "copper-lined kettle" in which he invests (37)—combined with his inheritance from his father, enable Lucas to amass what likely amounts to a larger fortune than that of Carothers "Roth" Edmonds, who owns the plantation Lucas inhabits. While the plantation economy held steady throughout the 1930s, by the 1940s it had begun to give way to a modern capitalist system, due to technological changes (Mandle 93). This shift, in addition to the alternative economy enabled by alcohol, leaves space for Lucas to be a more effectively subversive figure than those before him were able to be. Lucas's financial success and his McCaslin lineage (he is a direct descendant of the patriarch, old Carothers McCaslin) allow Lucas to destabilize the racial position granted to him by rigid plantation hierarchies.[16] Lucas represents the potential for something more—an alternative to the replication of destructive colonial ideologies—revealing the bootlegging associated with him as a disruptive force.

Like the characters of Popeye, Lee Goodwin, and Joe Christmas before him, Lucas is also racially ambiguous. Although he presents racially as black, he does not act in the way that southern whites at the time would prefer a black man—or, in Lucas's case, a biracial man—to act. Lucas does not defer to white men; he has "never once said 'sir' to [Roth's] white skin" (Faulkner, *Go Down, Moses* 126), even though he is a sharecropper on Roth's property, and he does not approach the main house through the kitchen door, as his position requires (44). Moreover, Lucas's defiant bootlegging provides him with cash, which lessens Roth's control over him as a sharecropper (Matthews 32), adding to his relative economic independence. The act of bootlegging figures differently in this novel, granting him more leeway than those in previous decades received as a result of the historical setting, which enables Lucas to refuse in a more direct manner the inferior social position granted to him by plantation racial hierarchies.

Additionally, Lucas is very aware of the racial stereotypes that he defies.[17] He manipulates racial perceptions and assumptions to get the reaction that he wants from Roth, performing according to stereotypes only when it suits his purpose: "Without changing the inflection of his voice and apparently without effort or even design Lucas became not Negro but nigger, not secret so much as impenetrable, not servile and not effacing, but enveloping himself in an aura of timeless and stupid impassivity almost like a smell" (Faulkner, *Go Down, Moses* 58). Lucas's conscious performances demonstrate his awareness of the constructed nature of race. Ironically, as a character, Lucas directly defies the stereotypes associated with black sharecroppers of the period: he is smart and industrious (outsmarting both Roth and the white salesman), an incredibly hard worker (laboring both day and night), and relatively rich.

As a result of 1940s setting, the plantation ideologies depicted in *Go Down, Moses* are increasingly tenuous, with both black and white characters at times consciously acting in opposition to them. For instance, although he ultimately sends her away, Roth Edmonds temporarily forms a family unit with his unnamed biracial relative in Mexico, and white lawyer Gavin Stevens takes seriously Mollie's atypical request to bring home the body of her executed grandson. If these subtle shifts can be viewed as social progress, then, for Lucas, bootlegging is uniquely positioned as a change agent. In addition to his privileged position on the plantation—resulting from his aristocratic lineage and white ancestry—his role in the economy of alcohol (and the wealth that results) is the essential factor for Lucas breaking the pattern of domination by whites.

Along with a number of Faulkner's other mixed-race characters, such as Sam Fathers, Charles Bon, and Joe Christmas, Lucas is a border figure inhabiting the line between whiteness and blackness. Through his refusal to let society define him, his racial ambiguity, and, of course, his bootlegging, Lucas is a destabilizing force that anticipates the breakdown of the southern plantation system. Lucas is the novel's most subversive figure—he is more combative and less servile than was expected of those before him. Through his depiction of Lucas, Faulkner leaves open the possibility for something beyond the hierarchical structures of plantation society.

Although it may be obscured beneath the weight of the same racial violence, discrimination, and sexual abuse that persisted into the postbellum era, Lucas serves as a reminder that some things are improving with time. While, on one level, Faulkner depicts traumatizing "planter masculinity with its toxic violations" as impossible to mourn or move beyond (Forter 98), at the same time, through characters like Lucas, he portrays a positive potential in challenging hierarchies. History is not simply the cyclical repetition of colonial crimes; it is simultaneously progressive in some ways, such as in technological developments (though advances may not always be in obvious increments).

Thus, the outcomes for each of Faulkner's racially ambiguous bootleggers improve with time. In the 1920s, Popeye gets away through having Lee Goodwin lynched and sexually violated in his place. A decade later, in the 1930s, Joe Christmas is castrated and killed by a representative of the community. Ultimately, in the 1940s, the decade during which "technological change finally resulted in the demise of the plantation economy" (Mandle 93), we find Lucas, Faulkner's final racially ambiguous bootlegger. Although he comes under fire in *Intruder in the Dust,* he is ultimately not lynched, and he survives to old age as "not only the oldest man but the oldest living person on the Edmonds plantation" (Faulkner, *Go Down, Moses* 36). The progression of these examples demonstrates the increasing complication of the set historical categories of race and class in the twentieth century, leaving room for new configurations that are made possible by the social subversion of racially ambiguous bootleggers like Lucas.

This is not to uncritically glorify bootlegging through its potential for social disruption. Many negatives accompanied the illegal production of alcohol during Prohibition: "Alcohol became more dangerous to consume; crime increased and became 'organized'; the court and prison systems were stretched to the breaking point; and corruption of public officials was rampant" (Thornton 1). However, in Faulkner's South, bootlegging also allowed for movement in the set social structures remaining from slavery. Bootlegging, combined with the subversive nature of racial ambiguity itself, exemplifies the potential for criminality to be a progressive force when directed against colonial ideologies and the status quo.

Notes

1. Moglen includes Faulkner among a list of "melancholic modernists" (28) who "produced literary works that are structured by the presumption that collective resistance to the damning forces of modernization was impossible, even unthinkable" (7). Forter focuses on Faulkner's use of the traumatic in expressing a melancholic project: "It is our fate—the human condition—to be traumatized by histories we cannot work through" (97–98). While I do not disagree that these aspects are present in Faulkner's work, I aim to show, through a focus on bootlegging, that progressive social tendencies are simultaneously apparent and should be taken into account.

2. Khalil Gibran Muhammad traces the "ideological currency of black criminality," which figures such as W. E. B. Du Bois and Ida B. Wells had attempted to decouple as early as the 1890s. The publication of the 1890 census represented the first time that prison statistics were used to position blacks as "a distinct and dangerous criminal population," ignoring the "race-conscious laws, discriminatory punishments, and new forms of everyday racial surveillance" that were institutionalized by that time (3–4).

3. McGirr also notes that "both African-Americans and whites were victims of indiscriminate and often deadly use of force" during the Prohibition period (81).

4. Other critics have linked criminality with race. Carlyle Van Thompson argues that Jay Gatsby in F. Scott Fitzgerald's *The Great Gatsby* (1922) should be read as a "'pale' black individual who passes for white" (75), as a result of his associations with jazz music, dancing, and black cultural production, in addition to bootlegging and other criminal activities. Van Thompson writes, "If the performance of racial passing delineates criminality, Fitzgerald's characterizations of Jay Gatsby's illegal activities reinforce this theme" (83). He also asserts that Fitzgerald draws on the association between criminality and racial passing in order to investigate Gatsby's hidden blackness. Ultimately, Gatsby's race only matters insofar as it can be used to illustrate how race and criminality construct each other. Faulkner challenges such stereotypical associations through the racially ambiguous bootleggers Popeye, Joe Christmas, and Lucas Beauchamp, the "uppity" biracial sharecropper (Faulkner, *Go Down, Moses* 124). Through these complex characters, Faulkner can expose stereotypical associations for what they are, demonstrating the potential for the fluidity of race and class distinctions to subvert the set power structures of the South.

5. According to Muhammad, during the early twentieth century "in a rapidly industrializing, urbanizing, and demographically shifting America, blackness was refashioned through crime statistics," becoming a more stable racial category juxtaposed against whiteness (5).

6. The social disruption made possible by the bootlegging enterprise is too much for one Alabamian bootlegger, who shoots an unsuspecting black cook as a result. "Once Aboard the Lugger" (I) and (II) (both 1928) depict bootleggers out of New Orleans during the mid-1920s Prohibition era. In "Lugger (II)," the fluid, borderless, nationless sea space allows for the reproduction and extension of the racial hierarchies of the plantation South. The bootlegging vessel that we follow in "Lugger (I)" is boarded by two hijackers: a "high voice," described by the narrator as "the wop," and a "flat Alabama voice," later matched with a man having "red hair and a long red face" with "chinacolored" eyes. The Alabamian is heavily invested in keeping racial roles strictly defined, to the extent that he shoots and kills the black cook of the enterprise, stating that the place "fer a nigger's behind a plow" (Faulkner *Uncollected Stories* 360–62). The cook disregarded what the Alabamian saw as his appropriate social position—agricultural laborer—and was killed for it.

The irony of this is apparent in an unpublished version of the tale in which the cook and the narrator share a moment of interracial connection over the fact that they both are country boys. The black cook reveals that his reason for taking the job aboard the ship is to save his money, return to the country, and buy a farm ("Once Aboard the Lugger—"). In other words, he plans to return to what the Alabamian considers his "place" as an agricultural worker (although the Alabamian likely would not have been pleased with the black cook owning property). Through his act of violence, the Alabamian erases whatever financial and social advancement the cook's role in the criminal enterprise made possible. In this case, bootlegging provides the black cook with an opportunity for advancement outside of the plantation economy, which the Alabamian considers a threat to the status quo. The Alabamian recognizes the social disruption as such and swiftly contains it.

7. During the 1920s and 1930s, the manufacture of liquor was a way for rural southerners to deal with rising taxes, with highland farmers and out-of-work miners relying on "corn culture and whiskey making" as a "strategy for coping with misery and overpopulation" (Kirby 205).

8. While we can see Lee Goodwin and Popeye destabilizing racial hierarchies in a way comparable to that of the black cook of "Lugger (II)," the combination of the cook's more apparent blackness and the lawlessness of the open sea lead to his swifter suppression.

9. Social scientists during the Progressive Era used "crime statistics to demonstrate the assimilability of the Irish, the Italian, and the Jew by explicit contrast to the Negro" (Muhammad 7).

10. Through the stereotype of hypersexuality and scientific racism, scholars attempted to prove that black women possessed not only "a 'primitive' sexual appetite but also the external signs of this temperament—'primitive' genitalia." They believed that if sexual parts and drives were different among the black race, then this could be taken as a sign that "blacks were a separate (and, needless to say, lower) race, as different from the European as the proverbial orangutan" (Gilman 213, 216). While they ultimately failed in this endeavor, there nevertheless was a conceptual split between the gender roles of black and white women in the eighteenth and nineteenth centuries (Abrahams 230), in which black women were viewed as inherently promiscuous or savage and white women were domesticated and desexualized, "the repositories of white civilization" (Jordan 77).

11. One of the lynchers states, in reference to Lee Goodwin's lawyer, Horace Benbow, "Do to the lawyer what we did to him. What he did to her. Only we never used a cob. We made him wish we had used a cob" (Faulkner, *Sanctuary* 296).

12. Lynching was a form of sexualized violence, given the nature of the assault, which frequently included castration and dismemberment—as in the case of Joe Christmas—along with other forms of torture, and should be seen as an inheritance from the institution of slavery.

13. The black rapist of the postbellum period was "'nearly always a mulatto,' with 'enough white blood in him to replace native humility and cowardice with Caucasian audacity'" (L. H. Harris, "A Southern Woman's View," quoted in Fredrickson 277). Thus, in the U.S. South, white racists associated biracial men with violent sexual tendencies due to what they saw as the mixture of blood and the resulting combined characteristics of both white and black men.

14. Tomey's Turl does not accept living separately from Tennie Beauchamp; he is constantly running away to be with her. Further, Turl is the dealer in the card game that determines his fate. Although he is depicted as disembodied hands dealing the cards (Faulkner, *Go Down, Moses* 26), it is hard to ignore the "hand" Turl has in his own fate.

15. While I agree with Thadious Davis that each time Lucas Beauchamp "constitutes himself as subject, his moves are contested" (138), I argue that more should be made of his attempts at disruption, given the forces against him in the postbellum South.

16. Lucas's social subversion is complicated slightly by the fact that he believes that his "white blood" and connection to Carothers McCaslin sets him apart on the plantation—a mind-set that simultaneously reifies the hierarchical structures in place.

17. Faulkner plays with racial categorizations through his portrayal of the biracial Lucas. According to Isaac McCaslin, Lucas is more like the plantation patriarch "old Carothers than all the rest of us put together, including old Carothers" (*Go Down, Moses* 114), even though, according to the one-drop rule, Lucas would have been considered black. Isaac also compares Lucas's face to "a composite of a whole generation of fierce and undefeated young Confederate soldiers" (114). This cross-racial comparison is striking in its bold emphasis of Lucas's stubborn, "fierce and undefeated" qualities over his race.

Works Cited

Abrahams, Yvette. "Images of Sara Bartman: Sexuality, Race, and Gender in Early Nineteenth-Century Britain." *Nation, Empire, Colony: Historicizing Gender and Race,* edited by Ruth Roach Piernon and Nupur Chaudhuri, Indiana UP, 1998, pp. 220–36.

Barr, Andrew. *Drink: A Social History of America.* Carroll and Graf, 1999.

Cooper, Frederick et al. *Beyond Slavery: Explorations of Race, Labor, and Citizenship in Postemancipation Societies.* Chapel Hill: U of North Carolina P, 2000.

Davis, James F. *Who Is Black?: One Nation's Definition.* Penn State UP, 2001.

Davis, Thadious. *Games of Property: Law, Race, Gender, and Faulkner's* Go Down, Moses. Duke UP, 2003.

Faulkner, William. *Go Down, Moses.* 1942. Vintage International, 1990.

———. *Intruder in the Dust.* 1948. Vintage International, 1991.

———. *Light in August.* 1932. Vintage International, 1990.

———. "Once Aboard the Lugger—." William Faulkner Papers, 1925–1950, Accession no. 9817, Albert and Shirley Small Special Collections Library, University of Virginia.

———. *Requiem for a Nun.* 1950. Vintage International, 1994.

———. *Sanctuary.* 1931. Vintage International, 1985.

———. *Uncollected Stories of William Faulkner.* Random House, 1979.

Forter, Greg. *Gender, Race, and Mourning in American Modernism.* Cambridge UP, 2011.

Fredrickson, George M. *The Black Image in the White Mind: The Debate on Afro-American Character and Destiny, 1817–1914.* Harper Torchbooks, 1972.

Gilman, Sander L. "Black Bodies, White Bodies: Toward an Iconography of Female Sexuality in Late Nineteenth-Century Art, Medicine, and Literature." *Critical Inquiry,* vol. 12, no. 1 (Autumn 1985), pp. 204–42.

Jordan, Winthrop D. *The White Man's Burden: Historical Origins of Racism in the United States.* Oxford UP, 1974.

Kirby, Jack Temple. *Rural Worlds Lost: The American South, 1920–1960.* Louisiana State UP, 1987.

Ladd, Barbara. *Nationalism and the Color Line in George W. Cable, Mark Twain, and William Faulkner*. Louisiana State UP, 1996.

López, Ian Haney. *White by Law: The Legal Construction of Race*. New York UP, 2006.

Mandle, Jay R. *Not Slave, Not Free: The African American Economic Experience since the Civil War*. Duke UP, 1992.

Matthews, John T. "Touching Race in *Go Down, Moses*." *New Essays on* Go Down, Moses, edited by Linda Wagner-Martin, Cambridge UP, 1996, pp. 21–48.

McGirr, Lisa. *The War on Alcohol: Prohibition and the Rise of the American State*. W. W. Norton, 2016.

Moglen, Seth. *Mourning Modernity: Literary Modernism and the Injuries of American Capitalism*. Stanford UP, 2007.

Mohammed, Patricia. "'But Most of All Mi Love Me Browning': The Emergence in Eighteenth- and Nineteenth-Century Jamaica of the Mulatto Woman as Desired." *Feminist Review*, vol. 65 (2000): 22–48.

Muhammad, Khalil Gibran. *The Condemnation of Blackness: Race, Crime, and the Making of Modern Urban America*. Harvard UP, 2011.

Okrent, Daniel. *Last Call: The Rise and Fall of Prohibition*. Scribner, 2010.

Picken, Conor. "Drunk and Disorderly: Alcoholism in William Faulkner's *Sanctuary*." *Mississippi Quarterly*, vol. 67, no. 3 (Summer 2014): 441–59.

Thornton, Mark. *Alcohol Prohibition Was a Failure*. Washington, DC: Cato Institute, 1991.

Tolnay, Stewart E., and E. M. Beck. *A Festival of Violence: An Analysis of Southern Lynchings, 1882–1930*. Champaign: U of Illinois P, 1995.

Van Thompson, Carlyle. *The Tragic Black Buck: Racial Masquerading in the American Literary Imagination*. Peter Lang, 2004.

Moonshine in the Sunshine State

Alcohol's Roots and Routes in Marjorie Kinnan Rawlings's South Moon Under *and Ernest Hemingway's* To Have and Have Not

CHRISTOPHER RIEGER

The premise of the present essay collection assumes that alcohol and the South have some type of unique bond or affinity, and in this essay I explore the key role that alcohol plays in defining place in a southern setting in the 1930s, as well as the ways in which gender is implicated in this construction. There is no shortage of southern stereotypes in popular culture that link alcohol to the South: beer-swilling rednecks acting crassly, white-suited gentlemen sipping mint juleps on verandas, and moonshine-smuggling hillbillies eluding lawmen in souped-up cars full of jugs of homebrew. Yet these reductive images are also quite distinct from one another in terms of alcohol type, class, geography, and era. While all of these images have some roots in historical reality, they also have taken on lives of their own through intertextual references that do not depend on any real original. Recent critical developments of the new southern studies and the turn toward the Global South have further distanced conceptions of southern literature from a defined geographic space. The "South," the argument goes, is more of an idea or set of (often competing) ideas, rather than any coherent historical entity. Or, as Michael Kreyling puts it, "the South" itself may be "always already a derivation, or . . . a derivation of a derivation" (*The South* 164).

Kreyling, in *Inventing Southern Literature* (1998), shows how the Agrarians created particular versions of the South and southern literature as defined against an outside Other. Scott Romine's *The Real South* (2008) further develops this notion of an invented or artificial South that "becomes the real South through the intervention of narrative" (9). Martyn Bone, in *The Postsouthern Sense of Place in Contemporary Fiction* (2005), takes issue with the idea that postsouthern literature rejects any relation to an actual, geographic place, "the

South," and argues that "a historical-geographical materialist approach might help us to recover the relation between postsouthern literature and the socio-spatial reality of the contemporary (post-) South" (45). He does not want to reject outright the concept of "place" in southern literary studies, even though he agrees in some ways with Romine's questioning of a "real South" that literature can represent.

Christopher Lloyd's *Rooting Memory, Rooting Place* (2015) makes this idea of a return to a real, physical, geographic South more of a central focus, and he takes issue with Kreyling, Romine, Bone, and "the postsouthern—and the interlocking discourses of the Global South and new southern studies" (2). "The South," he claims, "is more than the reproduced and reproducible articulation of it" (9). Bone, in a review of Lloyd's book, problematizes Lloyd's contention that new southern studies rejects a "real" South in favor of a postmodern, textual South: "He too often assumes that to take the transnational turn is (as with the postsouthern turn) to displace the regional" (543). While Lloyd does not take issue with the impetus to use postsouthern as a means to "talk about the region in nonexceptional, nontotalizing terms" (1), he seeks to use the idea of cultural memory as way to root "the South" to specific locations. He cites Thadious Davis's claim that "attention to the local . . . does not preclude today's dynamic global world," and he argues that "rooting and engaging the local must not be displaced from critical study, then, even while we explore transnational forces" (13).

In this essay, I want to suggest that a focus on alcohol provides a unique way both to root southern literature to a specific time and place, as well as to see a more global South. I will examine two novels set in Florida by authors originally from outside the South but living in Florida, both dealing with poor, rural white workers who turn to illegal alcohol in order to make ends meet during the Great Depression: Marjorie Kinnan Rawlings's *South Moon Under* (1933), a tale of Florida "crackers" in North Central Florida, near Rawlings's adopted home of Cross Creek; and Ernest Hemingway's *To Have and Have Not* (1937), the story of "conchs" in South Florida, in and around Hemingway's adopted home of Key West.

In examining the strikingly similar works of one author typically categorized as regional and southern and another more often labeled national and global, I hope to add to this critical conversation and, in particular, to suggest that rootedness in place is an important concept for assessing both novels and their versions of the South. While a "sense of place" has a long and notoriously vague role in defining southernness and southern literature, I want to define place more ecocritically in my usage by building off of Lloyd's titular phrase "rooting place." That is, "rooted" in this sense means that the characters of a work are situated in specific natural environments—landscape, flora, fauna, and ecosystems—and also in a particular socioeconomic and materialist milieu to which bootlegging responds.

Alcohol in these two novels is uniquely positioned as a material good to root Rawlings's characters to a specific southern geography while also illuminating a more global South being depicted in the international routes of Hemingway's novel. Alcohol plays such an integral role in the novels' conceptions of place because it is locally manufactured from materials in the surrounding environment; because it is consumed locally by family and friends but also is sold as a commodity in the wider marketplace, which connects the local to the global; and because it is illegal: homemade corn liquor in Rawlings's novel and smuggled rum in Hemingway's. This illegality is especially significant because it helps define each novel's setting as regional and southern. Because both forms of alcohol are illegal, they bring federal law enforcement into an adversarial role in both novels, thereby helping to define a regional identity for the South in opposition to an "outside" nation that acts to control and regulate alcohol in ways that threaten the livelihoods of people already on the brink of financial ruin. It is alcohol that, in a fundamental way, creates the notion of the South in these two novels, since the region is only defined in opposition to its binary term, "nation," an entity that is only actuated in the texts as an interfering, regulatory body for illegal alcohol.

Despite her identity as a writer being defined by her relationship to the South and to Florida, Rawlings was not a native of the state. She was born and raised in Washington, DC, before attending college at the University of Wisconsin and then moving to Rochester, New York. When she and her husband bought an orange grove and moved to Cross Creek, Florida, to run it, in 1928, Rawlings found subject matter for her fiction in the people and places surrounding her new home. Her novels and short stories about the "crackers" among whom she lived featured poor, rural southerners making a living through their relationships with a diverse and demanding natural environment. The Jacklin family of *South Moon Under* lives in the Florida scrub country, a distinctive, desertlike ecosystem of sandy soil, shrubs, and small trees found on coastal and inland ridges throughout Florida, especially around Rawlings's adopted home of Cross Creek and the Ocala National Forest.

Hemingway also moved to Florida in 1928, purchasing a house in Key West with financial assistance from Gus Pfeiffer, the uncle of his wife, Pauline (Baker 221). In many ways, both authors moved to the Sunshine State for a similar reason: to find solitude in nature that would allow them to focus on their writing. While Hemingway traveled away from Florida more than Rawlings did, much of this traveling kept him in the South, on extended boat trips around the Keys and frequent car trips to the Pfeiffer home in Piggott, Arkansas. Hemingway and Rawlings moved to Florida in the same year, but prior to the publication of their respective novels (in 1933 and in 1937), Hemingway had actually lived there nearly twice as long as the woman who would come to be synonymous with regionalism and with Florida literature.[1]

Hemingway spent long chunks of time in Bimini during 1935 and 1936, while working on *To Have and Have Not* (Baker 270–80), and we might also consider this location another of his southern haunts. Bimini is the westernmost district of the Bahamas and lies just about fifty miles east of Miami—much closer than Key West (or Cross Creek, for that matter). In June 1936, Rawlings and Hemingway, two Scribner's authors who worked with Max Perkins, met on the yacht of Rawlings's friend and host, Mrs. Oliver Grinnell, in Bimini (Silverthorne 115–17; Baker 286–90). Rawlings expressed an interest in returning to live in Bimini and to set a novel there, sensing a significant similarity between the island and her adopted home in the Florida scrub country: "Bimini caught at my throat the way the scrub does" (Tarr 246).

Both writers were attuned to place in a southern setting and experienced the Global South through Florida's international neighbors, while they similarly peopled their southern settings with characters based on local residents. Baker (among others) enumerates many real-life equivalents for Hemingway's characters in *To Have and Have Not* and suggests that "he also made good use of the Key West terrain, familiar now as the back of his hand after eight years of residence" (294). Rawlings would persuade locals to take her fishing, hunting, and trapping, and in a letter to Perkins she even describes her successful efforts to visit moonshine stills in her quest for accuracy in *South Moon Under*. Her fiction depicts a society and culture similar to those in which she lived, where neighbors work together for mutual benefit in times of deprivation and crisis.[2]

Although the two writers attempt to capture realistically the culture and places of their adopted homes, they also construct their settings quite differently. In contrast to Hemingway, Rawlings portrays characters with myriad roots to a specific southern location. Here, I am drawing on two meanings of "roots" in order to suggest a network of ecological, economic, and cultural ties between the land and its inhabitants, as well as a sense of familial roots that solidifies families' connections to a small geographic area through generations.

One of the most important of these material ties to place is the illegal moonshine that comes from a combination of natural and human-made elements: water, corn, sugar, fire, the homemade still, and so on. Rawlings's protagonist, Lantry Jacklin (usually called Lant), is successful at producing moonshine not only because of the quality natural ingredients on hand but also because he has access to the shared cultural memory of neighbors and relatives who instruct him in making, hiding, and selling his illegal product. Hemingway's Harry Morgan has no such extended kinship network, nor does he have any role in the production of the alcohol. His role is that of glorified delivery boy, an interaction that makes him merely a hired hand in a vast international economic enterprise. Not coincidentally, the natural world and settings of *To Have and Have Not* are much less specifically rendered, and the characters lack significant roots in their environments and communities.

In both novels, it is economic necessity that drives the characters to illegal alcohol. Often characterized as Hemingway's "proletarian novel," *To Have and Have Not* is an overt display of class consciousness focused on the divide between the exploitative idle rich and the disposable, hardworking poor of Key West and Havana. The opening paragraph of the novel depicts the deserted streets of Havana, zooming in on the Pearl of San Francisco Café, where Harry colludes with Spanish-speaking Cubans to smuggle Chinese men to the United States, suggesting continuities among locations in the Global South, such as disposable migrants who are valued only monetarily and the ways in which financial pressures on the poor can lead to ethical quandaries. Self-interest, mistrust, and competition, rather than a sense of community, pervade the novel, and when Harry loses money on a fishing trip, his only option to support his family is to smuggle either alcohol or men: "I was damned if I was going home broke" (28).

During this fishing trip, with Mr. Johnson, Harry is presented as more masculine than his wealthier client, established by Johnson's inability to land a marlin after refusing to follow Harry's advice. Harry displays the ability to read nature as he searches for marlin: "Those big flying fish are the best sign there is. As far you could see, there was that faded yellow gulfweed in small patches that means the main stream is well in and there were birds ahead working over a little school of tuna" (12). A tenuous solidarity exists among the working class, as well, early in the novel, as we see a fellow boat owner help steer Harry to possible work. Harry's assistant on the boat, Eddy, suggests that those from Key West are also united: "Us Conchs ought to stick together when we're in trouble" (43). Although they are in Cuba, Eddy does not suggest solidarity based on nationality but rather on a regional sense of identity that is defined by opposition to a larger (national) group.

The return to a Florida home after a failed attempt at human trafficking is presented as a respite from the chaos, violence, and immorality of the wider world, though the lack of description of the physical environment of Florida is notable for its contrast with Rawlings's work:

> Then we came to the edge of the stream and the water quit being blue and was light and greenish and inside I could see the stakes on the Eastern and the Western Dry Rocks and the wireless masts at Key West and the La Concha hotel up high out of all the low houses and plenty of smoke from out where they're burning garbage. Sand Key light was plenty close now and you could see the boathouse and the little dock alongside the light and I knew we were only forty minutes away now and I felt good to be getting back. (63)

Most of Hemingway's description of this return to the Keys is of human-made aspects of the environment, with the natural elements serving principally as landmarks, as navigational keys to the position of the boat, as opposed to having value or significance in their own right. Harry is happy to be returning home to his family, but the natural environment is rendered unimportant to the sense of home or place. Although early in the novel Hemingway shows Harry to be in tune with the natural environment when fishing, as the narrative progresses, the primary depictions of nature are of the ocean as a transition space between the home of the Keys and the economic world of Cuba. Nature, then, becomes an obstacle, something to be navigated and overcome in the pursuit of economic stability or in the quest to return home.

On a subsequent trip, when Harry and his assistant, Wesley, have both been shot while smuggling liquor to the United States, the notion of the southern landscape as protective space briefly returns. They hastily dump their illegal contraband in the water at the edge of a mangrove forest, using the protective trees as cover. Nonetheless, they are quickly spotted by a passing charter boat that happens to be carrying a federal government official, Frederick Harrison (modeled after the real-life Julius Stone, a regional director of the New Deal–era Federal Emergency Relief Administration), who wants to arrest Harry for the obvious bootlegging (Waitley 272). Only the protective intervention of a fellow conch who is piloting Harrison's boat, Captain Willie, protects Harry from prosecution.

In Rawlings's novel, the natural landscape itself is what protects the moonshiner from federal agents. Lant takes over his Uncle Zeke's still and hides it in "the swampy heart" of an island "a half-mile of tortuous travelling from the river" (217). Like Harry, Lant knows that illegal alcohol is the only financial tool he has to remain in his Florida home and support his family, and he uses his knowledge of his home territory to his advantage to outwit outsider government revenue agents, who lack the local knowledge to find the location of his still in the wilderness: "There were a dozen blind leads and only one true entrance. Time and again the water was so shallow, or ran over so obstinate an obstruction, that anyone would have turned back, refusing to believe there was an opening and an end" (218). Here, nature is an obstacle only to the revenuers, not to the locals. Knowing well the terrain and geography of this specific region is imperative to success as a bootlegger, and it is the alcohol that provides the impetus for learning the waterways, in the same way that hunting for food engenders deep knowledge of the wilderness of the hammock that surrounds their home.

This intimate knowledge of the landscape affords protection while also suggesting a kinship with the natural world. The forbidding and inhospitable environment of the scrub means that most people live on the other side of the Saint Johns River, but families like the Jacklins prefer the isolation and are able to survive by hunting, fishing, trapping, logging, subsistence farming, and moonshining. All of these activities are vital to the family economy in the midst of the Depression, and the residents of the scrub experience a bond with the natural world through these activities. Rawlings makes a point, for instance, of describing the methods of logging used by timber companies in language that asserts a relationship of masculine domination of a feminine landscape: "The noise of the timber outfit hummed in Lant's ears. He heard the shouts of men above distant axes and cross-cut saws. . . . The great cypress began to fall. Three hundred feet away he saw a trembling in the dark canopy that was the tree-tops over the swamp. There came a ripping, as woody cells, inseparable for a century, were torn violently one from another" (62–63).

Lant vows from this moment never to work for these companies, and when, as an adult, he turns to logging to make money, he raises the immense cypress logs discarded at the bottom of the river by the lumber companies, converting the waste products of the loggers into a marketable commodity with a method that suggests working *with* nature rather than exploiting it. This is similar to the use of "cane-skimmins," a waste product of cane syrup processing, to make moonshine (25).

Moonshining is presented in the novel as similar to hunting, trapping, and farming, as simply another way of living off the land and connecting humans to the local terrain and species. In his history of southern moonshine and its connections to NASCAR racing, *Driving with the Devil*, Neal Thompson says that "in the minds of many southern farmers, moonshining was just an extension of agriculture, and bootlegging no more than delivering a farm product to market" (61). Thompson also explains that corn liquor was very much a regional product, traditionally favored in the South, where it was made in home stills. Thomas Jefferson and George Washington had stills in their Virginia homes (55–56), and during the 1930s, Dawsonville, Georgia, was "the moonshining capital of the world" (51).

While critics in southern studies have rightly disposed of the Agrarians as arbiters of southernness, Rawlings published her novel just three years after the seminal *I'll Take My Stand* (1930), and her work dramatizes Andrew Lytle's call in "The Hind Tit," an essay in that collection, for "a return to a society where agriculture is practiced by most people" (203). The denizens of Rawlings's scrub country certainly fill the bill, and their moonshining is not only an extension of their agriculture but also an example of Lytle's appeal for a renewal of home manufacturing: "Any man who grows his own food, kills his own meat, takes wool from his lambs and cotton from his stalks and makes them into clothes, plants corn and hay for his stock, shoes them at the crossroads blacksmith shop, draws milk and butter from his cows, eggs from his pullets, water from the ground, and fuel from the woodlot, can live in an industrial world without a great deal of cash. Let him diversify, but diversify so that he may live rather than that he may grow rich" (244).

In *South Moon Under,* making their own liquor is part of what allows people to stay in their protected haven, remaining self-sufficient and free from the "industrial" world outside the scrub. Harry Morgan, too, just wants to make money and steer clear of the political disputes of the "outside" world. However, instead of manufacturing the alcohol at home, Harry is more of a cog in a machine, a disposable worker in an international trade network, who merely transports the rum, a spirit that Thompson says "had long been the preferred drink" in the North of the United States (56).

Rawlings's moonshiners are certainly more rooted to their home and to a specific place than are Hemingway's rumrunners. However, as the similarities to Lytle suggest, Rawlings's solutions to the financial pressures her characters face could be categorized as regressive, backward looking, even escapist in their intimations of a self-sufficient pastoral world free from the enervating and corrupting forces of capitalist America and the global marketplace. The seemingly isolated world of the scrub is repeatedly breached in the novel by "outside" forces of modernity, commerce, and technology, which are treated by Rawlings and her characters as unwelcome invasions. While the novel's happy ending suggests that freedom from this outside world is possible within the wilderness of the scrub, the rest of the novel shows that this separation is never that sharp.

Hemingway's novel offers a more sobering perspective of a southern enclave as part of the Global South and the world marketplace, as it shows Harry at the mercy of these "outside" forces, including corrupt government officials, anti-government Cuban revolutionaries, and human traffickers. His home is not a refuge, and the possibility of escape is never realistic. Harry, like his illegal alcohol, is only a commodity to be bought, sold, or, if necessary, dumped overboard in service of profit. Hemingway's depiction of an exploited laborer who must cross international borders illegally while battling government hypocrisy and corruption on both sides of the border anticipates the Global South of contemporary society and literature,[3] in contrast to Rawlings's backward glance. The role of water is illustrative of this difference between the novels. In *South Moon Under,* the water from local waterways is used to make the alcohol, then serves as a conduit for transporting it, while in *To Have and Have Not,* water is only the conduit that links the South to the wider world.

For Rawlings, the river is a border that can divide and unite simultaneously, providing an important conduit for those in the scrub to bring their goods to market. As Lant travels on this fluid, living boundary, history and culture seem to disappear, and his subjective identity fuses with the natural environment: "The river flowed interminably but as though without advance. The boy thought that he had been always in this still, liquid place. There was no change. There was no memory and no imagining. The young male restlessness that had begun to stir along his bones was quiet. If Piety and Cleve and Kezzy were really persons, instead of names, they lay drowned behind him. Nothing existed but the brown, clear water, flowing in one spot forever" (164).

Differences and boundaries are erased in water that is both brown and clear, always flowing but never advancing, blurring the line between the cultural and the natural. The reference to Lant's "young male restlessness" suggests that the distinction between masculine and feminine is similarly swallowed up, as even the fundamental split between humanity and nature is fused: "The river flowed, a dream between dreams, and they were all one, the boy and the river and the banks" (165).

Hemingway's novel also uses water as a boundary that both divides and connects, as Harry must navigate the waters of the Gulf of Mexico on his fishing trips and his smuggling runs between Key West and Cuba. The economic importance of the water is even more pronounced in *To Have and Have Not* than in *South Moon Under,* since the Morgan family's economic survival depends on Harry's ability to extract fish from the ocean for his tourist clients and to traverse its dangerous waters successfully as a smuggler. However, Rawlings's language of immersion and synthesis is countered by Hemingway's more adversarial descriptions of the human/nature relationship. During the fishing trip with Johnson, for instance, Harry uses language of domination and violence as he barks commands and narrates the hunt: "'Sock him!' I told him. 'Stick it into him. Hit him half a dozen times.' He hit him pretty hard a couple of times more, and then the rod bent double and the reel commenced to screech and out he came, boom, in a long straight jump, shining silver in the sun and making a splash like throwing a horse off a cliff" (Hemingway 16).

There is surprisingly little description of nature in the novel, considering that Harry spends most of the story in his boat, and when there is, the ocean is often depicted as a foe to be defeated in the pursuit of profit. This lack of connection to the natural environment is due, I argue, to the way alcohol functions here, compared to *South Moon Under.* In Hemingway's novel, rum-running is a substitute for Harry's more traditional, immediate interaction with nature and place: fishing. Thus, transporting alcohol is more akin to the practice of logging in *South Moon Under,* a purely profit-driven, even mercenary enterprise, likened by the novel to human trafficking. Lant does kill animals as a hunter and trapper, but he also plants crops and reuses natural resources, acting more as a member of a biotic community than a tourist trophy hunter, while Harry, at best, fails to steward environmental resources of his home and, at worst, destroys and exploits the natural world for short-term profit.

Rawlings's language of interdependence with nature breaks down traditional gender norms, while Hemingway presents a stereotypically masculine relationship of dominance over the natural world. As I have argued elsewhere,[4] Rawlings challenges conventional notions of both femininity and masculinity in her novel through her rendering of place and the natural environment. She depicts female characters who engage in physical labor alongside men and rejects a confining version of domesticity as the heroines of her work. When Lant has to choose between Kezzy, a more "natural" girl from the scrub, and Ardis, identified with the "artificial" world of stores, game wardens, and government revenuers, he finds Ardis unpalatable as a mate: "She was something he had bolted whole in his hunger and had spewed up" (282).

Lant engages in all of the traditional masculine activities of the men of the scrub country, but he is also nontraditionally masculine in his sensitivity, his shyness, his bonding with nature, and his cooking of moonshine. While a moonshine still is certainly a masculine preserve, Rawlings presents Lant's moonshining as a version of cooking, in an outdoor kitchen with a roof of thatched palm fronds (practically the only scenes of cooking in the novel). As Lant perfects his recipe, he feels a deep connection with the natural environment around him: "He liked the blue flame of the burning ash in the black of night, and the orange glow on the sweet-gum leaves. Here he liked the intimacy with the hammock. Its life washed over him and he became a part of it. . . . He and the scrub were one" (224). While he profits from his still, the activity of cooking itself is presented as communing with nature, along the same lines as hunting, rafting, and his version of logging, working with nature rather than exploiting it—a softer, kinder version of masculinity, which helps him head off in a rowboat with Kezzy to a happy ending.

Harry Morgan, on the other hand, rarely communes with nature. Instead, he fights a doomed battle to overcome it, as well as vast cultural and economic forces, in his attempt to fulfill his masculine role of breadwinner. His wife, Marie, is almost exclusively shown in the domestic space of their home in Key

West, where she is often pictured waiting anxiously for Harry to return safely and fretting about how the family will survive financially. He displays the conventional masculinity associated with all of Hemingway's code heroes: stoically enduring pain, doing physical battle with his enemies, and displaying his virility with women. Harry loses an arm in a gunfight but demonstrates that this symbolic castration will not weaken his potency: "You've got two arms and you've got two of something else. And a man's still a man with one arm or with one of those. . . . I got those other two still" (97). At moments like these, Hemingway seems to go out of his way to exaggerate Harry's masculinity and to refuse to "feminize" him in the way the Rawlings does with Lant.

Harry's individualism gets him nowhere. Masculine combativeness and competition defines his relationship to the natural world and the global marketplace. Rawlings presents a model of interdependence as an antidote to the financial pressures on the rural poor during the Depression. Alcohol provides two versions of the South in these novels. One is a more traditional notion, in which characters are rooted to place through economic and social activities that engender deep knowledge of the landscape. When viewed ecocritically, Rawlings's characters' ties to their home space are even progressive in terms of gender, though arguably escapist in their pastoral vision of eschewing society to live off the land.

The second version is a more postmodern, postsouthern notion of the South not as different or exceptional but as one node in a global network. Connections here, not only to place but among people, are tenuous. Hemingway's South is not one defined by ties to land or agriculture. It is more nebulous and free floating, and "place" is defined not by biological and ecological systems but by economic relationships to other places. It is a South that does the grunt work of the global economy while the larger nation aids and abets the exploitation.[5] Perhaps in this sense Hemingway's South is ahead of its time in its placelessness, its rootlessness, revealing troubling connections between the Great Depression and contemporary America.

In a way, alcohol functions as the lifeblood, the élan vital, of the community in the two novels. Follow the circulation of the alcohol and you can assess the health of the community. Rawlings presents a healthy community in the remote scrub region, able to balance its economic needs through limited trading of goods outside the community while primarily relying on an interdependent network of family and close neighbors for survival and prosperity, an optimistic portrayal that can be critiqued as backward looking and escapist. Alcohol is a homegrown product that can lubricate kinship networks as well as the wheels of global capitalism. Rawlings's version of the South is built through characters whose connections to place are more developed and more fully realized, as are those places themselves. Hemingway's thinly sketched southern environment seems less realistic, less detailed, less important—more of just an idea.

However, I would suggest that a South rooted in a realistic environment is not so different from a South based on an idea, as the critical disputes might suggest. An "authentic" connection can easily become untethered from an actual, specific place and become a simulacrum when narrative intervenes. One can imagine, for instance, the moonshine of *South Moon Under* becoming, in the twenty-first century, an artisanal craft liquor, with its handcrafted, small-batch qualities fetishized the point that its southernness becomes a postsouthern, nearly empty signifier of marketing terms: "down-home," "backwoods," "genuine."

Hemingway's novel, then, might be thought of as always already postsouthern, without any attempt to represent a "real" South but instead showing a rootless place of unbridled corruption, crime, and capitalism. When we follow the booze in *To Have and Have Not,* we find it ultimately on the megayachts of the rich, who are drinking to forget their problems of infidelity, impotence, closeted desires, and loneliness in the novel's closing chapters. Alcohol is another dead end, as opposed to a financial boon. Harry's death is unnoticed by the rich and by almost everyone else, indicating his inconsequence in the Global South. Humans are reduced to commodities, places to shipping routes, and communities to isolated individuals, as Harry's final words make clear: "A man alone ain't got no bloody fucking chance" (225).

Notes

1. *The Marjorie Kinnan Rawlings Journal of Florida Literature,* published by the University of Central Florida, makes Rawlings the avatar for all Florida literature.

2. In her autobiography, *Cross Creek* (1942), the similarities between Rawlings's real-life experiences and her fiction abound, especially in terms of local people who value their privacy and self-sufficiency yet often trade, barter, and work on one another's properties in a cooperative manner.

3. Cynthia Shearer's *Celestial Jukebox* (2005), for example, depicts emigrants from China and Mauritania in the Mississippi Delta; Monique Truong's *Bitter in the Mouth* (2010) and Robert Olen Butler's *A Good Scent from a Strange Mountain* (1992) examine the experiences of Vietnamese emi-

grants living in North Carolina and Louisiana, respectively; Tennessee native Madison Smartt Bell explores the Haitian Revolution in a trilogy of novels; and Cuban-born novelist Cristina Garcia connects Cuba and Florida in works like *Dreaming in Cuban* (1992), *The Aguero Sisters* (1997), and *King of Cuba* (2013).

4. See Rieger, *Clear-Cutting Eden,* chapter 2; and "Don't Fence Me In."

5. In 1935, Ernest Hemingway published an essay in the *New Masses* titled "Who Killed the Vets?," in which he blames the federal government for failing to evacuate World War I veterans working on a road project in Key West in advance of a hurricane. More than four hundred vets died, and fictional versions of the vets appear briefly in scenes in Freddy's Bar in *To Have and Have Not* (Baker 279–80).

Works Cited

Baker, Carlos. *Ernest Hemingway: A Life Story.* Charles Scribner's Sons, 1969.

Bone, Martyn. *The Postsouthern Sense of Place in Contemporary Fiction.* Louisiana State UP, 2005.

———. "Review of *Rooting Memory, Rooting Place: Regionalism in the Twenty-First-Century American South,* by Christopher Lloyd." *MFS Modern Fiction Studies,* vol. 62, no. 3 (Fall 2016), pp. 542–44.

Hemingway, Ernest. *To Have and Have Not.* 1937. Scribner, 2003.

Kreyling, Michael. *Inventing Southern Literature.* UP of Mississippi, 1998.

———. *The South That Wasn't There.* Louisiana State UP, 2010.

Lloyd, Christopher. *Rooting Memory, Rooting Place: Regionalism in the Twenty-First-Century American South.* Palgrave Macmillan, 2015.

Lytle, Andrew. "The Hind Tit." *I'll Take My Stand: The South and the Agrarian Tradition,* by Twelve Southerners. 1930. Louisiana State UP, 1977, pp. 201–26.

Rawlings, Marjorie Kinnan. *South Moon Under.* Charles Scribner's Sons, 1933.

Rieger, Christopher. *Clear-Cutting Eden: Ecology and the Pastoral in Southern Literature.* U of Alabama P, 2009.

———. "Don't Fence Me In: Nature and Gender in Marjorie Kinnan Rawlings's *South Moon Under.*" *Mississippi Quarterly,* vol. 57, no. 2 (Spring 2004), pp. 199–214.

Romine, Scott. *The Real South: Southern Narrative in the Age of Cultural Reproduction.* Louisiana State UP, 2008.

Silverthorne, Elizabeth. *Marjorie Kinnan Rawlings: Sojourner at Cross Creek.* Overlook, 1988.

Tarr, Rodger L., editor. *Max and Marjorie: The Correspondence between Maxwell E. Perkins and Marjorie Kinnan Rawlings.* UP of Florida, 1999.

Thompson, Neal. *Driving with the Devil: Southern Moonshine, Detroit Wheels, and the Birth of NASCAR.* Crown, 2006.

Waitley, Douglas. *Florida History from the Highways.* Pineapple Press, 2005.

Granny Fees for Apple Pie

Gender and the Settler South in Moonshine Cinema

JEROD RA'DEL HOLLYFIELD

This essay traces how the evolution of female roles in moonshine films and television over the past half century results from the failure of male moonshiner icons to adequately contend with the social and economic problems facing contemporary Appalachia in a settler colonial context. Focusing on John Frankenheimer's *I Walk the Line* (1970), Burt Reynolds's *Gator* (1976), and the second season of Graham Yost's cable series *Justified* (2010–2015), I examine how female characters have shifted from being pawns of male-dominated organizations to becoming savvy, independent partners and then figures of resistance against the transnational corporations attempting to exploit the region. Through this evolution, such female characters are able to transcend the renegade status of their male counterparts and to engage with both the paternalistic attitudes that have marginalized Appalachia and the "good ol' boy" traits of southern culture that lead to a sense of dual oppression for southern women. The women in these works position the region as colonized by global economic forces and domestic prejudices while they interrogate the multiple facets of the South's history responsible for the enduring popularity of the iconoclastic male moonshiner persona.

Moonshine to "Newshine": A Global Overview

When bootlegger Marvin "Popcorn" Sutton committed suicide, in 2009, to avoid transfer to a Georgia federal prison, he cemented his status as a moonshine icon. Already infamous for his perennially best-selling book *Me and My Likker* (1999) and a series of underground documentaries, Sutton became a catalyst for the tourism industries of East Tennessee and Western North Carolina. In 2010, Sutton's moonshine went legitimate when Hank Williams Jr. partnered with alcohol distributor J&M Concepts to market Popcorn Sutton's Tennessee White Whiskey, which was sold across the United States but distilled in Sutton's hometown of Cocke County, Tennessee (Cooper 2010).[1]

Sutton's niche industry and iconic status conform to what Scott Romine deems to be indicative of a South in which cultural production hinges on "an opposition between the real and the fake" that provides identity to a region marked by poverty and exploitation (17). Over the past decade, perhaps no form of cultural production has been more integral to Appalachia than renewed interest in and legitimization of moonshining. Four months after Sutton's suicide, Tennessee legalized whiskey distilleries throughout the state to spur job creation, expanding the industry and allowing entrepreneurs in East Tennessee's Appalachian counties to invest in moonshine production as long as they had a $500,000 tax bond and license (Yeldell). As a result, legal moonshine expanded rapidly, with distillers such as Ole Smoky Distillery, Short Mountain Distillery, and Sugarlands Distilling Company joining the ranks of Sutton and Piedmont Distillers in Madison, North Carolina—makers of Junior's Midnight Moon, the official moonshine of liquor runner turned NASCAR pioneer, Junior Johnson.

Such attention to the region's legacy as the most infamous distilling hub in the United States also dovetails with its recent shift to tourism, an industry that has grown in Appalachia at twice the rate of the United States' gross national product but has continued to lag behind the rest of the nation in the income it generates (Drake 199). Discussing the increased tourist activity in Sutton's hometown over the past half decade, Emelie K. Peine and Kai A. Schafft place its emphasis on moonshining within the greater context of Appalachia: "Cocke County happens to be surrounded by tourist towns, and the marketing of the 'hillbilly' image is explicit. Tourists come to the area for several reasons, including outlet malls, Dollywood, and the Great Smoky Mountains National Park, but they also come because of nostalgia. They want to see and experience what they have been led to believe is a disappearing way of life, and this includes moonshining" (103–4). Despite this heritage tourism's reliance on timeless nostalgia, its widespread adoption in smaller Appalachian communities is primarily an attempt to transition a flagging economy away from dormant industries such as coal and toward participation in global capital markets.

This "newshine" boom began a resurgence of moonshine in popular culture. Max Watman published his book *Chasing the White Dog*, in 2010, as the Discovery Channel announced plans for its reality show *Moonshiners* (beginning in

2011). As *Moonshiners* neared its one hundredth episode in 2016, WGN America premiered *Outsiders* (2016–2017), a scripted series following the Farrell family in the hills of Kentucky. In contrast to the hillbilly vogue of the 1960s, which saw Appalachian representations dominating the airwaves, from Mountain Dew advertising campaigns to the runaway success of *The Beverly Hillbillies* (1962–1971), this recent fascination with moonshine culture is not simply a response to Appalachia's construction as a "problem region" in the mid-twentieth-century public consciousness, stemming from War on Poverty rhetoric and the founding of the Appalachian Regional Commission in 1965 (Harkins 202). Rather, it is an example of what Deborah E. Barker and Kathryn McKee refer to as the southern imaginary: "The result has been a critical recognition of the U.S. South as fully implicated in the process of national self-creation. That southerners themselves have been active participants in alternately rejecting and embracing, and continually reinventing, understandings of themselves likewise complicates any effort to offer a fixed summary of what it means to claim a southern identity today" (3).

Despite the enduring popularity of shows like *The Beverly Hillbillies* in Appalachia, this new iteration of moonshine popular culture provides not only an increased agency of actual southerners involved in the industry and artistry of the distilling process but also a tendency toward global dissemination of its iconography. As the international popularity of *Moonshiners* grew, its breakout star, Tim Smith, went legitimate and began manufacturing Climax Moonshine, a product with such high demand that a 2015 episode of the series revolved around his attempts to produce enough to meet a massive order from Poland. Likewise, Ole Smoky Moonshine developed a partnership with WGN America in 2017, a few months before the cancellation of *Outsiders,* to produce Farrell Shine, a version of the "Farrell Wine" that characters consume on the show, which continues to be available "in a unique, commemorative mason jar" ("Ole Smoky").

Given that the show is produced by Japan-based Sony Entertainment, the international circulation of both the series' images and its "made in Appalachia" tie-ins position it as directly applicable to contemporary debates about globalization and neocolonial politics. Although moonshining may appear to be removed from international popular culture and geographically bound to the Appalachian hills, it is indicative of, in the words of James L. Peacock, a "grounded globalism" that "speaks not just of merging local and global, but of grounding, building a groundwork in which global meanings and issues enter our life worlds" (42).

In locating representations of moonshining within the realm of globalization, it is helpful to apply postcolonial theory to the Appalachian region and to understand bootlegging not as an isolated cultural activity but as a method of resistance to hegemonic forces. Such an approach differs from moves in U.S. southern studies that offer postcolonial critiques of the plantation economy, such as Jon Smith and Deborah Cohn's landmark collection *Look Away!*.[2] Given that the invasion of Ireland in the late sixteenth century was Britain's first attempt at large-scale colonization, for instance, the Irish heritage of Appalachia becomes even more relevant to a postcolonial reading of the region in which the urban centers of New England and Washington, DC, exploit the area's resources and culture while relegating its inhabitants to the status of irredeemable Others in need of uplift, who are bound to hopeless poverty and caricatured by Hollywood and Madison Avenue as shoeless yokels (Wood 79).

However, while the United States' policies and perceptions situate white Appalachians in an imperial framework, Appalachia's colonial legacy must be distinguished from that of other marginalized groups in the region, including African American migrants and the Native American tribes who originally inhabited the land. In the aftermath of Donald Trump's election and the runaway success of J. D. Vance's 2016 memoir *Hillbilly Elegy*, historians such as Elizabeth Catte have revisited the positioning of the region as an internal colony, a pioneering characterization first made famous in the 1978 book *Colonialism in Modern America: The Appalachian Case* (Lewis et al.), which, as Catte indicates, also excuses Appalachians from the region's own role in structural racism and oppression (121).

Yet, while locating Appalachia seamlessly into a colonized/colonizer dichotomy elides white Appalachians' relationships to African Americans and displaced native populations, discussing the region within the context of colonial settler identity preserves the potency of the internal colony model while fostering a space for less-represented Appalachians and their oft-neglected history. As Pal Ahluwalia writes, "For the post-colonial white settler subjects, there is a dual burden—not only do they have to recover their own narratives but they must also recognize that they have blocked the narratives of the indigenous populations which they rendered invisible. It is this double inscription of resistance and authority which constitutes the settler subject" (508).

For white Appalachian settlers, moonshining serves as an attempt to assert heritage while resisting U.S. hegemony by evading federal control and preserving tradition. According to Peine and Schafft:

> The relationship of moonshiners to the federal state and the role of that relationship in the construction of the Appalachian ideal can be traced back as far as the *usquebaugh* (spirits distilled from grain) of the Scottish highlands and "colonization" of the Ulster region of Catholic Northern Ireland by Scottish Protestants when whiskey became synonymous with individual freedom and autonomy from the authority of the state. . . . During this "colonization" the English Parliament instituted an excise tax on liquor in order to finance the suppression of the civil war. The black market in liquor that this tax helped to create soon eclipsed the revenue generated for the crown. (96–97)

The original Appalachian moonshiners, who were largely Ulster Scottish, preserved the distilling culture of their homelands while extending its imperial critique to a settler nation that reproduced a similar colonial situation for those outside the dominant Anglo-Saxon Protestant culture (Thompson 76). The result is a transnational resistant force, made even more global when moonshiners modified the original corn recipes, using sugar from Barbados, Haiti, and Jamaica, to create a hybrid postcolonial product that was positioned to engage with other subservient regions bound to the triangular trade with Britain, which served as the foundation of the colonial economy of the United States (xxviii).

Although moonshine has dominated cultural representations of Appalachia for centuries, a curious exclusion of women exists in moonshine narratives. With the exception of the protagonist of Sherwood Anderson's novel *Kit Brandon* (1936), hypermasculine bootleggers such as Sutton, Burt Reynolds's 1970s antiheroes, and Robert Mitchum in *Thunder Road* (1958) have traditionally dominated moonshine culture, despite the fact that women are as involved in tending mash and running liquor as men.[3] Such an absence is all the more peculiar given that nineteenth-century women such as Katherine Sherwood McDowell and Mary Murfree were some of the first and most successful writers to depict Appalachia (Drake 124).[4]

Even when they were not directly involved in the craft, women acted as intermediaries between local moonshiners and federal agents during crackdowns on the region. Ora Harrison, an Episcopal missionary in Endicott, Virginia (the "moonshine capital of the world"), served as the pivotal character witness for the men indicted in the Great Moonshine Conspiracy trial of 1935, despite their early resentment of her and her mission (Thompson 93). While Appalachian women historically assumed roles as caretakers for their children, they also were essential to creating and maintaining with their husbands the networks of small farms and, by extension, the moonshining operations that kept them afloat during lean years (Toplovich 73).

Similar to Oyèrónké Oyêwùmí's hierarchy of colonialism as divided by gender, in which "the creation of 'women' as a category was one of the very first accomplishments of the colonial state" (342), Appalachian females involved on the margins of the moonshine economy provide relevant insight into the gender dynamics of a settler colonial Appalachia. In this postcolonial framework, depictions of women in moonshining culture are at the center of understanding Appalachian identity, their roles fluid but marginalized by remnants of colonialism and globalization.

Over the past forty years, cinematic depictions of bootlegging have begun to focus more on women, as such figures of rugged southern individualism as *Thunder Road*'s Doolin clan and Burt Reynolds's iconic Bandit become less relatable. As a result, the women of Appalachia-set films steeped in moonshine iconography provide a fruitful space for examining the complexities of this unique settler colonial formation.

I Walk the Line, Tarnished Icons, and Female Capital

A nearly forgotten product of the American film renaissance of 1968 to 1975, *I Walk the Line* saw director John Frankenheimer (a representative of the New York School of social realism) tone down the singular action style that made him famous for *The Manchurian Candidate* (1962) and *Seconds* (1966) and move his setting to the hills outside Knoxville, Tennessee.[5] Based on Agrarian writer Madison Jones's 1967 novel *The Exile,* the film follows the small-town Sheriff Tawes (Gregory Peck) as he falls in love with Alma McCain (Tuesday Weld), the daughter of abusive moonshiner Carl McCain (Ralph Meeker), and uses his political clout to protect her family's business from his suspicious deputy, Hunnicutt (Charles Durning), and a federal revenue agent, Bascomb (Lonny Chapman).[6] Although R. Barton Palmer and Murray Pomerance call Frankenheimer

"arguably postwar Hollywood's most politically engaged and astute writer/
director" (1), critics have largely neglected *I Walk the Line*, concentrating much
of their attention on Johnny Cash's eight-song score and the troubled production, which was a critical and commercial failure and saw Peck receive some of
the worst reviews of his career. Yet, while the film lacks the direct political engagement of *The Manchurian Candidate* or Frankenheimer's prison drama *Bird-
man of Alcatraz* (1961), its keen insight into Appalachia's shifting landscape and
its nuanced interrogations of moonshine's economic role in the region serve as
sharp contrasts to the pop-culture representations of hillbillies dominating the
airwaves at the time of its release.

Though Peck's Sheriff Tawes and his midlife crisis occupy most of the narrative arc, the film's emotional and thematic core belong to Alma as she attempts
to forge her own identity in a world of Appalachian men who, at best, objectify
her for personal and economic advancement and, at worst, abuse her physically and sexually. Frankenheimer imbues the narrative with a cohesive incest
subtext through numerous scenes of Carl and his adolescent sons, Clay (Jeff
Dalton) and Buddy (Freddie McCloud), leering at Alma as she lies in bed or in
various states of undress. While the film clearly offers an implicit criticism of
their misogynistic behavior, it also contextualizes their masculine desperation
through its depiction of the dwindling prospects in the unincorporated landscape on the outskirts of the fictional town of Sutton, Tennessee.[7]

Though critics such as Stephen B. Armstrong view Tawes as a springboard
for Frankenheimer's antiauthoritarian satire of the police (147), which was common in films of the era such as Norman Jewison's *In the Heat of The Night* (1967)
and Dennis Hopper's *Easy Rider* (1969), such categorizations overlook the film's
multifaceted depiction of Appalachia and of the toll that the region's systemic
oppression takes on Tawes's stability. Neglecting his wife, Ellen (Estelle Parsons), and their children, Tawes spends most of his patrol time looking out
over the lake forged by the creation of a Tennessee Valley Authority dam, which
flooded his childhood home—an event he succinctly relates to Alma by telling
her, "They took us from it."

In contrast to his signature role as Atticus Finch in *To Kill a Mockingbird*
(1962), Peck constructs Tawes as a man broken by the South and obsessed with
possessing the innocence of youth, rather than as a bastion of wisdom and ethics integral to guiding a young woman through the region's seamier elements.

With the population of his town in decline, Tawes spends much of his time protecting the few remaining families—many of whom are bootleggers—from federal agents. Throughout the film, Tawes writes in a thick ledger that contains the names and addresses of all known moonshiners under his jurisdiction, tearing out a page with information about the McCain family when Bascomb first pays him a visit. As he tells Carl during one of his calls on Alma, "There's a federal man involved now. There's no choice."

Frankenheimer's depiction of the community in Tawes's charge is a direct reflection of the issues facing areas like Sutton at the time of the film's release. The postwar era saw a migration of more than three million Appalachian families from their homelands to major Midwestern cities to escape the crushing unemployment caused by the mechanization of the coal industry. There, they regularly encountered job ads saying "Southerners need not apply" and pejoratives such as "hillbilly" or "SAM"—Southern Appalachian migrant (Harkins 175).

Despite the lingering influence of New Deal programs such as the Tennessee Valley Authority dam that flooded Tawes's home and a host of War on Poverty initiatives, those who stayed in the region were left to turn to illicit trades such as moonshining to, as Thompson writes, keep "people on their own land for a generation or two longer" (xxix). Consequently, local law enforcement and judges often shared in the persistent attitude that federal agents were northern "invaders," not only letting moonshiners off with reduced sentences but also charging revenuers with local crimes, to such an extent that the U.S. Supreme Court eventually mandated changes in venue when a federal agent was charged (Birdwell 212).

Exemplifying such tensions, McCain's moonshine operation in the film appears as a direct response to Appalachia's political context of the late 1960s. Occupying an abandoned, ramshackle farmhouse near the Smoky Mountains, the McCain still is an enormous and professional operation. Yet, despite its size, the family continues to live in poverty, only getting by because of Tawes's love for Alma.

Thus, according to Linda Ruth Williams, Alma serves the function of "both reward and collateral exchanged in an unspoken agreement between criminal and lawman" (158). Williams cites Alma as a prototype for the erotic thrillers featuring teenage "*filles fatale*" that would dominate the 1980s and 1990s. Yet Alma's responsibility to her family's livelihood and her role as a catalyst to curtail Tawes's existential crisis frame her as more a victim of patriarchy and federal policy (158–59).

Frankenheimer structures much of the narrative around scenes of Alma's labor—both domestically and as an intermediary for the moonshine operation. When Tawes first meets Alma, after pulling her and Buddy over for reckless driving, she slinks out of her father's jalopy and sits on the industrial-size sack of sugar in the truck bed, distracting Tawes by not so subtly showing him her legs. The sequence is immediately followed by a scene of her cooking for the family as Carl interrogates her about the interaction. Likewise, the film often juxtaposes scenes of the male characters initiating transactions with her that will further their livelihoods: Carl lingers over her bed, offering to buy her new dresses as compensation for seducing Tawes; Hunnicutt suggests that his connection to the Miss Knoxville pageant could win her an Atlantic City trip in exchange for information that will soil Tawes's reputation and allow Hunnicutt to become sheriff—a scene Frankenheimer blocks and executes as the precursor to a sexual assault.

In perhaps the most potent moment in the film, Tawes kneels in the stairway of the McCain home, begging Alma to go away with him. While Frankenheimer shoots the scene through the bannisters, making Tawes appear as if he is in a prison cell, Alma's reaction is framed with both in the foreground, resulting in a visual motif that highlights Tawes's stasis and Alma's inability to evolve beyond her role as economic asset. As Alma drives away with her family at the film's end, rebuffing Tawes's advances by stabbing him with a scythe, Frankenheimer makes it clear that the move is lateral; her family is migrating to a new town in which more men will exploit her youth and body to preserve some semblance of agency in a region mired in poverty and lacking opportunity.

Gator, Good Ol' Boys, and the Liberated Woman

As one of the ten highest-grossing stars from 1973 to 1984 and the top-grossing movie star from 1978 to 1982, Burt Reynolds used his good ol' boy charm and stunts like his 1972 nude *Cosmopolitan* spread to become a quintessential southern icon (Smith 21).[8] Much of Reynolds's appeal resulted from his ability, in the words of Jacob Smith, to act as a star who "merges the Right and Left Cycle" of American cinema by combining the rebellion and antiauthority spirit of films such as *Bonnie and Clyde* (1967) and *MASH* (1972) with the reinforcement of traditional values implicit in works like *Dirty Harry* (1972) and *Walking Tall* (1973) through self-reflexive play with his persona (23). By the mid-1970s, Reynolds's star power was so strong that he shifted to directing for five films, beginning with *Gator* (1976).[9]

A sequel to Joseph Sargent's *White Lightning* (1973), *Gator* features Reynolds reprising his role as Georgia Appalachian moonshiner Gator McKlusky, who, after taking down the corrupt small-town Georgia sheriff J. C. Connors (Ned Beatty) to avenge the murder of his social activist brother in the first install-ment, is forced by the federal government to go under cover in Florida to ex-pose a crime ring run by his childhood best friend, Bama McCall (Jerry Reed).[10] While the film insinuates that McCall, too, came to prominence through boot-legging, his business has expanded beyond the "granny fees" paid to local law enforcement and into the realms of prostitution and drug running, a common trend in the late 1960s, when the moonshine trade began to wane in the face of marijuana and other drug production (Birdwell 224).

Although Reynolds's persona has resulted in a career fraught with critical scorn—his lauded performances in Alan J. Pakula's *Starting Over* (1979) and Paul Thomas Anderson's *Boogie Nights* (1997) notwithstanding—he depicts the South of *Gator* as a dynamic, diverse, and unique region that does not shy away from introspective critique of its problematic history. Although *Gator* displays an open hostility to the federal agents who force its hero into undercover work by threatening his daughter (Lori Futch), the film also does not endorse the state or local governments, as both are corrupt and embody a small-minded, self-serving South. In the opening sequence, the governor (Mike Douglas) laments his inability to clean up McCall's home base of Dunston County, ranting to his underlings about how he's "eaten so much crow" he will never fulfill his ambi-tions to run for president.[11] As the film cuts to Gator's introduction, a cadre of two dozen police cars creates a roadblock and Reynolds commences a nearly ten-minute boat chase sequence that finally ends in Gator's capture and reluc-tant acquiescence. For Reynolds, only a figure who possesses a moonshiner's renegade spirit while retaining the playful authenticity of a southern gentleman can take down McCall.

However, Gator's successful restoration of order in Dunston County hinges much more on his partnership with local television reporter Aggie Maybank (Lauren Hutton) than on his idealized southern masculinity. Unlike *I Walk the Line*'s Alma, Aggie is an independent career woman, more dedicated to fighting corruption than Gator. Though the two eventually develop a romantic relationship, Gator views Aggie as an equal in a union against McCall, refusing to perceive her as just a romantic double. In their first scene of banter, Aggie tries to convince Gator to talk to the press about the police officers on McCall's payroll, telling him that "he's a lot smarter than he looks" and calling him a "schmuck." She whistles to get Gator's attention as he walks away muttering, "All I'm trying to do is not get killed. All I want to do is stay out of the slammer."

After Aggie, with an impassioned speech, convinces him to help her, Gator takes her arm and cracks a smile, remarking, "Women's lib. I love it," a seemingly dismissive line that their subsequent partnership proves is genuine sentiment. Comfortable with seeing Aggie as an ally who can assume responsibilities that he cannot, Gator embodies the potential of a tolerant, cooperative South that values individual freedom, forming a team that includes Aggie, the northeastern Jewish federal agent Irving Greenfield (Jack Weston), and the female liberal activist turned government whistle-blower Emmeline Cavanaugh (Alice Ghostley) that is eventually successful in exposing corruption and dispatching McCall.

Regardless of the success of their coalition and their clear affection for each other, Gator and Aggie do not end the film in a romantic union. In the wake of her investigative report on the McCall machine's demise, Aggie receives a job offer at a major network in New York City. After Gator speaks his final words to Aggie—"I learned a lot from you"—Reynolds includes a shot reverse shot that shows both crying as they part ways. As an outsider, Aggie retains the upward mobility and opportunity to pursue her career goals, possessing an agency to bring Alma's dreams to fruition. With his moonshiner status and lifelong ties to the region, Gator remains an enlightened good ol' boy driving off in McCall's convertible, presumably back to his still in Appalachian Georgia, a defender of a forward-thinking South but bound by the region's history of poverty and cultural marginalization.

Conclusion: Justifying a Global Moonshine Matriarch

Though *I Walk the Line* and *Gator* present complicated depictions of southern women complicit in moonshine culture, both narratives remain insular, neglecting Appalachia's global ties and moonshine's transnational history. However, the rise of prestige television in the mid-2000s and the reinvigoration of moonshine iconography opened a space for a female moonshiner who represents the global scope of the contemporary South: Mags Bennett, on the FX series *Justified*.[12]

Detailing the return of maverick U.S. Marshall Raylan Givens (Timothy Olyphant) to his hometown of Harlan, Kentucky, the series centers on Raylan's negotiation of his duties to uphold the law and to maintain his family ties. The premiere of the second season introduces Bennett, the matriarch of a clan of boys, including Dickie (Jeremy Davies), Coover (Brad William Henke), and Police Chief Doyle (Joseph Lyle Taylor), who reignites a Prohibition-era blood feud with the Givens family over an accident Raylan caused that left Dickie disabled in high school.

While Bennett assumed the family moonshine operation after her husband's death and shifted to becoming a marijuana grower, general store owner, and community investor, she still makes "apple pie" for residents of Harlan County, using bad runs of liquor as poison for those who oppose her. As she tells Walt McCready (Chris Mulkey) after giving him a lethal dose of apple pie for farming marijuana on her land without permission and for involving authorities after a child molester, James Earl Dean (Billy Miller), who works for her as an enforcer, threatens McCready's daughter, Loretta (Kaitlyn Dever): "Oh, this is the bad part, but it doesn't last long. Mixture's all natural, from up in the hills. All kinds of knowledge up in the hills. Something my grandmama taught me. She learned it from her grandmama."

Though the Harlan of *Justified* is clearly sensationalized, Mags anchors the second season's complex portrait of the region. As is true of the moonshiners under Tawes's jurisdiction in *I Walk the Line*, it is a lack of economic opportunity that has led to the Bennett clan's multigenerational involvement in the bootlegging industry. At the same time, Mags eschews hillbilly stereotypes of the Snuffy Smith variety, proving to be a ruthless and intimidating force in the region, whose quest for monopoly over Harlan's underground economies has allowed her to fill a power vacuum caused by the waning coal industry.

Even her murder of McCready is entrenched with ambivalence. McCready's unforgivable affront was neither squatting on her land nor crossing one of Mags's enforcers to protect Loretta. She makes this clear when she allows Raylan to arrest Dean and tells her victim, in his final moments, that she will raise Loretta as her own daughter: "Don't you think that'll be better for her? Than the way it's been around here with you and your sadness. All the troubles of your hard life, it's all gone now." Instead, for Mags, McCready's murder is inevitable because he went above the local police that she controls through Doyle's position as chief and involved the state and federal authorities that have served as outside threats to Appalachia for generations. Raylan's dual status as the embodiment of federal authority and as the Givens responsible for her resuscitating the family blood feud makes McCready's indiscretion an even greater violation.

Lacking the mobility that allowed Alma and Aggie to uproot their lives for better economic opportunity, Mags remains firmly rooted in the region. As a result, she absorbs the localism and fiercely regional identity typically associated with male moonshiners like Gator and Popcorn Sutton. In Yost's twenty-first-century Appalachia, the conflict between Mags and Raylan does not center on a federal lawman asserting a seemingly colonial authority over Appalachian identity but on the idea that a son of Appalachia would betray his own identity and align himself with federal authorities in Lexington, mimicking a culture that Mags has vowed to preserve by any means necessary only when it is convenient for him.

Justified is a series immersed in local color but challenging pervasive stereotypes of the region. Its premise relies on Raylan's exile to the hometown and culture he spent his career escaping, after a bloody and very public showdown with a Miami drug lord in the series pilot leads to his transfer back home. While Raylan shares the antiauthority spirit customary of the moonshining hillbilly, he opts to fashion his identity as a contemporary cowboy to such an extent that his oversize hat becomes a running gag throughout the series. According to Kylo-Patrick R. Hart, the hat "functions as a recurring visual element of iconography in order to regularly call to mind the series' Western undertones" as well as its genesis as a late-career project for pulp writer Elmore Leonard (292).[13]

As a result, regardless of Raylan's hard masculinity, job effectiveness, and ties to the region, the native Kentuckians on both sides of the law regard him as either a ladder climber who desires to flee to more cosmopolitan areas or, in Mags's case, as a traitor to his people. Such views are typified by an exchange between Raylan and his boss, Art Mullen (Nick Searcy), early in the second season, as they discuss the Bennett clan. Raylan coolly claims, "I know my people," to which Art deadpans, "You're like the hillbilly whisperer. We oughta put you on Oprah," a chiding that calls into question Raylan's grasps at authenticity. As is true of his relationship with childhood friend cum archnemesis, Boyd Crowder (Walton Goggins), which serves as the core of the series' narrative over its six seasons, Raylan's contentious dealings with Mags expose him as a failed performative Appalachian whose goals to return from exile in Harlan can only be achieved by imposing the force of federal law and exterminating the underground economies of a region ravaged by the whims of entities in Washington and beyond.

Despite the series' emphasis on Raylan's exploits, the primary conflict of the second season is a struggle between two women: Mags and Carol Johnson (Rebecca Creskoff), an executive of the global Black Pike conglomerate that wants to secure mineral rights from the town's citizens. Though framed as a "big bad," in television parlance, Mags becomes a resistant force to the season's real villain, the transnational corporation bent on establishing a neocolonial power dynamic in Harlan. Accordingly, Mags personifies Appalachia's oft-neglected history as a region of resistance to corporate and federal control. This is especially important to her hometown of Harlan, which saw the infamous Harlan County War between labor and coal companies during the 1930s and the resurgence of this conflict during the 1970s, most famously depicted in Barbara Kopple's 1976 documentary *Harlan County USA*. As Catte writes of Appalachia, and of Eastern Kentucky in particular, "Rebellious activists didn't transplant radical action against corporate interest to the mountains. That radical action originated here" (102).

With her deep knowledge of the landscape and her familiarity with the discourse of global power, Mags is a fictionalized successor to the female activists integral to fighting for Appalachia, from Eula Hall, founder of the Mud Creek Clinic, who faced arson and violence in her quest to provide health care to struggling Appalachians; to the dedicated miners' wives Kopple features in her documentary; to the iconic Mary G. Harris "Mother" Jones, who was central to the fight for mine unionization in the region (Catte 107–9). As Raylan's investigation closes in on the Bennett clan, Mags initially brokers a deal with Johnson that is both favorable to Harlan's residents and forward-thinking about the region's relationship to the globalized economy. The deal would allow the Bennett family to gain a legitimacy that its bootlegging legacy would never allow, positioning it as a Harlan iteration of the Kennedy dynasty, which could bring sustainable growth to the area. The deal falls through, however, when Crowder reveals that he has bought land out from under Mags and Black Pike, forcing her to fight for the preservation of her family and her monopoly over Harlan's illicit economy. Before personal gain and greed ultimately compromise her intentions and lead her both to sell out the people of Harlan and to commit suicide via the apple pie that has defined her family for generations, Bennett acts as an authentic manifestation of grounded globalism.

Appalachia and its white, working-class hillbilly voters continue to serve as subjects of poverty porn and objects of ridicule in post-2016 America. However, the evolving role of women in depictions of moonshining serves as a counter-narrative that positions the region within the context of settler colonialism and networks of domestic and international marginalization. As the narratives under discussion indicate, even texts that conform to the masculine iconography of moonshine create narrative roles for women that provide depth and insight into Appalachian struggles while illustrating an inchoate series of viable political solutions.

Although Alma remains both victim and commodity in *I Walk the Line,* her resistance to Tawes and her futile grasps at independence serve as prototypes for Aggie's cooperation with Reynolds's "good ol' boy" to confront the toxic and provincial masculinity that dominates Dunston County in *Gator.* Opposing Alma's and Aggie's desire to abandon the region, *Justified*'s Mags Bennett ultimately embodies a twenty-first-century model for moonshining that resists authority, preserves her home, and contends, albeit unsuccessfully, with a globalized economy that is as potentially harmful to contemporary Appalachia as its colonial legacy or the federal policy decisions that continue to haunt the region.

Notes

1. Marvin "Popcorn" Sutton's moonshine was the subject of a trademark infringement lawsuit with Tennessee distiller Jack Daniel's in 2013. See Schreiner.

2. The South's relationship to settler colonialism is also explored in Benson Taylor's *Disturbing Calculations* (2008) and *Reconstructing the Native South* (2012).

3. In field research, I have come across several examples of women involved in the moonshine economy, including a woman in Cosby, Tennessee, who, to protect her livelihood, fled from the police while pregnant. Although I knew that my paternal great-grandparents were the most prominent moonshiners in Letcher County, Kentucky, during the Great Depression, my own grandmother and her sister kept my great-grandmother's role in bootlegging a secret until 2012, when they finally revealed that she was responsible for most of the business and, when caught, refused to take the fall for her boyfriend unless he agreed to marry her.

4. Katherine McDowell's *Dialect Tales* (1883) and Mary Mufree's *In the Tennessee Mountains* (1884) both are touchstone works on Appalachia and include depictions of the moonshine trade.

5. Shooting took place in Tennessee and in Colusa County, California.

6. Charles Durning is also a recurring supporting player in the films Burt Reynolds directed, with roles in *Sharky's Machine* (1981), *Stick* (1985), and *The Final Hit* (2000), as well as in *Starting Over* (1979), the Alan J. Pakula divorce drama that saw Reynolds shave his trademark mustache and receive the critical acclaim that eluded his films set in the South.

7. Although there is no evidence that the town's name is an allusion to Popcorn Sutton, the time of the film's release coincided with his early career as a moonshiner.

8. *Smokey and the Bandit* was the highest-grossing film of 1977 after *Star Wars*.

9. Reynolds's five films as a director are *Gator* (1976), *The End* (1978), *Sharky's Machine* (1981), *Stick* (1985), and *The Final Hit* (2000). He also directed many episodes of his TV shows *B. L. Stryker* and *Evening Shade* (1989–1994) and the TV movies *The Man from Left Field* (1993) and *Hard Time* (1998).

10. Ned Beatty also played the Atlanta canoer raped by hillbillies in John Boorman's *Deliverance* (1972). While *Deliverance* made Reynolds a star, it became infamous for its demonization of hillbillies and, as Anthony Harkins writes, "accentuated the idea of the mountaineers' utter degeneracy" (208). Jerry Reed would become most famous for his role as Reynolds's sidekick Cledus in *Smokey and the Bandit* and for performing its chart-topping theme song, "East Bound and Down."

11. The governor is a clear parody of Jimmy Carter, a figure that James L. Peacock sees as embodying the idea of grounded globalism.

12. The role of Mags Bennett earned Margo Martindale a Primetime Emmy Award for Outstanding Supporting Actress in a Drama Series in 2011.

13. Raylan Givens first appeared in Elmore Leonard's novels *Pronto* (1993) and *Riding the Rap* (1995) before he took on a central role in the short story "Fire in the Hole," from Leonard's 2002 short story collection, *When the Women Come out to Dance*. In the wake of *Justified*'s success, Givens later appeared as the central character in Leonard's 2013 novel, *Raylan*.

Works Cited

Ahluwalia, Pal. "When Does a Settler Become a Native?" *Postcolonialisms: An Anthology of Cultural Theory and Criticism*, edited by Gaurav Desai and Supriya Nair, Rutgers UP, 2005, pp. 500–513.

Armstrong, Stephen. *Pictures about Extremes: The Films of John Frankenheimer*. McFarland, 2008.

Barker, Deborah E., and Kathryn McKee. "Introduction: The Southern Imaginary." *American Cinema and the Southern Imaginary*, edited by Deborah E. Barker and Kathryn McKee, U of Georgia P, 2011, pp. 1–23.

Benson, Melanie R. *Disturbing Calculations: The Economics of Identity in Postcolonial Southern Literature, 1912–2002*. U of Georgia P, 2008.

Benson Taylor, Melanie. *Reconstructing the Native South: American Indian Literature and the Lost Cause*. U of Georgia P, 2011.

Birdwell, Michael E. "'There's a Lot of Nourishment in an Acre of Corn': Upper Cumberland Moonshine." *People of the Upper Cumberland: Achievements and Contradictions*, edited by Michael E. Birdwell and W. Calvin Dickinson, U of Tennessee P, 2015, 203–36.

Catte, Elizabeth. *What You Are Getting Wrong about Appalachia*. Belt, 2018.

Cooper, Peter. "Hank Williams Jr. Helps Continue Popcorn Sutton's Moonshine Legacy." *Tennessean*, 12 November 2010.

Drake, Richard B. *A History of Appalachia*. U of Kentucky P, 2001.

Gator. Directed by Burt Reynolds, MGM, 1976.

Harkins, Anthony. *Hillbilly: A Cultural History of an American Icon*. Oxford UP, 2004.

Hart, Kylo-Patrick R. "The (Law)Man in the Cattleman Hat: Hegemonic Masculinity Redux." *Journal of Men's Studies*, vol. 21, no. 3 (Fall 2013), 291–304.

I Walk the Line. Directed by John Frankenheimer, Columbia, 1970.

Justified: The Complete Second Season. Directed by Graham Yost, Fox, 2011.

Lewis, Helen, Linda Johnson, and Donald Askins, editors. *Colonialism in Modern America: The Appalachian Case*. Appalachian State University, 1978.

"Ole Smoky Distillery & WGN America's Co-Branded Moonshine Is Now Available Online." *PRWeb*, 27 February 2017, prweb.com/releases/2017/02/prweb14087848.htm.

Oyěwùmí, Oyèrónké. "Colonizing Bodies and Minds: Gender and Colonialism." *Postcolonialisms: An Anthology*, edited by Gaurav Desai and Supriya Nair, Rutgers UP, 2005, pp. 339–61.

Palmer, R. Barton, and Murray Pomerance. "Introduction: Why Don't You Pass the Time by Playing a Little Solitaire?" *A Little Solitaire: John Frankenheimer and American Film*, edited by R. Barton Palmer and Murray Pomerance, Rutgers UP, 2011, pp. 1–12.

Peacock, James L. *Grounded Globalism: How the U.S. South Embraces the World*. U of Georgia P, 2011.

Peine, Emelie K., and Kai A. Schafft. "Moonshine, Mountaineers, and Modernity: Distilling Cultural History in the Southern Appalachian Mountains." *Journal of Appalachian Studies*, vol. 18, no. 1 (Spring/Fall 2012), 93–112.

Romine, Scott. *The Real South: Southern Narrative in the Age of Cultural Reproduction*. Louisiana State UP, 2008.

Schreiner, Bruce. "Jack Daniel's in Legal Fight with Small Distiller." Associated Press, 25 October 2013, www.yahoo.com/news/jack-daniels-legal-fight-small-distiller -151734616.html.

Smith, Jacob. "Showing Off: Laughter and Excessive Disclosure in Burt Reynolds' Star Image." *Film Criticism*, vol. 30, no. 1 (Fall 2005): 21–40.

Smith, Jon, and Deborah Cohn, editors. *Look Away!: The U.S. South in New World Studies*. Duke UP, 2004.

Thompson, Charles D., Jr. *Spirits of Just Men: Mountaineers, Liquor Bosses, and Lawmen in the Moonshine Capital of the World*. U of Illinois P, 2011.

Toplovich, Ann. "'A Woman's Work is Never Done': Achievements of Women in the Upper Cumberland." *People of the Upper Cumberland: Achievements and Contradictions,* edited by Michael E. Birdwell and W. Calvin Dickinson, U of Tennessee P, 2015, pp. 53–80.

Vance, J. D. *Hillbilly Elegy: A Memoir of a Family and Culture in Crisis.* HarperCollins, 2016.

Watman, Max. *Chasing the White Dog: An Amateur Outlaw's Adventures in Moonshine.* Simon and Schuster, 2010.

Williams, Linda Ruth. "Walking the Line with the *Fille Fatale.*" *A Little Solitaire: John Frankenheimer and American Film,* edited by R. Barton Palmer and Murray Pomerance, Rutgers UP, 2011, pp. 157–69.

Wood, Ellen Meiksins. *Empire of Capital.* Verso, 2005.

Yeldell, Cynthia. "Ground Zero for Whiskey: Law Allows Production of Distilled Spirits in State." *Knoxville News Sentinel,* 5 July 2009, archive.knoxnews.com/business /ground-zero-for-whiskey-law-allows-production-of-distilled-spirits-in-state-ep -409860713-359327571.html.

The Bourbon Street Hustle

Midcentury Tourism in John Kennedy Toole's
A Confederacy of Dunces

ROBERT REA

Near the end of *A Confederacy of Dunces,* John Kennedy Toole gathers together a rotating cast of characters for a burlesque show gone horribly wrong. The evening begins with a striptease by Harlett O'Hara, the Virgin-ny Belle, and ends in a state of near-riot as an unruly crowd spills onto Bourbon Street. Mayhem ensues after Toole's bumbling hero, Ignatius Reilly, joins the party, convinced the act is a "brilliant satire on the decadent Old South being cast before the unaware swine in the Night of Joy audience" (254). There is a grain of truth in what he says, of course, because the Night of Joy wraps the traditional offerings of Bourbon Street—sex and alcohol—in nostalgia for the southern past to sell them better.

Toole's cult classic takes readers inside a fictional world that Jean Baudrillard, Frederic Jameson, and others characterized some time ago as the postmodern condition. Like popular historical novels and big-budget Hollywood epics, the tourism industry uses a vivid mixture of fact and fiction as a device for trademarking New Orleans as the pleasure capital of the South. Scott Romine, in *The Real South,* claims that "through the intervention of narrative . . . the South is increasingly sustained as a virtual, commodified, built, themed, invented, or otherwise artificial territoriality" (9).[1] Romine briefly notes how the Night of Joy reconstructs Tara "at the threshold of emergent economies based on spectacle, tourism, image manipulation, built environments, and themed space" (42). But there is something else about the novel as a whole—something Romine, for all his close study of the culture industry, overlooks—and this is how Toole redraws the map of the city's oldest neighborhood along the blurred lines between simulation and reality.

What started out as a campaign to preserve French Quarter heritage morphed into a marketing template for hosting a nonstop party. Restoration of its architecture—including roofs, facades, and courtyards—began in the 1920s, after downtown had deteriorated and was threatened with demolition. Renewal efforts transformed the formerly funky district, inhabited mostly by immigrant workers and bohemian types, which laid the groundwork for a midcentury boom in tourism. "After the 1930s, Bourbon Street would look only backward in time for its architectural inspiration," writes Richard Campanella, author of *Bourbon Street: A History*. "That structural framework would form a perfect space from which the social memory of New Orleans's historical hedonism could be commoditized and sold" (115).

The Night of Joy participates in the heritage-industrial complex by rebranding itself as a feudal world where cotton is king. Anthony Stanonis explains, in *Dixie Emporium*, "As mass-produced goods and travelers unfamiliar with local customs increasingly penetrated the region . . . the South became as much an evolving set of images as an actual place" (5). After one of the servers auditions for the show, we are told, "Lana [the owner] screamed in the best tradition of the director in a musical movie. She had always enjoyed the theatrical aspects of her profession: performing, posing, composing tableaux, directing acts" (Toole 190). Thus, in Toole's hands, Bourbon Street becomes a kind of theme park that sells more than just sex and alcohol. Turning a profit involves storytelling—in this case, a story that attempts to convert heritage into a nostalgic getaway from the tourist's normally hectic life.

A Confederacy of Dunces has long been celebrated as a faithful portrait of New Orleans.[2] The time frame for the novel is a throwback to a bygone era when upscale nightclubs were the main attraction. "Bourbon Street from the late 1930s to the mid-1960s was campy. [Burlesque shows] were proudly proffered by impresarios as exemplars of stylish eroticism. People dressed to the nines and patronized Bourbon clubs craving the velvety cultural cachet that such clubs convincingly delivered. We laugh at them in retrospect, but they were not produced to be ridiculed; they were produced to dazzle. Midcentury Bourbon Street nightclubs presented themselves with enough decorum and pizzazz to make the kitsch campy" (Campanella 302).

The Night of Joy falls far short of the deadpan dazzle cultivated by Bourbon Street tastemakers, though Lana aspires to compete for the suit-and-tie set. That this low-rent gin joint needs a face-lift is evident from the opening episode. Ignatius and his mother, Irene, duck into an empty barroom after being harassed by a cop outside a department store on Canal Street. Ignatius collapses onto a bar stool and orders "chicory coffee with boiled milk," to which the bartender responds, "Only instant" (Toole 8).

More often than not, indifferent owners struggle to stay afloat because, in addition to serving alcohol, bar success on Bourbon requires a creative marketing concept. Tropical Isle owner Earl Bernhardt told Campanella, "A lot of people think if you come to Bourbon Street and open the doors, the money's going to roll in, but it's *not* . . . If you don't have something to offer the public and you don't know how to market it, you're going to fall flat on your face" (261). Not serving café au lait signals a missed opportunity by an uninspired owner, at the very least, and poor management skills, at the very worst. Lest any doubt remain, a conversation between two employees sums up the downscale vibe: "Don't knock yourself out cleaning up this dump," Darlene advises her newly hired workmate, Burma. "I never seen it really clean since I been here. And it's so dark in here all the time, nobody can tell the difference. To hear Lana talk, you'd think this hole was the Ritz" (Toole 31).

The Reillys hang around until nightfall, the start of typical drinking hours for anyone not from New Orleans: "Outside, Bourbon Street was beginning to light up. Neon lights flashed off and on, reflecting the streets dampened by the light mist that had been falling steadily for some time. The taxis bringing the evening's first customers, Midwestern tourists and conventioneers, made slight splashing sounds in the cold dusk" (15). Still, not a single thirsty customer crosses the threshold. Bourbon Street patrons in those days, according to Campanella, "would not have strolled back and forth in promenade fashion because the action was indoors in the clubs, not in the public space as it is today. There were no to-go drinks; the whole idea of going to Bourbon Street in this [postwar] era was to make an entry into a stylish club or restaurant and be treated like someone special" (127). Yet the Night of Joy furnishes none of the amenities top-tier clubs used to entice tourists. To make matters worse, Lana chases off her few paying customers: "Beat it. Trade from people like you is the kiss of death" (Toole 21).

The "people like you" at whom Lana turns up her nose are locals. The clientele for what appears to be an average night at the Night of Joy consists of mother and son, an unassuming gambler hunched over a racing form, and a chain-smoking dapper dresser who waves off a round of daiquiris from Mrs.

Reilly, adding, "I think I'm in the wrong bar anyway" (16). Ignatius and his mother live in the Irish Channel, an uptown neighborhood with blue-collar bona fides. The gambler most likely bets on horses at the New Orleans Fair Grounds, a sprawling racetrack tucked away in Mid-City. The other man, Dorian Greene, reappears later in the novel and, as it turns out, relocated from Nebraska to settle in a city that has always harbored a vibrant gay community.

More to the point, Lana looks to draw the tourist crowd, not French Quarter regulars, and she blames Darlene for soliciting the amenable group of undesirables: "I try to explain to you the kind of clientele we want in here. Then I walk in and find you eating crap off my bar with some old lady and a fat turd. You trying to close down my business? People look in the door, see a combination like that, they walk off to another bar" (29–30). Whether Lana can regroup depends on whether she can find a more effective marketing strategy than the rage, bluster, and disdain she has mustered up to this point.

What Lana has failed to note so far is that her competitors sell a distinct local offering. Paradise Vendors, for one, builds its brand by commodifying the past and selling iconic images of the place that tourists want to visit. In his "Journal of a Working Boy," Ignatius bristles at the dress code enforced by his employer, Mr. Clyde: "The vendor who formerly had the Quarter route wore an improbable pirate's outfit, a Paradise Vendor's nod to New Orleans folklore and history, a Clydian attempt to link the hot dog with Creole legend" (196). The service Mr. Clyde provides—fast food—is simply the stage for the heritage that he is really selling.

Other French Quarter points of interest in the novel—Pirate's Alley and Lafitte's Blacksmith Shop, to cite just two examples—traffic in the same nostalgia for a venerable icon from Old New Orleans. A nineteenth-century pirate and smuggler, Jean Lafitte led a colorful life in New Orleans and, according to legend, buried gold in the outer swamps and bayous. Surely, Mr. Clyde regrets hiring his bloated employee, since the latter ingests far more product than he moves. But even so, the Clydian marketing gimmick is spot-on. Ignatius chronicles a telling incident in his treatise on how not to get a job.

A group of tourists wandered along the streets, their cameras poised, their glittering eyeglasses shining like sparklers. Noticing me, they paused and, in sharp Midwestern accents which assailed my delicate eardrums like the sounds of a wheat thresher (however unimaginably horrible that must

sound), begged me to pose for a photograph. Pleased by their gracious atten-
tions, I acquiesced. For minutes, they snapped away as I obliged them with
several artful poses. Standing before the wagon as if it were a pirate's vessel,
I brandished my cutlass menacingly for one especially memorable pose, my
other hand holding the prow of the tin hot dog. As a climax, I attempted to
climb atop the wagon, but the solidity of my physique proved too taxing for
that rather flimsy vehicle. (198–99)

We laugh because the misadventures of a hot dog–peddling pirate juggles two
seemingly irreconcilable moments in time. But, upon closer inspection, the
heritage that Mr. Clyde offers is just as ultramodern and prepackaged as the hot
dog. Paradise Vendors serves its bland street fare wrapped in a tale of seafaring,
swashbuckling adventure. Worse still, the Night of Joy already stocks a similar
line of heritage-based products in the cooler behind the bar. Mrs. Reilly, before
plowing her Plymouth into the base of a wrought iron balcony, downs a half
six-pack of Dixie 45 (8).

Brand names do more than just advertise; they have symbolic meaning that
says something about identity and values. Dixie Brewing Company, as it bills on
its website, "captures the essence of its proud southern traditions." Apart from
an ice-cold beverage, Dixie promotes its product as a link to the past. Karen
Cox, who has written extensively on Dixie imagery in consumer culture, points
out, "On both sides of the Mason–Dixon line, businessmen sought to capitalize
on the marketing and consumption of a Dixie that incorporated the mythology
and traditions of a southern past" (51). On the surface, Mrs. Reilly's drink of
choice forecasts the myth touted in the disastrous burlesque show. At a deeper
level, though, it illustrates how marketing and advertising target consumers by
sugarcoating the southern past. After all, Dixie brand conveniently passes over
the history of enslaving black Americans in its "proud" toast to tradition.

Toole further develops his running critique of the tourism industry with
the Night of Joy's botched makeover. Fashionable nightclubs "brought together
entertainment and alcohol (legal or otherwise) in dark, stylized spaces scented
with the possibility of sex" (Campanella 105). Lana runs an illegal pornography
racket on the side yet somehow is slow to reap the financial rewards of the legal sex trade. Unlike modern-day strip joints with sleazy sex shows, burlesque
houses with "thematic decor, usually imaginative and sometimes garish, aimed
to evoke swankiness or exoticism" (Campanella 105).[3]

At first, Lana considers rebranding the bar with a tropical theme. Darlene, all too aware of her employer's struggle to make ends meet, shows up in a hand-sewn costume and auditions with her pet cockatoo: "I been practicing in my apartment. It's a new angle. He grabs at those rings with his beak and rips my clothes off. . . . I'm telling you, Lana. It's gonna be a smash hit sensation" (146). Toole, in all likelihood, lifted his story line from an exotic dancer named "Yvette Dare, whose parrot was trained to steal her sarong (the secret was a tomato slice entwined in the knot)" (Campanella 167). Island-themed souvenirs and attractions remain a fixture of Bourbon Street nightlife, with the Tropical Isle, for instance, serving one of the most notorious frozen cocktails on the entire thoroughfare. With every oversize cup of sugar-infused booze, the Hand Grenade evokes the leisurely pace of paradise, whether real or imagined, that travelers look for in tropical destinations.

None of this seems relevant to the carefully preserved architectural heritage, and therefore it facilitates and enhances a setting that can only be described as postmodern in its jarring blend of geographic differences. Even more mind-bogglingly, Lana eventually settles on an Old South theme, without ditching the parrot as a prop. In an ironic twist, Burma triggers the half-baked concept after she orders him to sweep the floor. "Right away, Scarla O'Horror," he snaps from behind a cloud of tobacco smoke (Toole 190).

As a result, the novel uses a script deeply familiar to midcentury movie-goers to take down the sort of heritage tourism for which the French Quarter is so often known. "Tara," Romine persuasively argues, "stands positioned, as a kind of ur-simulacrum, at the threshold of the South's entrance into the culture industry and its subsidiaries—the heritage industry, the nostalgia industry, the tourist industry, and so forth—by distinctively mixing memory and desire. More specifically, *Gone with the Wind* enacts—and in enacting, constitutes—the commodification of southern culture, reproducing the South not as *home* (inhabited place), but as *homesickness,* as an object of nostalgia in both the spatial and temporal senses of the word. . . .Tara is the sim-plantation that all real plantations of the tourist industry strive to reproduce" (28–29, emphasis Romine's). Lana's stage (re)production of *Gone with the Wind* not only adapts a cultural icon that keeps the past alive in the present but also reproduces the South as a free-floating image, created by Hollywood, without a referent. A primary question, then, must be how does Toole's Tara-like nightclub promise to whisk customers to a faraway time and place?

First of all, the Night of Joy puts on a glaring display of the heritage that the tourism industry converts into an "object of nostalgia." Old South mythology in the marketplace conveys ideas about "a rural rather than urban society, an agricultural rather than industrial economy, and an antimodern rather than modern worldview" (Cox 55). Lana goes on to detail her plan during a dress rehearsal that whips us from palm trees and sandy beaches to wide porches with white columns. She proposes:

> *Now* see this act. You're gonna be a southern belle type, a big sweet virgin from the Old South who's got a pet bird on the old plantation. . . .We get you a big plantation dress, crinoline, lace. A big hat. A parasol. Very refined. Your hair's on your shoulders in curls. You're just coming in from a big ball where a lot of southern gentlemen were trying to feel you up over the fried chicken and hog jowls. But you cooled them all. Why? Because you're a lady, dammit. You come onstage. The ball's over, but you still got your honor. You got your little pet with you to tell it good night, and you say to it, "There was plenty beaux at that ball, honey, but I still got my honor." Then the goddam bird starts grabbing at your dress. You're shocked, you're surprised, you're innocent. But you're too refined to stop it. Got it? (190–91)

In examining the business of catering to lust, the ill-conceived adaptation draws on the perceived ideals of antebellum life. Darlene's belle-at-the-ball routine demystifies clichés about southern charm and womanly virtues, on the one hand, while also deconstructing the consumer culture that reached the South with *Gone with the Wind*. For those "Midwestern tourists and conventioneers" arriving on Bourbon Street, the South is a version of paradise. "For the ad men who sought to brand the region, the South increasingly represented a respite from the afflictions of modernity. If, for northerners, 'paradise' was never where they were, then 'Dixie' was paradise, even if the reality did not match the myth. Only the idea of Dixie was needed to make it seem real, and the nation's consumers ate it up with a spoon" (Cox 66). The Harlett O'Hara bit appeals to nostalgia for hospitality, a life of leisure, and the code of chivalry often associated with the genteel class. It implies, by contrast, a lifestyle different from a modern way of life without manners, time for leisure, or any ties to the past.

In a far more toxic manner, however, the Night of Joy appeals to what some people would like history to be, without the more difficult aspects of what life was actually like in the past. *Gone with the Wind* glorified the plantation as an idyllic estate where docile slaves and benign mistresses lived together in peace and harmony. To fill the shoes of the faithful slave, Lana turns to Burma: "You gonna be out front on the sidewalk. We're gonna rent you a costume. Real Old South doorman. You attract the people in here. Understand? I wanna see a full house for your pal and her bird" (Toole 192).

As much as Toole counts on exaggeration for comic effect, black workers commonly held demeaning positions steeped in racial stereotypes: "Blacks on Bourbon Street were excluded from the conversation, and physically banned from the bars and clubs. . . . relegated to the roles of the bowing doorman, devoted servant, obsequious entertainer, stereotyped prop, or sidewalk busker. The Famous Door Bar, for example, boasted in 1946 that it featured 'the best small combo of Negroes in the entire state of Louisiana for entertaining, and special jive tunes.' One block away, 'Uncle Tom,' described as an 'aged Negro,' entertained Old Absinthe House patrons with banjo music and guided them on tours of its secret mezzanine" (Campanella 149).

Club owners treated black labor as bit players in Bourbon Street theater and, in doing so, shamelessly dressed up segregation in down-home(sick) attire. Disarming racial caricatures, moreover, attracted a broad customer base because "these faithful servants projected the image of leisure to which white middle-class consumers aspired" (Cox 62). To this same end, Burma becomes a prop in Lana's sanitized celebration of the slaveholding South. In this version of (white) paradise, the Confederate cause was never lost and chattel slavery never outlawed. But this is satire, so Toole uses laughter to drag North America's largest slave market out from the shadows and into the spotlight.[4] Under his breath and out of earshot, Burma protests that his employer "ain exactly hire me. She kinda buyin me off the auction block" (Toole 30). Ultimately, the past intrudes on this nostalgic rendition of itself, for Burma is no Uncle Tom—a fact underscored when he sets in motion a full-scale insurrection against his cruel mistress.

The myth of down-homeness begins to unravel when, a few days before Darlene's debut, Burma spots Ignatius outside the bar and urges him to crash the premiere. As the plot comes full circle, the chaotic sequence of events jumps abruptly from Old South nostalgia to a handful of other subcultures, all of them completely unrelated. Stuffed into his pirate outfit (naturally), Ignatius stops by the club solely because he mistakes Darlene for an avid reader of medieval philosophy. Meanwhile, Burma stands out front, underselling the show with a scalding sales pitch: "Hey! All you peoples draggin along here. Stop and come stick your ass on a Night of Joy stool . . . Night of Joy got genuine color peoples workin below the minimal wage. Whoa! Guarantee plantation atmosphere, got cotton growin right on the stage right in front your eyeball, got a civil right worker getting his ass beat up between show. Hey" (281)! Ignatius, having been tossed out once already, wonders aloud, "The Nazi proprietress is gone, I hope" (281).

Adolf Hitler, Boethius, Richard Pryor, and Captain Hook walk into a plantation-themed bar . . . It sounds like the setup for an obscene punch line, but the scene is no joke. The Night of Joy quotes the South™ to tell—and, indeed, to sell—a history-rich spectacle to sightseers, with little concern that its relapse into myth embraces the horrors of modern history as a source of profit and pleasure.

With so much space- and time-hopping, we wonder not only where are we but when. The opening night festivities unspool a dizzying narrative that is radically disconnected from any particular time or place. Yet, despite its broken logic, the baffling mix of Nazis, pirates, and planters clarifies Toole's point about Bourbon Street. As Romine concludes, "My understanding of the basic work of narrative in the age of cultural reproduction . . . is not as a means to weld a discontinuous reality into a coherent whole . . . but as a more contingent register of negotiating and reproducing reality's seams as they are confronted in time and space—more specifically, in the received time–space fusion called 'the South'" (Romine 23).

If coherence amounts to a betrayal of the postmodern condition, *A Confederacy of Dunces* exposes how that strip of adult Disney World overwhelms the ability to absorb anything at all. Ignatius wanders onto a historic site so overloaded with referents that it short-circuits any conditions for a grand narrative about culture, heritage, or history. What Toole shows us, among other things, is that Bourbon Street immerses tourists in a drinking destination where there is nothing to anchor reality—it is, instead, an alternate reality where time and place no longer apply.

In 1966, Walt Disney unveiled a brand-new replica of the French Quarter inside his Southern California theme park—but with less vomit. Toole took his life three years later, after having failed to find a publisher for his novel, but the unpublished manuscript he left behind tapped into much of what contemporary America was becoming. His Pulitzer-winning masterpiece takes aim at the neon-lit tourist traps that deliver the sort of reality-altering experience usually reserved for science fiction. But rather than a distant future or a faraway galaxy, Toole flashes a comic grin at the fantasyland in his own backyard. *A Confederacy of Dunces*, in this way, breaks with romantic clichés of New Orleans that dwell on its storied past.

Perhaps no literary figure has shaped the popular perception of New Orleans more than Tennessee Williams. An incurable romantic, he once remarked, "America is no longer a terribly romantic part of the world, and writers . . . are essentially romantic spirits—or they would not be writing. Now there are only two cities left in America with a romantic appeal, however vestigial, and they are, of course, New Orleans and San Francisco. Our industrial dynamism has dispelled whatever magic the other great cities may have once possessed" (29–30). New Orleans was distinct from other cities, in his view, because it had avoided the homogenizing effects of mass commerce.[5]

But the era when cheap rents and its shabby-genteel charm lured artists like Williams had long since passed by the time Toole wrote his novel. The French Quarter, by then, resembled more closely the Las Vegas Strip, where a mishmash of adult entertainment and history-themed attractions merely simulates the magic for tourists. Toole's slightly more skeptical take leans closer to that of writer and resident Richard Ford: "New Orleans deludes itself more than any city I've ever lived in, and I've lived in most of the major cities in the U.S. It deludes itself that it's 'the city that care forgot,' it deludes itself into believing that it's 'the Big Easy,' it deludes itself into sort of somehow living up to all of its sobriquets. The fact is it's a great big urban complex with a theme park in the middle, and everything else about New Orleans is just like every other city in America" (quoted in Guagliardo 190).

What defines New Orleans for Ford—as it does for Toole—is not its old-school character but rather its postmodern planning. Although it caters to those who seek out the past, Bourbon Street is the urban equivalent of an all-you-can-eat buffet, inviting partygoers to sample all kinds of times and places, which are removed from any sense of context and whose only aim is pleasure.

As for the swift decline of the Night of Joy, Toole leaves us with one final glimpse of its owner tempting passersby with stories of southern grandeur. By this time of night, Darlene should be onstage, performing to a packed house, but the club is mired in a permanent state of disarray, with tables overturned, glasses shattered on the floor, and Ignatius lying in the street after almost getting hit by a bus. Nonetheless, Lana clings to her dream of tavern renewal with one last call: "Well, folks, now that you're all here, how's about coming into the Night of Joy? We got a class show." She beckons to a throng of onlookers fascinated by the spectacle of disaster. The Night of Joy promises customers a fantasy world dipped in moonlight and magnolia, all for the price of a few watered-down drinks. The "crowd, however, was craning at the white mound, which was wheezing loudly, and declined the invitation to elegance" (286).

Notes

1. Other scholars have proposed similar theories about the postmodern South. Tara McPherson, *Reconstructing Dixie,* begins with the assertion, "The South today is as much a fiction, a story we tell and are told, as it is a fixed geographic space below the Mason–Dixon line" (1). See also Yaeger.

2. For instance, W. Kenneth Holditch finds "the enthusiastic reception accorded *A Confederacy of Dunces* by readers in New Orleans . . . somewhat surprising, since a large percentage of its residents are not particularly interested in literature. . . . What exactly do New Orleanians like about the novel?" he asks. "They are, I believe, amused and bemused by the author's grasp of and credible representation of local customs—social, ethnic, and culinary—and his ability, probably a gift from his mother, for identifying residents of particular neighborhoods and for capturing their voices" (112–13).

3. Campanella's research on midcentury Bourbon Street backs this up with one particularly compelling example. "Names of clubs in this halcyon era reflected the thematic moods that the dons of Bourbon Street sought to produce," he observes (139). Some themed clubs included the exotic El Morocco Lounge, the erotic Club Slipper, the rustic Old Barn, the native Mardi Gras Lounge, and the ironically named Dunce Cap Bar.

4. Once again, Romine hits the mark, noting—as does John Lowe—that the theme of modern slavery "insists on the continuity of plantations old and new, a continuity that extends to the Night of Joy, where Burma Jones is forced to endure 'modren [sic] slavery' in order to avoid arrest as a vagrant" (Romine 45).

5. This is not to say that Tennessee Williams romanticized New Orleans or French Quarter life. The distressed conditions near the Kowalskis' apartment in *A Streetcar Named Desire* thoroughly expose urban poverty and ethnic strife in the Quarter.

Works Cited

Campanella, Richard. *Bourbon Street: A History.* Louisiana State UP, 2014.

Cox, Karen L. "Branding Dixie: The Selling of the American South, 1890–1930." *Dixie Emporium: Tourism, Foodways, and Consumer Culture in the American South,* U of Georgia P, 2008, pp. 50–67.

Guagliardo, Huey, editor. *Perspectives on Richard Ford.* UP of Mississippi, 2000.

Holditch, W. Kenneth. "Another Kind of Confederacy: John Kennedy Toole." *Literary New Orleans in the Modern World,* edited by Richard S. Kennedy, Louisiana State UP, 1998, pp. 102–22.

Lowe, John. "The Carnival Voices of *A Confederacy of Dunces.*" *Louisiana Culture from the Colonial Era to Katrina,* edited by John Lowe, Louisiana State UP, 2008, pp. 159–90.

McPherson, Tara. *Reconstructing Dixie.* Duke UP, 2003.

Romine, Scott. *The Real South: Southern Narrative in the Age of Cultural Reproduction.* Louisiana State UP, 2008.

Stanonis, Anthony, editor. *Dixie Emporium: Tourism, Foodways, and Consumer Culture in the American South.* U of Georgia P, 2008.

Toole, John Kennedy. *A Confederacy of Dunces.* Louisiana State UP, 1980.

Williams, Tennessee. *Where I Live: Selected Essays.* New Directions, 1978.

Yaeger, Patricia, editor. *The Geography of Identity.* U of Michigan P, 1996.

Jim Crow, Mardi Gras, and the Ojen Cocktail

HANNAH C. GRIGGS

In the late 1980s, liquor distributors in New Orleans found themselves in a crisis: a small distillery in southern Spain, the only distiller left that produced the anise-based liqueur Ojen, was going to shut down (Price, "Last Bottle").[1] Though production of the liqueur originally began in 1830 in Ojén, a small town in the province of Malaga, Spain, Ojen (sans tilde) had been wildly popular in twentieth-century New Orleans. Generally, it was made into a cocktail by mixing it with a few drops of Peychaud's Bitters and a splash of seltzer water over cracked ice. The Ojen Cocktail was served at New Orleans's most upscale restaurants and became inextricably connected with Mardi Gras and the Krewe of Rex, one of the city's oldest Carnival organizations, whose members traditionally drank Ojen on Fat Tuesday.[2] Ojen was sweet and anise flavored and had a delicate "one note" taste that distinguished it from other anise-based liqueurs, such as Herbsaint and Pernod (Price, "Last Bottle").

The 1989 crisis that beset Ojen's New Orleans distributors was narrowly averted when Martin Wine Cellar, one of the city's largest liquor distributors, convinced Manuel Fernandez, owner of the Ojen distillery, to produce one last batch of the liqueur. The two parties agreed that Martin would have to purchase all five hundred cases of the run, which amounted to about six thousand bottles (Price, "Last Bottle").

When word got out that Ojen would no longer be produced, locals flocked to purchase their own personal supply. As one French Quarter bartender remarked, "When we found out they were going to stop making it, we went out and bought every bottle we could find" (Bruno). The Krewe of Rex also supposedly hoarded enough cases for several Carnival seasons (Price, "Last Bottle").

Though bottles of Ojen became increasingly difficult to find, it wasn't until April 2009 that the last bottle of that 1989 batch officially sold, and when it did, New Orleans mourned. Kevin O'Hara of Martin Wine Cellar lamented, "There's nothing quite like it" (Price, "Last Bottle"). It had been sipped by New Orleanians as long as anyone could remember. When the liqueur was featured at the 2008 New Orleans Food and Wine Experience, one of the moderators commented, "Ojen is an old-school New Orleans drink," adding that older locals, in their seventies, had memories of their parents drinking Ojen (J. Walker).

In fact, collective memory of Ojen seems to begin at Brennan's, an upscale restaurant in the French Quarter that opened in 1946. Brennan's originally featured an Ojen Frappé on its breakfast and brunch menus, advertising the drink as the "absinthe of the Spanish aristocracy" (Brennan's).[3] In February 2015, Jack Maxwell of the Travel Channel's *Booze Traveler* visited Brennan's for an ostensibly rare treat: restaurant management had recently discovered a small stash containing a few bottles of Ojen, supposedly hidden in the wine cellar. Of the discovery, owner Ralph Brennan said, "It was like finding gold, it really was" (Maxwell).[4]

Nonetheless, all hope was not lost when Martin Wine Cellar sold its last bottle of Ojen. The cocktail's popularity in New Orleans was so widespread that the Sazerac Company, a distillery headquartered just outside the city, decided to reproduce Ojen as part of its New Orleans Specialty Brands collection (Simonson). Sazerac had been "tossing around recreating Ojen for a few years," and it debuted the remade liqueur in January 2016, less than ten years after Martin's stash had run dry (Griggs). Kevin Richards, a marketing director for the Sazerac Company, said, "This is an old, storied New Orleans brand that needed someone to bring it back to life" (Price, "Another Round").

Because the role of nostalgic cultural appeal was so crucial to the reproduction of Ojen, and because the history of the Ojen Cocktail in New Orleans has never been fully or formally documented, this essays maps out how Ojen arrived in the city during the late nineteenth century and unravels the origins of Ojen's rise to popularity in New Orleans cocktail culture through the twenty-first century.[5] In addition, because issues of race and class have been absent from recent conversations about the return of Ojen, I hope to raise questions about the formation of cultural identity among New Orleans drinking cultures, particularly among the city's white upper classes, who deliberately excluded themselves and their places of leisure from both lower-class and nonwhite communities. I also hope to provide some insight into the connection between Ojen and Mardi Gras, an association that has served to restrict access to Ojen to a small group of wealthy whites.

Though depictions of Ojen can be found scattered through various literary texts,[6] I largely focus on how Ojen was depicted in the print and ephemera of the late nineteenth and twentieth centuries—in advertisements, menus, cocktail manuals, and travel narratives. The Ojen Cocktail was not New Orleans's most widely consumed drink, nor its most famous, but its stature as an "old-school" cocktail and its resurrection by the Sazerac Company resulted from the cultural and political circumstances surrounding the post-Reconstruction and Jim Crow eras. Much of the scholarship on southern foodways asserts that food could be used "to find a sense of commonality" in a region scarred by racial conflict (Latshaw 103); however, Ojen's place in culinary culture troubles that notion because, like much of consumer culture in the post-Reconstruction South, the consumption of Ojen was "predicated on the logic of segregation" (Szczesiul 132). Ojen came to the city during a time when the propagation of culinary traditions and Creole[7] culture worked to reinforce the "racial and patriarchal status quo of the Jim Crow regime," and that legacy continued in varying and complex ways until the last bottle was sold (Stanonis 209).

OJEN! OJEN!

In 1883, a businessman named Paul Gelpi ran a monthlong advertisement in the *Daily Picayune*—a newspaper that eventually merged with the *Times-Democrat* to become the *Times-Picayune* still distributed today—publicizing fifty newly imported cases of Ojen. This was the first time that Ojen was advertised publicly in the city. In 1874, Gelpi and his brother, Oscar, had started Paul Gelpi and Bro., a liquor distribution company specializing in imported wines and spirits ("Copartnership").

Paul and Oscar were following in the footsteps of their father, Pablo Gelpi, who immigrated to New Orleans from Spain in the early nineteenth century to open a similar business, founding an enterprise that would become a New Orleans dynasty and last nearly 150 years.[8] According to his grandchildren, Pablo was descended from generations of Spanish winemakers and sellers, and he wanted to bring his prosperous family business to the recently purchased Louisiana Territory ("Gelpi Family").[9] Because of Ojen's connection to Spain, the liquor served as a personal link between family and business interests for the Gelpi brothers.

By the time Ojen was first imported into New Orleans for commercial and retail sale, in 1883, Paul Gelpi and Bro. had become "one of the principal houses" of the French Quarter (Morrison 146). The brothers located their business on the corner of Decatur and Canal Streets—a stone's throw away from where their father had first established his company sixty years prior ("Gelpi Family"). This corner would have been the ideal spot for a successful business in the late nineteenth century. It straddled the division between the more commercial American district of Canal Street and the old residential Creole district of the Vieux Carré. Canal, a street frequented by both locals and tourists alike, served as New Orleans's hub of social and commercial activity. Within ten blocks stood the Grand Opera House, the Art Union, the customhouse, and the New Orleans Cotton Exchange. Running perpendicular to Canal and heading downriver, Decatur Street served as an artery to Esplanade Avenue, passing Café Du Monde, the bustling French Market, and the shipping docks along the way, destinations essential to the commercial life of New Orleans (Jackson, *New Orleans* 12–13).

Gelpi maintained his father's transatlantic connections abroad to import to New Orleans a diverse array of wines and spirits from Europe and the Caribbean (Morrison 146). The ad for the newly imported Spanish Ojen is plain but spacious and attention-grabbing. It ran in the *Daily Picayune* between May 20 and June 19, 1883, and read "OJEN! OJEN! 50 Cases of OJEN of Majorca. Superior to ABSINTHE as an Appetizer and Tonic." The words jump out on the page like a headline featuring breaking or exciting news, wholly indicative of the flurry of commerce that had recently come to the city.

The local economy was finally on the mend after the commercial stagnation of the 1870s. A new government had just been elected in 1880. Property values had doubled between 1880 and 1881. The price of cotton rose to pre–Civil War levels and the Southern Pacific Railroad had just been completed, linking New Orleans to California. However, the decade of the 1880s was also an era of mixed blessings (Jackson, *New Orleans* 4–5). The demographics of New Orleans were changing profoundly. Two hundred years of Creole dominance was being rapidly usurped by an ever-increasing population of middle-class Americans who did not have roots in Louisiana. A proliferation of culinary and cultural traditions filtered in from the North and other parts of the nation, causing anxiety among locals that the unique culture of New Orleans was being threatened into extinction by the deluge of tourism and the commodification of New Orleans and Creole culture.

Because of these demographic and economic shifts, advertising Ojen as "superior to absinthe" was a clever move by Gelpi. By comparing the two spirits, Gelpi appealed to local drinking habits. For native New Orleanians, absinthe had, during the 1870s, been a "bourgeois refinement" too expensive for most to afford (Adams 220). But the subsequent decade's economic "boom"—as it had been called colloquially—allowed more New Orleanians who "wanted to forget the misery of war and Reconstruction" to afford the potent green drink, as well as other, more costly liquors (Morrison 7; Adams 220). Moreover, declaring Ojen to be imported "from Majorca," Spain, and associated with the French tradition of consuming absinthe propped up the myth that the roots of the city's Creole heritage were firmly Western European, whitewashing the African, Caribbean, and Native American roots that contributed much—if not most—to New Orleans's palate.

Nonetheless, Gelpi's first advertisement set the stage for the cultural production of drinking Ojen. Gelpi's ad runs counter to the notion that southern foodways were "an accessible medium to use in finding cohesion or creating a context for the celebration and performance of southern identity" (Latshaw 103). Rather, drinking culture in late nineteenth-century New Orleans was exceptionally exclusionary. The ad appealed to New Orleans's middle and upper classes—those who could afford absinthe—who were anxious to claim New Orleans's multiracial and multilingual culture as white, European, and Anglophone. Above all, by maintaining a secure image of an Ojen drinker as an elite white Creole, Gelpi's ad is an attempt to quell growing fears of miscegenation among his white consumers.

Gelpi also advertised at the height of tourist season, feeding into New Orleans's notoriety for its egregious alcohol consumption. While the city of New Orleans continued to consume large quantities of alcohol, Gelpi, as a liquor importer, would have been privy to the prohibitionist rhetoric growing in other parts of the country and the expanding influence of the temperance movement. Advertising Ojen as a safer, healthier "appetizer and tonic" than absinthe appealed to tourists wary of trying the real stuff.

As visitors from around the country and the world poured into New Orleans, they endeavored to immerse themselves in the Creole culture that was at "the heart of New Orleans's tourism narratives," which often perpetuated false notions of white Creole superiority (Ferris 220). For many visitors, that included having a drink at the infamous Absinthe House on the corner of Bourbon and Bienville Streets, whose popularity mushroomed when the "Parisian style" of dripped absinthe was introduced in 1869 (Adams 220). Just like locals, visitors imbibing absinthe nodded to its sophisticated European past, which "connoted New Orleans's unique flavor and authenticity" but erased the contributions of its nonwhite and non-European inhabitants (Ferris 220).

With such sharp business acumen, Gelpi found much success in both his commercial and his personal endeavors. In 1885, Andrew Morrison wrote, in *The Industries of New Orleans,* that Paul Gelpi and Bro. was "a most excellent example of the mercantile houses of the city of New Orleans, and one that should have a high place allotted in a work of this sort" (146). Indeed, it is quite telling that the only advertisement that Gelpi ever released for Ojen was between May and June of 1883.

As he became increasingly prominent and successful, Paul Gelpi served as a board member for a number of the city's powerful and influential organizations, including several Carnival associations, the New Orleans Sewerage and Water Board, the Louisiana Historical Society, and, most notably, the Boston Club ("Who's Who" 96). Named after a card game popular in the antebellum period, and often shortened to "the Boston," the Boston Club was an elite and exclusively white gentlemen's organization founded in 1841.[10] During the 1880s, the Boston was frequented by New Orleans's leading Creole elite; Gelpi was inaugurated as a member in 1886 (Landry 229).

Though it's unclear exactly what role Gelpi played in introducing Ojen to members of the Boston, it was at the Boston Club that the Ojen Cocktail, by adding two dashes of Peychaud's Bitters and soda water, was born. By the early 1900s, the Ojen Cocktail had become the Boston's most popular drink (Fuller). The Ojen Cocktail had, by word of mouth and by association with Gelpi, become "one of the drinks that made New Orleans famous," and its influence resonated through the twentieth century and until the present day (Washburne 93).

During the late nineteenth and early twentieth centuries, Creole culture also began to transform "to include ambitious white citizens who invented their own self-styled royalty and pageantry, which culminated in the city's annual Mardi Gras festival," and these upper-class sensibilities were intertwined with the tradition of drinking Ojen during Mardi Gras season (Ferris 220). This connection between Ojen and Mardi Gras also began with Gelpi. In fact, the Boston Club is the nexus through which four generations of Ojen drinkers can be traced. The Ojen Cocktail became *the* Mardi Gras drink because the king of Carnival used to toast his queen at the Boston Club, a practice that was abandoned in the 1990s due to time constraints. Many Krewes, but most notably the Krewe of Rex, drank Ojen before the parades began (Griggs). This practice endured through the late twentieth century. In a 1981 *Times-Picayune* editorial that highlighted local Carnival traditions, a New Orleans woman relays that, at Mardi Gras, Ojen is just "another New Orleans tradition," and that Ojen has "been a Mardi Gras drink for as long as [she] can remember" (Peck). Though Ojen would not come to be *exclusively* affiliated with Carnival until one hundred years later, it was Gelpi who set in motion the tradition of drinking Ojen on Fat Tuesday.

Because of the Club's wide-reaching social sphere, Ojen was often featured on the menus of high-class parties and banquets throughout the city, associating the drink with exclusively white events and wistful allusions to the Old South.[11] The cocktail also appeared in travel narratives through the 1910s. A 1919 issue of *The Photo-Engravers Bulletin*, published just before the advent of Prohibition, describes the Southeastern Photo-Engravers Conference, hosted in New Orleans. Before the conference began, a committee of seven people waited at the train station to greet the president of the association, E. C. Miller, who was arriving from Chicago. After his train arrived, the committee could not locate Miller, so they went to his hotel, where they found that he had already checked in. Upon knocking on his hotel room door, they were greeted by the association's commissioner and found Miller drunk in his bathtub, with "a Sazerac cocktail in one hand, a Ramos gin fizz in the other, and a[n] Ojen cocktail in his shaving cup." The narrator quipped in reflection, "He seemed to become acclimated almost immediately" (Flader 44).

Drinking an Ojen Cocktail was directly identified with the kind of bourgeois debauchery often associated with New Orleans. Furthermore, the name of the author of the *Photo-Engravers Bulletin* article, "Marse Henry," is meant to be a tongue-in-cheek nod to the colloquial title for a slave master. This pseudonym not only reveals nostalgia for the plantation economy but also demonstrates how the culture of imbibing Ojen actively worked to maintain the racial hierarchy of Jim Crow policies (Adams 217).

Ojen's favor at the Boston Club coincided with its burgeoning popularity in early twentieth-century New Orleans, and, as a result, the Ojen Cocktail became intertwined with perceptions of elite whiteness. Mentions and appearances of the Ojen Cocktail were almost exclusively featured in ephemera utilized by white local and tourist consumers, which exalted white, upper-class sensibilities. Consequently, the Ojen Cocktail began making its way into popular cocktail and drink-mixing manuals targeted at predominantly white readers.

After absinthe was banned in 1912, New Orleanians looked for other anise-based alternatives, such as Pernod, L. E. Jung's Greenopal, and Herbsaint (known as Legendre Absinthe before Prohibition), which rose to popularity during this period. Just as when it was first imported into the city, Ojen became a popular alternative to absinthe. According to a 1914 cocktail recipe book, *Beverages De Luxe*, a "guide to connoisseurs" of cocktails, Ojen was "for people who like absinthe" (Washburne and Bronner 9, 93). The Ojen Cocktail is featured in the 1914 cocktail manual *Drinks*, by Jacques Straub, the wine steward for the upscale Blackstone hotel in Chicago. He writes in the book's introduction that it "contains about seven hundred accurate directions for mixing various kinds of popular and fancy drinks served in the best hotels, clubs, buffets, bars and homes of the civilized world" (Straub 1).

A fixation on the *upper* class also filtered into cocktail and drinking culture in New Orleans. A 1910 issue of the *Lumber Trade Journal* recounts the annual convention of the Southern Cypress Manufacturers Association, held in New Orleans that year. Attendees were treated to lavish luncheons and banquets accompanied by orchestras and prominent speakers. During the convention's closing dinner banquet, guests dined on an elaborate menu of Creole dishes, including gumbo and soft-shell crab bouillabaisse, served with café brûlot and Ojen Cocktails as after-dinner digestifs.

Diners were entertained by the speech of a Creole "dialectician" named Jac Lafiance, "a vanishing type of the old 'Acadian' Creole, opposed to all innovations, heedless of money, . . . whose life is governed by his ancestral post, and takes no note of modern progress." The author of the article transcribes Lafiance's short speech in dialect: "I got mo' regard fo' the requirement of hospitality, me, than hurt yo' feeling by tell you my h'opinion of yo'self, me, mes amis, no. I wish to say, I ver' happy fo' h'extend to you' the good wish of the Creole h'en this h'occasion, me, an' at the sem time fo' h'express my felicitation at yo' h'early departure, yes, f'om the place w'eh yo' come to the place w'eh yo' b'long—w'ich I glad fo' say I don't live theh myse'f, me" (Boyd 42F). Rather than declaring his presumably negative opinion of the guests, Lafiance, "heedless of money," privileges "the requirement of hospitality"—one of the few phrases that stands oddly out of dialect in his speech—extending "the good wish of the Creole h'en this h'occasion."

The event characterizes how notions of Creoleness had transformed: while hosts portrayed New Orleans as "a friendly land of perpetual welcome to white nonsoutherners," the culture of "lower-class" Louisiana was "tarted up and trotted out" for visitors to be entertained by, enjoy, mock, and, more importantly, pay to see (Szczesiul 133; Long 6). White New Orleanians, who had now colonized the moniker of Creole, were dedicated to safeguarding the patriarchal racial and class structure of the Jim Crow South, and this meant celebrating New Orleans's culinary traditions and Creole heritage—of which Ojen was now inseparably a part—as an exclusively white tradition.

The ways in which Ojen was used to privilege whiteness was, of course, not limited to tales of inebriated tourists. White Creoles who remained in New Orleans after Reconstruction—those who could supposedly trace their heritage to French and Spanish settlers, and many of whom were members of the Boston Club—along with newcomers eager to appropriate New Orleans's past as their own, "insisted that 'Creole' referred to pure-blooded whiteness" (Fertel 14). This is no better exemplified than by a December 1911 *Daily Picayune* article featuring recipes for the holiday season. The article suggests dishes for the ideal "Anglo-Saxon Yuletide feast"—with the Ojen Cocktail at the top of the menu ("*Picayune*'s Christmas Menu").

Kickless, but Tasteful

Despite New Orleans's prosperous cocktail culture, the city saw encroaching restrictions on liquor consumption during the early twentieth century, which eventually led to Prohibition. In 1909, the Louisiana legislature passed the Gay–Shattuck law, which not only segregated black and white citizens in bars, pubs, and saloons but also forbade women from entering establishments where liquor was sold. The two exceptions to this, however, were restaurants and hotels that served meals. This meant that "respectable," wealthy, and mostly white men and women could be served alcohol in higher-end restaurants, but establishments without food service were required by law to forbid women and socialization across the color line. Though ostensibly intended to police New Orleans's red-light district, Storyville, the Gay–Shattuck law was the beginning of a number of attempts to control how New Orleanians consumed their alcohol and with whom they imbibed.

A decade later, on the night of June 30, 1919, large crowds gathered in bars, saloons, and hotels across the city "to imbibe what they hoped were not their last drinks" (Jackson, "Prohibition" 265). Much to the chagrin of the vast majority of its populace, New Orleans would spend the next thirteen years attempting to undermine and evade Prohibition laws. Many restaurants, bars, and saloons continued to serve alcohol openly, despite the threat of federal raiding, from which no establishment was exempt. Both Commander's Palace and Arnaud's, two of New Orleans's oldest restaurants, fell victim to raids by the mid-1920s. Even the Boston Club made headline news, in 1924, when the doorman was caught selling a bottle of whiskey to the chauffeur of one of its members. The president and seven board members of the Boston were immediately arrested ("Head of Boston Club Charged").

The liquor industry in New Orleans panicked. Paul Gelpi, now in his seventies, had passed down his business to his seven children. Anticipating financial ruin when it became clear that Prohibition would not be promptly repealed, the Gelpis left the liquor industry after more than one hundred years in the business. They instead went into candy making, selling high-quality candies and bonbons until Prohibition was repealed. The company's treasurer, A. J. Gelpi, released a statement on this decision in a *Times-Picayune* interview in 1919: "We are through with the liquor business. Our firm has been engaged in this business for more than fifty years but the handwriting on the wall is plainly visible . . . the field where wholesale liquors may be distributed has dwindled perceptively" ("Liquor Firm"). Less than a year later, in 1920, Paul Gelpi passed away at the age of seventy-two ("Funeral").

Others in the liquor industry reinvented their businesses to profit within the confines of Prohibition, trying their hands at creating nonalcoholic versions of New Orleans cocktails. One of these companies was New Orleans–based manufacturer L. E. Jung & Wulff, often shortened to J&W. Famous for the manufacture of absinthe substitutes, most notably Greenopal, they also were known for a less favored anisette called Milky Way. Jung, also a prominent liquor merchant, entered the New Orleans liquor business around the same time as Gelpi. In *Industries of New Orleans,* Morrison profiled Jung in the entry just above Gelpi's, characterizing his business, Baumann and Jung, as having a reputation "obtained by the strictest attention to the quality of their goods for long years" (146). Gelpi and Jung most certainly knew each other; in the mid-1880s, their offices stood just down the street from each other, and they both were members of the Boston Club.

In fact, Jung's company was dedicated to the production and distribution of Ojen. In 1933, just before Prohibition was repealed, J&W published a promotional cocktail manual, "offering this booklet of Recipes in the hope that Sanity in Drinking will shortly return." Its cover featured a large-bellied, mustachioed "Old Time Bartender . . . now many years gone" dressed in a stark white suit, pouring a red liquid between mixing cups (figure 2). The manual dedicates an entire page to Ojen and the Ojen Cocktail, stating, "It is our firm belief that this

FIGURE 2. The front cover of L. E. Jung & Wulff's promotional cocktail manual. *The Mixologist: How to Mix the Makings*, L. E. Jung & Wulff, 1933.

drink, one of the most delicious of modern day liqueurs, will shortly become immensely popular with the American people." The pamphlet even suggests that Jung or his company had invented the Ojen Cocktail, asserting that the "Ojen Cocktail . . . was originally developed by this firm" (*Mixologist* 4). Though Jung died in 1925 and his company eventually liquidated in 1940, J&W carried the Ojen-soused torch through the bitter dry days of liquor outlaw. When the Volstead Act was enacted and Ojen could not long be legally imported into New Orleans from Spain, Jung began manufacturing a "kickless, but tasteful" nonalcoholic version of the Ojen Cocktail—the first time that "Ojen" had been manufactured in the city of New Orleans.

In 1923, Jung & Wulff rebranded itself as the "trustees of Southern traditions." Their most common advertisement featured a young white man dressed in formal ballroom regalia (see figure 3). He sits alone at a dining table covered by a white cloth, upon which rests a small cocktail glass, a cocktail shaker, and a bottle of an unidentified liquor. In his right hand, which rests carefully on the table, the figure holds a white napkin. In his left hand, he delicately holds the stem of a small, frail cocktail class. His facial expression is somber, focused, and controlled. He gazes intently at the items on the table, though his emotions are ambiguous—perhaps nostalgic, perhaps content, or both. His pose exudes an air of sophistication. While, at first glance, the ambiguity of his location seems to demonstrate the widespread appeal of the ad, it in fact speaks to the exclusivity of the target audience. Whether he sits at a restaurant or in his home is unclear, suggesting that wealth and tradition can be accessed regardless of environment. In fact, his confidence and poise imply that he dominates all of the spaces he occupies ("When J. & W.").

The text of these advertisements consistently appeals to those "bon vivants" who "disregard price for quality." They were often accompanied by small blurbs selling Peychaud's Bitters, used to get that "old Creole taste" in cocktails and recipes. The ad transforms the interracial and multicultural Creoleness that once defined New Orleans into a commodified relic. "Creole" now referred exclusively to the city's unique cuisine and the haughty culture that surrounded it. Jim Crow had been in effect for more than thirty years, and the Gay–Shattuck law continued to segregate places that sold alcohol. Now that Ojen had "been the standard with the best families of the South for 40 years," the term "best families" referred exclusively to New Orleans's wealthy white elite.

Figure 3. An advertisement for Jung & Wulff's nonalcoholic Ojen cocktail. "When J. & W. Mean OJEN," *Times-Picayune*, 30 September 1923, p. 7.

Post-Reconstruction New Orleans was a tangled, complex web of racial, political, and class conflict. The manner in which Ojen was imbibed, and by whom, is reflected in the major social shifts of the late nineteenth and early twentieth centuries: the rise in the population of middle-class Americans in New Orleans, the commodification of New Orleans Creole culture, and the exclusionary policies of Jim Crow. The legacy of the Ojen Cocktail survived because elite white Creoles sought to prolong and preserve the racial and class hierarchy of Jim Crow. As a result, Ojen became a part of the southern social and culinary customs that played a critical role in upholding racial segregation.

Notes

Portions of this essay first appeared in the February 23, 2017, issue of *The Atlantic* as "How New Orleans's Favorite Mardi Gras Cocktail Was Saved From Extinction."

1. Ojen is pronounced *oh-hen,* though Ray Bordelon told me in an interview some used to pronounce it *oi-yen.*

2. A "krewe" refers to an organization that puts on parades and balls during Carnival.

3. Brennan's also established the tradition of drinking Ojen as a morning or brunch drink. In the 1984 edition of *The Commander's Palace New Orleans Cookbook,* the instructions for preparing the Ojen Cocktail read that the drink "turns a pretty pink when put on ice and has a subtly sweet licorice taste. We like it before lunch" (Brennan et al. 6). Later, the Ojen Cocktail was served at a number of different restaurants in New Orleans, including Kolb's German Tavern (Kolb's 2) and Begue's. In 1969, Begue's wrote in its restaurant operating philosophy that the bar "will be fully equipped and fully stocked with all the known brand beverages of our day . . . however, we will project this outlet as a CREOLE BAR featuring Creole beverages," followed by a list of drinks that includes a number of absinthe cocktails, the New Orleans gin fizz, a Sazerac, and an Ojen Cocktail (Begue's 3). Brennan's first breakfast menu is viewable online via the Louisiana Menu and Restaurant Collection.

4. Jack Maxwell later reminisced on the experience: "Ojen is one of, if not the, rarest alcohols in the world. I got to try it thanks to the wonderful hospitality of Ralph Brennan and his family. Kind of sums up the Big Easy—rare but inviting and hospitable!" (quoted in D. Walker).

5. Some informal attempts have been made to document the history of the Ojen Cocktail (see, for instance Hémard or "Classic New Orleans"), but "for reasons no one can explain," Ojen made its way across the Atlantic and came to be a New Orleans tradition (Price, "Last Bottle").

6. Perhaps most famously in Ernest Hemingway's 1937 novel, *To Have and To Have Not,* in which protagonist Arthur Gordon knocks back three glasses of Ojen in a Havana gambling room.

7. "Creole" is a loaded word. Though it originally referred to "the historical interaction of Native Americans, Europeans, enslaved Africans, and their descendants, including free persons of color in New Orleans and the Lower Mississippi" (Ferris 220), the term has evolved to contain multiple, often overlapping meanings. "Creole" can refer to New Orleans's diverse racial history, the city's African heritage, its unique cuisine, or the social standing of a particular person or group. Marcie Cohen Ferris also notes that the term eventually referred to "the cultural products, including cuisine, born of the voluntary and forced contact among New Orleans's eclectic citizenry."

8. It is unclear whether Paul and Oscar Gelpi inherited the establishment from their father or started a completely new business. The announcement of their firm ("Copartnership") makes no mention of their father, but sources from the 1940s claim that, by the time of Prohibition, the business had been "operated by the Gelpi family for one and a quarter century without interruption" ("Gelpi Family").

9. Pablo Gelpi's ventures in New Orleans were later romanticized during the 1940s by one of his grandchildren, who claimed that Pablo sailed into the Port of New Orleans in 1815 on a clipper ship full of casks filled with "old rare wines," with the intention of entering the business of importing and selling fine liquors ("Three Generations").

10. Many of the Confederacy's most powerful men had often visited the Boston Club, until it was closed during the Civil War. Jefferson Davis, for example, was known to frequent the club during visits to New Orleans (Kendall 693).

11. The Ojen Cocktail, for instance, was found on the menu of the annual banquets of the Louisiana Bar Association from 1912 to 1919 (*Report*) and also was served at the annual meetings of the Louisiana Engineering Society through the 1910s (*Proceedings*).

Works Cited

Adams, Jad. *Hideous Absinthe: A History of the Devil in a Bottle.* U of Wisconsin P, 2004.

Arthur, Stanley Clisby. *Famous New Orleans Drinks & How to Mix 'Em.* Pelican, 1937.

"Begue's Creole Restaurant and Bar Image Interpretations and Operating Philosophy." Louisiana Menu and Restaurant Collection, Howard-Tilton Memorial Library, Tulane University, digitallibrary.tulane.edu/islandora/object/tulane%3A17586.

Boyd, James, editor. "Entertainment for the Visitors." *Lumber Trade Journal,* June 1910, pp. 42E–42H. babel.hathitrust.org/cgi/pt?id=pst.000055552363.

Brennan, Ella, Dick Brennan, and Lynne Roberts. *The Commander's Palace New Orleans Cookbook.* Clarkson N. Potter, 1984.

"Brennan's Restaurant Menu." Louisiana Menu and Restaurant Collection, Howard-Tilton Memorial Library, Tulane University, digitallibrary.tulane.edu/islandora/object/tulane%3A17913.

Bruno, R. Stephanie. "A Room That Can Hold Its Liquor." NOLA.com, 22 July 2012, www.nola.com/entertainment_life/home_garden/article_7b630214-67b5-5d1b-b756-9dd55c08135f.html.

"Classic New Orleans: A Brief History of Ojen." *La Fille de la Ville,* 1 April 2009, filledelaville.wordpress.com/2009/04/01/ojen.

"Copartnership." *Daily Picayune,* 21 April 1874, p. 5.

Engelhardt, Elizabeth. "Redrawing the Grocery: Practices and Methods for Studying Southern Food." *The Larder: Food Studies Methods from the American South,* edited by John T. Edge, Elizabeth Engelhardt, and Ted Ownby, U of Georgia P, 2013, pp. 1–6.

Ferris, Marcie Cohen. *The Edible South: The Power of Food and the Making of an American Region.* U of North Carolina P, 2014.

Fertel, Rien. "'Everybody Seemed Willing to Help': *The Picayune Creole Cook Book* as Battleground, 1900–2008." *The Larder: Food Studies Methods from the American South,* edited by John T. Edge, Elizabeth Engelhardt, and Ted Ownby, U of Georgia P, 2013, pp. 10–31.

Flader, Louis, editor. "Side Notes on the Southeastern Photo-Engravers Conference." *Photo-Engraver's Bulletin,* May 1919, p. 44. babel.hathitrust.org/cgi/pt?id=uiug.3011 2087877780.

Fuller, Margaret. "The Secret Life of Liqueurs." *Times-Picayune/States-Item*, 24 July 1986, pp. G1–G2.

"Funeral of Prominent New Orleans Man Is Private, at His Residence." *Times-Picayune*, 17 October 1920, sec. 5:14.

"Funeral Services Held for L. E. Jung." *Times-Picayune*, 24 December 1925, p. 20.

"Gelpi Family Wine Importers since Year 1815." *Times-Picayune*, 9 October 1941, p. 23.

Griggs, Hannah C. "How New Orleans's Favorite Mardi Gras Cocktail Was Saved from Extinction." *The Atlantic*, 23 February 2017, www.theatlantic.com/technology/archive/2017/02/ojen-mardi-gras/517605.

"Head of Boston Club Charged by Dry Agents." *Times-Picayune*, 22 May 1924, p. 1.

Hémard, Ned. "Banana Republics and *Ojen* Cocktails." *New Orleans Nostalgia*, New Orleans Bar Association, 2007, www.neworleansbar.org/uploads/files/OjenUpdate.3-2.pdf.

Jackson, Joy J. *New Orleans in the Gilded Age: Politics and Urban Progress, 1880–1896*. Louisiana State UP, 1969.

———. "Prohibition in New Orleans: The Unlikeliest Crusade." *Louisiana History: The Journal of the Louisiana Historical Association*, vol. 19, no. 3, 1978, pp. 261–84.

Kendall, John Smith. *History of New Orleans*. Vol. 2, Lewis Publishing, 1922.

"Kolb's German Tavern Restaurant Menu." Louisiana Menu and Restaurant Collection, Howard-Tilton Memorial Library, Tulane University, digitallibrary.tulane.edu/islandora/object/tulane%3A18004.

Landry, Stuart O. *History of the Boston Club*. Pelican, 1938.

Latshaw, Beth A. "The Soul of the South: Race, Food, and Identity in the American South." *The Larder: Food Studies Methods from the American South*, edited by John T. Edge, Elizabeth Engelhardt, and Ted Ownby, U of Georgia P, 2013, pp. 99–127.

"Liquor Firm Going into Candy Making." *Times-Picayune*, 25 July 1919, p. 11.

Long, Alecia P. *The Great Southern Babylon: Sex, Race, and Respectability in New Orleans, 1865–1920*. Louisiana State UP, 2005.

Maxwell, Jack, performer. "Dead in New Orleans." *Booze Traveler*, season 1, episode 12, Travel Channel, 9 February 2015.

The Mixologist: How to Mix the Makings, L. E. Jung & Wulff, 1933.

Morrison, Andrew. *The Industries of New Orleans: Her Rank, Resources, Advantages, Trade, Commerce and Manufactures, Conditions of the Past, Present and Future, Representative Industrial Institutions, Historical, Descriptive, and Statistical*. J. M. Elstner, 1885. babel.hathitrust.org/cgi/pt?id=loc.ark%3A%2F13960%2Ft1gjo871v.

"Ojen! Ojen!" *Daily Picayune*, 20 May 1883, p. 5.

Peck, Renee. "Party Pleasers for Mardi Gras." *Times-Picayune/States-Item*, 26 February 1981, p. 8.

"The *Picayune*'s Christmas Menu, by Famous Louisiana Chef." *Daily Picayune*, 17 December 1911, p. 7.

Price, Todd A. "Another Round of Ojen: Sazerac Reintroduces Carnival Favorite." *Times-Picayune*, 29 January 2016.

———. "Last Bottle of Locally Popular Ojen Spirit Sold." *Times-Picayune*, 10 February 2015.

Proceedings of the Louisiana Engineering Society. Vol. 2, Louisiana Engineering Society, 1916.

Report of the Louisiana Bar Association for 1912–1913. Vol. 14, E. P. Andree, 1913.

Simonson, Robert. "Ojen, a New Orleans Favorite, Is Back in the Liquor Cabinet." *New York Times*, 29 January 2016, www.nytimes.com/2016/01/29/dining/ojen-liqueur .html.

Stanonis, Anthony Joseph. "Just Like Mammy Used to Make: Foodways in the Jim Crow South." *Dixie Emporium: Tourism, Foodways, and Consumer Culture in the American South*, U of Georgia P, 2008, pp. 208–33.

Straub, Jacques. *Drinks*. Hotel Monthly, 1914. babel.hathitrust.org/cgi/pt?id=uc1.31175 012996842.

Szczesiul, Anthony. *The Southern Hospitality Myth: Ethics, Politics, Race, and American Memory*. U of Georgia P, 2017.

"Three Generations of Gelpis Have Carried on the Tradition Of America's Oldest Liquor Importing House." *Times-Picayune*, 25 January 1937, p. 18.

Walker, Dave. "*Booze Traveler* Visits New Orleans for Halloween Celebration." *Times-Picayune*, 9 February 2015, www.nola.com/tv/index.ssf/2015/02/booze_traveler_visits _new_orle.html.

Walker, Judy. "N.O.W.F E. Seminar Participants Will Be Saying 'Ole!'." *Times-Picayune*, 22 May 2008, www.nola.com/food/index.ssf/2008/05/nowfe_seminar_participants _wil.html.

Washburne, George R., and Stanley Bronner, editors. *Beverages De Luxe*. Wine and Spirit Bulletin, 1914. babel.hathitrust.org/cgi/pt?id=chi.73572013.

"When J. & W. Mean Ojen." *Times-Picayune*, 30 Sept. 1923, p. 7.

Who's Who in Louisiana and Mississippi. *Times-Picayune*, 1918. babel.hathitrust.org/cgi /pt?id=wu.89072980022.

W's Good Time

JENNIE LIGHTWEIS-GOFF

Q: What's the southern woman's mating call?
A: I'm sooo drunk.
—An overheard joke, circa 1992

Too Drunk to Fuck

Nola. Her name evokes excess, decadence, the smell of hurricanes and hand grenades: those that intoxicate as well as those that deposit shrapnel in the human gut.[1] On a short walk through this web of associations, one finds New Orleans's distinctive archive of sexual frisson: the quadroon ball, the strip club, the zipless fuck of flash and bead when you're inclined to get Bourbon-faced on Shit Street, to paraphrase the T-shirt. It is certainly not an archive of sex, fibrillating as it does between two vernacular critiques of sexual display. Imagine Jello Biafra howling about getting "too drunk to fuck" and Frank Zappa assuring us that there is no sex on television, just titillation. I would revise only to note that there is no sex on Bourbon Street, and that the titillation is mainly for the bored and the boring.

Perhaps those of us who are pro-sex—that is, passionately invested in the flesh, not the flash, committed to consummation, not commodification—can sigh with relief that it is sex for at least one of the involved parties, generally the hegemonic male, for whom so much "sex" in public remains legal, even as queers get rounded up for cruising, gendered bodies are banished from public streets by catcalls and threats of rape, and sex workers are all but branded for so-called crimes against nature ("Louisiana"). Goddess deliver me from actually existing sex and to the sexual culture that is not yet here, from the "prison-house. . . . [of the] here and now" (Munoz 1) to the erotic utopia that is, I swear, possible.

I wrecked it. I ruined it. As complementary language to nailing and screwing and cutting, the verbs have a curious resonance for people who have lived in the cool shadow or the hot miasma of disaster. The great sage of the Jewish American experience, Lenny Bruce, once said, "If you live in New York or any other big city, you are Jewish. It doesn't matter even if you're Catholic; if you live in New York you're Jewish" (5). Perhaps those residents of the battered tropics ignored by an indifferent America are women even when they are men.

Apres le deluge, the human-made disaster that followed the natural disaster of Katrina, the city that had spent so much of its life—and, in the postindustrial period, so many of its resources—showing America a good time was told that the tourist's good time must be recovery's highest priority. First, there were the left partisans deploying the post-Katrina metaphor of an "American Venice"— that is, comparisons to a shrunken, sinking city that swells nightly when the cruise ships dock and the packaged tours park ("Can Ruined City Become an American 'Venice'?"). That analogy acknowledged that New Orleans possessed a cultural influence far surpassing its diminutive size. But then there was George W. Bush, standing on a tarmac, telling the nation about how he had, as a young man enjoyed himself, "occasionally too much," within the city's porous, fragile boundaries. Once he left the tarmac, he went to Jackson Square to promise repair, then spent the rest of his presidency extolling the virtues of a "surge" in another gulf. For all of his various deficiencies, Dubya sure knew when to hit it and quit it.

The man was a coke-addled, drunken pledge chair whose legacy will be repaired only by the election of a spectacularly unqualified reality show host and pussy-grabbing misogynist. Bush rose to prominence as the macho enfant terrible trust fund kid of a famously controlled and controlling patrician family. For all his purported failure to care about black people—not a personal animus but a seeming indifference to the "group-differentiated vulnerability to premature death" (Gilmore 28) in either Gulf—we might also consider his asymmetric, dimorphic relationship to geographies of disorder: his Gulfs, his Delta. They showed him a good time; he showed them the back of his hand.

All of which is to say that Bush's evocation of New Orleans's drinking culture and drunken tourism made the so-called Katrina hangover as inevitable as a difficult morning after a dozen daiquiris. Making tourism the priority of repair ensured that the neighborhoods and communities lying beyond the map, but nonetheless serving the industry with laboring bodies, would struggle under the weight of an imagined "resilience" at and beyond the storm's tenth anniversary. And all of these conditions—the city as eminently quit-able good time, as receptacle for drunken excess, as repository of flexible service work, as vulnerable geography on the periphery of civilization—gendered and raced the city in durable, diffuse, determinative ways that far exceed Wolf Blitzer's declaration that the city was "so poor and so black" (CNN, September 1, 2005). These delineations emerge, in no small part, from an archive of American stories about New Orleans as both wife and mistress, a necessary safety valve formed from a superfluous rib. Over the course of this essay, I evoke the drunken ramble, the associative link, the almost literary polysyndeton, to reveal (but not expose) the New Orleans of Bush's fantasy, rooted in myth and history that reveal the sharp link between drunken excess and exploitation.

Three Scenes of Les Demoiselles d'Orleans

All over the Quarter and the Marigny, a graffito's rendering of an apocryphal Tennessee Williams quote assures the *flaneuse* that she can see the whole country by strolling through only three of its cities: New Orleans, San Francisco, and New York. The rest of this broad continental expanse is just . . . Cleveland. (News that will surprise no city so much as it surprises Cleveland.) Other figures of the midcentury deployed the same cities as metonym, though their sense of each place's value certainly differed. New York's "immensity and diversity" and San Francisco's "gateway to the Orient" set them apart. But it was New Orleans's typicality that mattered; it "embod[ied] the myths of the Old South" while "creat[ing] a mythology of its own" (Reinders xiii).

It seems almost impossible to imagine such an argument offered in 2017. Today, we are accustomed to thinking about New Orleans as a perpetual outsider: it is the South of Brazil, not the South of the Southern Baptist Convention, a "city-sized act of civil disobedience" against national norms (Baum xiii). The city masons this difference at the foundation of its tourist economy. The partisans deploy it to argue for the city's resilience and repair. The musicians and artists and chefs offer it to explain either their authenticity or their needful migration, depending upon their nativity. After Hurricane Katrina, the city at once signified a kind of foreignness and a forgotten here-ness in the American project. And throughout so many stories about Katrina, a certain kind of iconicity abounded. New Orleans was not America. It was not the South. It was something much smaller than either region or nation. New Orleans was a woman. A black woman (Harris-Perry 17–19).

The stories that America tells itself about itself—legends of cowboys and frontiersmen, of soldiers and presidents, of rugged individualism and the glories of the frontier—are interrupted, excepted, and sometimes contested in sites like New Orleans, supplanted by bohemias and planned gridscapes, global cities and multiracial fugitive communities. Writing in the two decades before the Civil War, Americans tended to attribute conflict to problems of regional character, positing northerners as descended from Puritans (who resisted royal authority in England), while southerners were descended from Cavaliers (who supported the monarchy after the English Civil War). In *Cavalier and Yankee*, William R. Taylor suggests that this led to a revolutionary ethos among New Englanders and to a socially stratified promotion of aristocracy in the South (21). By the late eighteenth century, it was not unusual to encounter descriptions of southerners— even the men—as torpid, gluttonous, and effete, supported as they were by un-free labor (Greeson 75).

Three centuries later, tourists *still* travel to the South looking for its feminine servility, for its complementary virtues to the place from which they travel. Whether they come from Pyongyang or Pittsburgh, Cyprus or Seattle, their imagined South emerges from centuries of framing the region as either incompletely integrated to national (political, moral, and sexual) conventions or as reconstituting lost national ideals. Simultaneous savagery and gentility— the violence of slavery, the indolence it produced in the white elite—are civilized and contained by the forward-looking, acquisitive strivings of the equally imagined North. The regional relationships are thus sustained by the always *real* complementarity of slavery's loom and the lash, of Puritan sobriety and Cavalier debauchery, of the fingerprint of England and the lure of Otherness, and the imagined complementarity of masculine and feminine—an ideology of necessary difference that, when assigned to the matter of gender, reaffirms the heterosexual pairing as the dominant mode of social organization. When projected onto space, such complementarity reveals and obscures: exceptionalism is a myth that enables arguments for both New Orleans's obsolescence and the urgency of its repair.

In the city, the paradigm of regional complementarity was thrown into sharp relief by "race"—an endlessly flexible term that could encompass differences between English and French national characters, and the high visibility of the enslaved in the city. In the three "scenes" that follow, I consider the multifaceted feminine face of New Orleans. These women—marked by race and gender, asked to bear the burdens of emotional labor—become the receptacle for national notions of the city as hooker, nursemaid, waitress, and slave.

SCENE 1: THE BELLE

Before Scarlett broke hearts and box office records, there was *Jezebel* (1938), directed by William Wyler. Starring Bette Davis, it at once cashed in on the highly marketable plantation story and activated extant interest in New Orleans, which had been the site of debates about historical preservation, resulting in the formation and juridical empowerment of the Vieux Carré Commission by city and state governments, in 1936. After decades of genteel bohemian decline, New Orleans was once again a tourist attraction and site of urgent repair. Some of that power emerged from cinematic cultures of spectacle. Though it has never been as famous as David O. Selznick's *Gone with the Wind* (1939), *Jezebel* exceeded it in critical acclaim, earning Davis the Oscar and driving people back to New Orleans in search of what remained after an earlier disaster: the brutal yellow fever epidemic of 1851. From 1941 to 1969, a train called the *Southern Belle* ran from Kansas City to New Orleans, marketing New Orleans as a destination personified with and by feminine bodies, signifying nostalgia in seeming tension with hypermodern, luxurious rail travel.

Both Davis's Julie Marsden and the eponymous train—impositions of the twentieth century on the nineteenth—rely on the spectral plantation, a rural spatial phantasm that scarcely graphs onto New Orleans, one of the few planned cities in the United States. Dense urban blocks and unfree agricultural labor existed within spitting distance of one another, a condition still visible on the deltoid arpent lines in the old riverfront neighborhoods where French plantation allotments share blocks with row houses and service space. New Orleans did not begin as a series of farms, only to conurbate into a city during Sun Belt expansion. Nor was it a trading outpost that became a metropolis, like New York. Like very few other cities—and most of them southern places, such as Savannah, Charleston, and Mobile—it is the product of eighteenth-century urban planning.

Yet, at the beginning of a half-century period of suburbanization, during which white Americans left cities in droves, urban tourism to New Orleans was framed as a regression to plantations embodied in a female form that was never so elite and white as Vivien Leigh's Scarlett O'Hara or Bette Davis's Julie Marsden. The women of early New Orleans were indigenous, enslaved, or deported from prisons and insane asylums in Paris. The bleached belle is not a legible or recognizable metonym for the city.

SCENE 2: THE QUADROON

If we began to list the writers who chased the frisson of interracial sex in antebellum New Orleans, our roll call would include high modernist masters like William Faulkner, feminist abolitionists like Harriet Martineau, a former mayor of New York City (Abraham Oakey Hall), and the man who designed Central Park. Frederick Law Olmsted traveled South as a young man, attempting to save himself from the world of work as a travel writer. Scholars have since demonstrated that these writers frantically copied one another. One writer would describe a slave auction of a light-skinned woman (as Solomon Northrup did in *Twelve Years a Slave*), another would plagiarize, a third would assume that every light-skinned woman he encountered on the street was kept for the sexual pleasure of an elite white man.

Here is the problem with the myth of the quadroon (or "the placage complex," as Emily Clark calls it): travelers impose their perspective on women who they never quote, never ask, never interview (148). Bound by the intersecting ideologies of sexism and racism, travelers were not interested in the effect of sexual slavery on the women who were sold, only in the comfort of those who bought—and the titillation of those who looked at her and guessed at her history. This elision ought to remind us of post-Katrina rhetoric, characterized as it was by an urgency to repair the city for the tourist to enjoy himself . . . occasionally *too* much.

The social distance of tourism complicated the moral claim of abolitionism, and it is that social distance that threads through Bush's post-Katrina declaration of good-time sentiments. The Katrina hangover—the expiration of sympathies following the return of crime and social disorder, and the imposition of disaster capitalism—was, by the end of a low, dishonest decade, inevitable. It is impossible to read the history of New Orleans as separate from tourism within its borders. Those who are not native might recall their first visit, might remember the tourist mythologies and economies that magnetically drew them to the mouth of Mississippi.

In 2002, I arrived armed only with the tourist guidebooks, which urged their reader to handcuff herself to a hotel shower rail for the duration of travel to avoid the various dangers promised on the borders of the Quarter—pickpockets and voudons crouching behind tombs in Saint Louis Cemetery—and farther afield, in a now obsolete list of bars it urged were only for Kevlar-encased veterans of foreign travel. Younger and accustomed to a more orderly southern city—Atlanta—I took its advice, and sought a tour.

After a miasmic stroll in Saint Louis Cemetery no. 1, the tour guide—a woman in her forties who had found her way to New Orleans from Arizona—took the assembled tour to the cottage on Saint Ann Street where, she claimed, voodoo queen Marie Laveau had lived. A few blocks away, the guide began a rambling, free-associative monologue about the relationships between voodoo and interracial eroticism. On the sidewalk opposite us, a woman walked from Rampart Street toward the heart of the Quarter. She was young, light skinned, African American, beautiful, and gorgeously dressed for an evening out. In a stage whisper, the tour guide said, "That's what the quadroon brides looked like."

More than a decade ago, on a trip to look at graduate schools, the comment offered me a glimpse at another potential career. I imagined myself carrying an umbrella stamped with the legend "Cranky Tours." I would belligerently knock people like this guide off of the sidewalk. I would correct bad history, even if I had to shout at retreating horses and buggies. Failing that, I offer you this tale in the hope of leveling the logic of substitution, which replaces the violence of slavery with an elegant myth of fabricated consent.

SCENE 3: STORYVILLE

In 1897, New Orleans Councilman Sidney Story created the boundaries of a red-light district in the city's Fifth Ward. It straddled the French Quarter. The most profitable of its brothels stood taller than Saint Louis Cathedral. Photographer and native New Orleanian E. J. Bellocq committed the women of "Storyville" to posterity, posing them in brothels and "cribs," the smaller sites where they sold sex.

Today, an elegant bar on New Orleans's Lee Circle brands itself Bellocq's. Louis Malle's film *Pretty Baby* (1978) stars Keith Carradine as a highly fictionalized version of Bellocq. In 2013, New Orleans jazz musician Meschiya Lake posed as the lady in the stockings for the cover of her album *Lucky Devil*. People who would hurriedly close a PornHub tab if you walked toward their open laptop might, considering Bellocq's seeming respectability in nonpornographic popular culture, display his photographs on their coffee tables. The glamorization of these images and of Storyville more broadly—the post hoc creation of a "golden age" of prostitution—is seemingly designed to make us forget the current moment, in which sex workers remain vulnerable and unprotected by legal labor regimes (Grant 2014).

The golden age did not take place. In her time as well in as ours, the woman in striped stockings had no protected legal status. Prostitution was never legal inside of Storyville; the idea of its legality emerged because penalties for selling sex outside of the district were far worse than they were for selling sex inside of it. The district housed violent crime and dramatic health risks; a contemporary Dutch time traveler would not recognize it as kin to *De Wallen*. When the district died, in 1917—in part because of moral panics surrounding the possibility of soldiers and sailors finding their way to legal brothels before deployment— prostitution shifted to private sites, presumably maintaining much of its danger (Landau 204). Though these glamorous images create a romanticized image of the past, we ought not forget that Lulu White, who owned the brothel that dwarfed Saint Louis Cathedral, died as a panhandler on Basin Street, sometimes supporting herself with lower-status sex work (140). When the district was mowed over, the dangers of criminalized prostitution abided.

Afterwards, Storyville became the Iberville housing projects. Before it was shuttered in Katrina's wake—for political, not fluvial, reasons—75 percent of its heads of household were women. The city subsequently converted subsidized housing to a voucher system, in which people paid private landlords with public moneys, thus leaving its most vulnerable residents at the mercy of private actors who discriminated against recipients of social spending (Henrici et al.). The Iberville projects dodged demolition but were transformed into high-rent condominiums.

We might wonder the same thing that people asked at the end of Storyville: Where did its residents go? A public housing unit might not be a woman's first choice. Neither is a brothel. But both have the benefit of four walls and a roof.

These paragraphs locate New Orleans exceptionalism in its gendered form. Among its sins is the assumption that places and positions can be seen most acutely from the outside, by men with a *marvelously* unbiased sense of gender, by whites with a refreshingly honest view of people of color, by tourists who can tell—with a single sniff of the trash runoff on Bourbon Street—everything that residents do wrong in their own city. That all of these marked identities (woman, black, subordinate) converge in the body of the displaced New Orleanian reveals something of the limitation of the city's all–bachelor party economy: that the people who staff it are seemingly shingled by layers of presumption, of objectification, of imposed definition. Under those layers, they might never be seen, but from the inside out and the bottom up, they are nonetheless capable of rebuilding. Such an effort requires bravery; its residents have the comfort of knowing that this city is flooded with liquid courage, and that in abundance.

Note

1. For their stories of evacuation and exile, I thank myriad neighbors, friends, and folks who shared a square foot of the sidewalk or neutral ground on the parade route. For revision suggestions, I thank Matt Dischinger. For institutional and financial support, I thank the Monroe Fellowship at the New Orleans Center for the Gulf South at Tulane University. For much else, I thank Phillip Lightweis-Goff, Katie Van Wert, and Burke Scarbrough.

Works Cited

Baum, Dan. *Nine Lives: Mystery, Magic, Death and Life in New Orleans.* Spiegel and Grau, 2010.

Bruce, Lenny. *How to Talk Dirty and Influence People.* Touchstone, 1992.

Bush, George W. "Remarks on Hurricane Katrina Recovery Efforts in Kenner, Louisiana," 2 September 2005. *American Presidency Project,* www.presidency.ucsb.edu/node/216360.

"Can Ruined City Become an American 'Venice'?" *Wall Street Journal,* 6 September 2005.

Clark, Emily. *The Strange History of the American Quadroon: Free Women of Color in the Revolutionary Atlantic World.* U of North Carolina P, 2013.

Gilmore, Ruth Wilson. *Golden Gulag: Prisons, Surplus, Crisis, and Opposition in Globalizing California.* U of California P, 2007.

Grant, Melissa Gira. *Playing the Whore: The Work of Sex Work*. Verso, 2014.

Greeson, Jennifer Rae. *Our South: Geographic Fantasy and the Rise of National Literature*. Harvard UP, 2010.

Harris-Perry, Melissa. *Sister Outsider: Shame, Stereotypes, and Black Women in America*. Yale UP, 2013.

Henrici, Jane M., Chandra Childers, and Elyse Shaw. "Get to the Bricks: The Experiences of Black Women from New Orleans Public Housing after Hurricane Katrina." Institute for Women's Policy Research, 2015.

Landau, Emily Epstein. *Spectacular Wickedness: Sex, Race, and Memory in Storyville, New Orleans*. Louisiana State UP, 2013.

"Louisiana: Repeal 'Crime Against Nature' Laws." *Human Rights Watch*, 22 April 2014, www.hrw.org/news/2014/04/22/louisiana-repeal-crime-against-nature-laws.

Munoz, Jose Esteban. *Cruising Utopia: The Then and There of Queer Futurity*. New York UP, 2009.

Reinders, Robert. *End of an Era: New Orleans, 1850—1860*. Pelican, 1964.

Taylor, William R. *Cavalier and Yankee: The Old South and American National Character*. Harvard UP, 1979.

Vieux Carré Commission. "About Us: History of the Vieux Carré Commission." City of New Orleans, www.nola.gov/vcc/about-us.

Zappa, Frank. *Crossfire*. CNN, 28 March 1986.

CONTRIBUTORS

ALISON ARANT is associate professor and chair of English at Wagner College in Staten Island, New York City. She teaches courses in U.S. Southern Literature, American Literature, and African American Literature. She is the coeditor of *Reconsidering Flannery O'Connor* (forthcoming), and her work has appeared in *Flannery O'Connor Review, Modern Fiction Studies*, and *Southern Literary Journal*.

KATHARINE A. BURNETT is associate professor of English and coordinator of the Gender Studies Program at Fisk University in Nashville, Tennessee. Her book *Cavaliers and Economists: Global Capitalism and the Development of Southern Literature, 1820–1860* (2019) examines the relationship between economics and fiction published in the U.S. South before the Civil War. Her essays have appeared in *PMLA, College Literature, Southern Literary Journal*, and *Global South*.

DAVID A. DAVIS is associate professor of English, director of fellowships and scholarships, and associate director of Southern Studies at Mercer University. He is the author of *World War I and Southern Modernism*, which won the Eudora Welty Prize in 2018. He has published essays and reviews in *African American Review, American Quarterly, Journal of American Studies, Mississippi Quarterly, Modern Fiction Studies, Mosaic, Southern Quarterly, Southern Literary Journal*, and other journals. He edited a reprint of Victor Daly's novel *Not Only War: A Story of Two Great Conflicts* (2010) and a reprint of John L. Spivak's novel *Hard Times on a Southern Chain Gang* (2012; originally published as *Georgia Nigger*, 1932). He coedited with Tara Powell *Writing in the Kitchen: Essays on Southern Literature and Foodways* (2014).

MATTHEW DISCHINGER is a lecturer in the department of English at Georgia State University, where he teaches courses in American Literary and Cultural Studies, Postcolonial Studies, and first-year writing. His work has appeared in *South Asian Review, Global South, Mississippi Quarterly, Virginia Quarterly Review, North Carolina Literary Review,* and edited collections examining race, region, and popular culture.

CALEB DOAN is a doctoral candidate in the department of English at Louisiana State University. He published "From *Typee's* Tommo to *Moby-Dick's* Ishmael: Gift Exchange in the Capitalist World System" (2016) in *Atlantic Studies* and was the editorial assistant for the *Oxford Handbook of Edgar Allan Poe* (2019). He will defend his dissertation, "Pacific Crosswinds: Antebellum American Fiction and the Transpacific World," in spring 2020.

HANNAH C. GRIGGS is a writer, researcher, and critic from New Orleans. She is currently pursing a PhD in English at Emory University.

JEROD RA'DEL HOLLYFIELD is associate professor of Communication and Film at Carson-Newman University. His book *Framing Empire: Postcolonial Adaptations of Victorian Literature in Hollywood* was published by Edinburgh University Press in 2018, and his other work has appeared in *Settler Colonial Studies, Atlantikos, CineAction, Film International,* and several edited collections. He is also a filmmaker, whose short, *Goodfriends,* played at international and Oscar-qualifying film festivals and was endorsed by national disability organizations. Hollyfield is the creator of the *Assisted Stories Project,* a collection of video essays that aims to preserve and promote the narratives of the American South's elder population.

J. GERALD KENNEDY is the Boyd Professor of English at Louisiana State University and the author of *Strange Nation: Literary Nationalism and Cultural Conflict in the Age of Poe* (2016). A former president of the Poe Studies Association, he has also published *Poe, Death, and the Life of Writing* (1987) and *Imagining Paris: Exile, Writing, and American Identity* (1993). His edited books include the *Historical Guide to Edgar Allan Poe* (2001) and (with Jerome McGann) *Poe and the Remapping of Antebellum Print Culture* (2012). His latest book, coedited with Scott Peeples and with Caleb Doan as editorial assistant, is *The Oxford Handbook of Edgar Allan Poe* (2019).

CARA KOEHLER is a doctoral candidate in the department of Literary and Media Studies at the University of Bamberg. Before moving to Germany, she studied English Literature and French Language at DePaul University, Chicago. Her research interests include American literature of the nineteenth century, the graphic novel and teen culture, theories of adaptation, and American visual culture.

ELLEN LANSKY teaches Literature, Composition, and Creative Writing at Inver Hills Community College in Minnesota. Her essays on literature and addiction have appeared in several anthologies and journals, including *Literature and Medicine* and *Dionysos*. She has written about alcoholism in the work of Ernest Hemingway, Djuna Barnes, Paul and Jane Bowles, Dorothy Parker, Katherine Anne Porter, F. Scott and Zelda Fitzgerald, Tennessee Williams, and Carson McCullers. She is also a fiction writer and has published several short stories, a novella, and two novels, *Golden Jeep* and *Suburban Heathens*. She attended St. Catherine University (BA), Binghamton University (MA), and the University of Minnesota (PhD).

JENNIE LIGHTWEIS-GOFF is an instructor of English at the University of Mississippi and Invited Professor at North China University of Technology. She teaches American ethnic, regional, and national literatures of the past three centuries as well as film studies and feminist theory. In 2010, she received her PhD in English and Graduate Certificates in both Gender and Africana Studies from the University of Rochester. The monograph based on her dissertation research, *Blood at the Root: Lynching as American Cultural Nucleus*, won the SUNY Press Dissertation/First Book Prize in African American Studies and was published by SUNY Press (2011). Presently, she is at work on several projects that place southern cities at the center of U.S. urban studies. Articles from these projects have appeared in *American Literature, Minnesota Review, Signs*, and the edited collection *Small-Screen Souths: Region, Identity, and the Cultural Politics of Television* (2017).

MONICA C. MILLER is assistant professor of English at Middle Georgia State University. Her work focuses on the relationship between gender and region in American literature. Her first book, *Being Ugly: Southern Women Writers and Social Rebellion*, is available from Louisiana State University Press.

CONOR PICKEN is assistant professor of English at Bellarmine University in Louisville, Kentucky. His teaching and research focus on American literature, southern literature, modernism, and social change. His work has appeared in *Mississippi Quarterly, Faulkner and History, Critical Insights: American Multicultural Identity,* and *Faulkner and Warren.*

ROBERT REA is the deputy editor and web editor for *Southwest Review.* His scholarly work has appeared in *Southern Literary Journal, Mississippi Quarterly,* and *Southern Quarterly.* He also has published essays in the *Oxford American, The Millions,* and the *Los Angeles Review of Books,* among others. He currently teaches courses in American Literature at the University of Mississippi.

CHRISTOPHER RIEGER is the director of the Center for Faulkner Studies and Professor of English at Southeast Missouri State University. He is the author of *Clear-Cutting Eden: Ecology and the Pastoral in Southern Literature* and the coeditor of five essay collections, including *Faulkner and Hurston* (2017) and *Faulkner and Hemingway* (2018).

JENNA GRACE SCIUTO is associate professor of English at the Massachusetts College of Liberal Arts. Her current book project, under contract with the University Press of Mississippi, examines literary representations of sexual policing of the color line across spaces with distinct colonial histories and constructions of race: Mississippi, Louisiana, Haiti, and the Dominican Republic. Her work has appeared in *Journal of Commonwealth and Postcolonial Studies, ariel,* and *Faulkner and the Black Literatures of the Americas* (from the University Press of Mississippi).

JOHN STROMSKI is an independent scholar. He received his PhD in English from the University of Tennessee and has worked as a Visiting Assistant Professor at Marshall University. His research interests focus on the relationship between slavery, labor, and nineteenth-century American literature.

MATTHEW D. SUTTON is a postdoctoral fellow at East Tennessee State University and holds a PhD in American Studies from the College of William and Mary. His essays on U.S. South literature and music have most recently appeared in *Mississippi Quarterly, Studies in American Culture, Popular Music and Society, a/b: Auto/Biography Studies,* and the edited collection *Country Boys and Redneck Women: New Essays in Gender and Country Music* (2016).

ZACKARY VERNON is assistant professor of English at Appalachian State University. In both his teaching and writing, he focuses on American literature, film, and environmental studies. His research has appeared in a range of scholarly books and journals, and he is a coeditor of and contributor to *Summoning the Dead: Essays on Ron Rash* (2018) and editor of *Ecocriticism and the Future of Southern Studies* (2019).

SUSAN ZIEGER is professor of English at the University of California, Riverside, and the author of *The Mediated Mind: Affect, Ephemera, and Consumerism in the Nineteenth Century* (2018) and *Inventing the Addict: Drugs, Race, and Sexuality in Nineteenth-Century British and American Literature* (2008). Her articles have appeared in *American Literature, PMLA, Genre, Victorian Studies, Modernism and Modernity,* and other journals. She is currently researching and writing *Logistical Life.*

INDEX